MW00786265

HANDBOOK ON CONTEMPORARY
AUSTRIAN ECONOMICS

In memory of my two teachers in Austrian Economics:
Hans Sennholz (1922–2007) and Don Lavoie (1951–2001)

Handbook on Contemporary Austrian Economics

Edited by

Peter J. Boettke

George Mason University, Virginia, USA

Edward Elgar
Cheltenham, UK • Northampton, MA, USA

Published by
Edward Elgar Publishing Limited
The Lypiatts
15 Lansdown Road
Cheltenham
Glos GL50 2JA
UK

Edward Elgar Publishing, Inc.
William Pratt House
9 Dewey Court
Northampton
Massachusetts 01060
USA

A catalogue record for this book
is available from the British Library

Library of Congress Control Number: 2009941412

Mixed Sources
Product group from well-managed
forests and other controlled sources
www.fsc.org Cert no. SA-COC-1565
© 1996 Forest Stewardship Council

ISBN 978 1 84720 411 0 (cased)

Printed and bound by MPG Books Group, UK

Contents

PART IV   CONCLUSION

Contributors

Scott A. Beaulier is the BB&T Distinguished Professor of Capitalism and Department Chair of Economics at Mercer University (Macon, Georgia). He is also the faculty director of the Laffer Center for Global Economic Growth at Mercer University. He received his PhD in Economics from George Mason University in 2004. He has written extensively on property rights economics, and his research in the areas of Austrian economics, development economics, economic education, and law and economics has been published widely.

Peter J. Boettke is the BB&T Professor for the Study of Capitalism at the Mercatus Center at George Mason University, Virginia and a University Professor of Economics, also at GMU. Professor Boettke is the author of several books on the history, collapse, and transition from socialism in the former Soviet Union as well as books and articles on the history of economic thought and methodology. In 1998, Boettke assumed the editorship of *The Review of Austrian Economics*. Prior to assuming that editorship, Boettke was the editor of *Advances in Austrian Economics*. Besides GMU, Boettke has held faculty positions at London School of Economics, Hoover Institution at Stanford University, and New York University.

Christopher J. Coyne is an Assistant Professor of Economics at West Virginia University. He is also the North American Editor of *The Review of Austrian Economics*, a Research Fellow at the Mercatus Center at George Mason University and at The Independent Institute, a member of the Board of Scholars for the Virginia Institute for Public Policy, and Distinguished Scholar for the Center for the Study of Political Economy at Hampden-Sydney College. In 2008, he was named the Hayek Fellow at the London School of Economics. He obtained his PhD in Economics from George Mason University, Virginia.

Anthony J. Evans is currently Assistant Professor of Economics at ESCP Europe Business School. His research interests are in corporate entrepreneurship, monetary theory, and transitional markets. He has published in journals such as *Eastern European Economics, Constitutional Political Economy* and *The Review of Austrian Economics*, and his recent co-authored book *The Neoliberal Revolution in Eastern Europe: Economic Ideas in the Transition from Communism* was published in 2009 by Edward Elgar. Anthony received his MA and PhD in Economics from

George Mason University, USA, and a BA (Hons) from the University of Liverpool, UK.

Peter T. Leeson is Visiting Professor of Economics at the University of Chicago's Becker Center on Chicago Price Theory and BB&T Professor for the Study of Capitalism at George Mason University, Virginia. Formerly, he was a Visiting Fellow in Political Economy and Government at Harvard University and the F.A. Hayek Fellow at the London School of Economics.

Stephen C. Miller is an Assistant Professor of Economics at Western Carolina University. His research focuses on the role bias and irrationality play in forming voters' political and economic beliefs. Miller received his PhD from George Mason University, Virginia and his BA degree from Towson University, Maryland.

Benjamin Powell is an Assistant Professor of Economics at Suffolk University, Boston, Massachusetts, a senior economist with the Beacon Hill Institute at Suffolk University, and a research fellow with The Independent Institute. Professor Powell is the editor of *Making Poor Nations Rich: Entrepreneurship and the Process of Development* (Stanford University Press, 2008), co-editor of *Housing America: Building Out of a Crisis* (Transaction, 2009) and author of more than 30 scholarly articles and policy studies. He earned his BS in Economics and Finance from the University of Massachusetts at Lowell, and his MA and PhD in Economics from George Mason University.

Frederic Sautet is an economist at the Mercatus Center at George Mason University. He holds a doctorate in economics from the University of Paris and studied, as a post-doctorate fellow, under the auspices of Prof. Israel Kirzner, Peter Boettke, and Mario Rizzo at New York University. Dr Sautet teaches a course on entrepreneurship theory and policy in the Masters program in economics at George Mason University. He has widely published on the topic of entrepreneurship and is the author of *An Entrepreneurial Theory of the Firm* published in 2000 by Routledge.

Virgil Henry Storr is a Senior Research Fellow and the Director of Graduate Student Programs at the Mercatus Center and the Don C. Lavoie Research Fellow in the Program in Philosophy, Politics and Economics, Department of Economics, George Mason University. He holds a PhD in Economics from George Mason University and did his undergraduate work at Beloit College, Wisconsin. Virgil is the author of *Enterprising Slaves & Master Pirates* (Peter Lang, 2004) and his writings in political economy have been published or are forthcoming in *Rationality &*

Society, the *Journal of Urban Affairs*, the *Cambridge Journal of Economics*, the *American Journal of Economics and Sociology*, the *Review of Austrian Economics* and several other scholarly publications.

Edward P. Stringham earned his PhD from George Mason University in 2002. Stringham is the Shelby Cullom Davis Visiting Associate Professor at Trinity College in Connecticut, editor of the *Journal of Private Enterprise*, editor of two books *Anarchy and the Law* (Transaction, 2006) and *Anarchy, State, and Public Choice* (Edward Elgar, 2006) and author of more than 40 articles and book chapters in outlets including *The Review of Austrian Economics*, *Quarterly Journal of Austrian Economics*, *Journal of Institutional & Theoretical Economics*, and *Public Choice*.

J. Robert Subrick is Assistant Professor of Economics at James Madison University, Virginia. He earned a BA and BS from the University of Delaware and received a PhD in Economics from George Mason University. Prior to joining JMU, he was a Research Associate for the Center for the Economic Study of Religion at George Mason University and the Center for Institutional Reform and the Informal Sector at the University of Maryland. His research has focused on the political economy of development, especially in sub-Saharan Africa, and the economics of religion.

Introduction*
Peter J. Boettke

The Austrian school of economics was founded in 1871 with the publication of Carl Menger's *Principles of Economics*. Menger, along with William Stanley Jevons and Leon Walras, developed the marginalist revolution in economic analysis. Menger dedicated *Principles of Economics* to his German colleague William Roscher, the leading figure in the German historical school, which dominated economic thinking in German-language countries. In his book, Menger argued that economic analysis is universally applicable and that the appropriate unit of analysis is man and his choices. These choices, he wrote, are determined by individual subjective preferences and the margin on which decisions are made. The logic of choice, he believed, is the essential building block to the development of a universally valid economic theory.

The historical school, on the other hand, had argued that economic science is incapable of generating universal principles and that scientific research should instead be focused on detailed historical examination. The historical school thought the English classical economists mistaken in believing in economic laws that transcended time and national boundaries. Menger's *Principles of Economics* restated the classical political economy view of universal laws and did so using marginal analysis. Roscher's students, especially Gustav Schmoller, took great exception to Menger's defense of "theory" and gave the work of Menger and his followers, Eugen Böhm-Bawerk and Friedrich Wieser, the derogatory name "Austrian school" because of their faculty positions at the University of Vienna. The term stuck.

Since the 1930s, no economists from the University of Vienna or any other Austrian university have become leading figures in the so-called Austrian school of economics. In the 1930s and 1940s, the Austrian school moved to Britain and the United States, and scholars associated with this approach to economic science were located primarily at the London School of Economics (1931–50), New York University (1944–), Auburn University (1983–), and George Mason University (1981–). Many of the ideas of the leading mid-twentieth-century Austrian economists, such as Ludwig von Mises and F.A. Hayek, are rooted in the ideas of classical economists such as Adam Smith and David Hume, or early-twentieth-century figures such as Knut Wicksell, as well as Menger, Böhm-Bawerk, and Friedrich von Wieser. This diverse mix of intellectual traditions in economic science is even more obvious in contemporary Austrian school economists, who have been influenced by modern figures in economics. These include Armen Alchian, James Buchanan, Ronald Coase, Harold Demsetz, Axel Leijonhufvud, Douglass North, Mancur Olson, Vernon Smith, Gordon Tullock, Leland Yeager, and Oliver Williamson, as well as Israel Kirzner and Murray Rothbard. While one could argue that a unique Austrian school of economics operates within the economic profession today, one could also sensibly argue that the label "Austrian" no longer possesses any substantive meaning. In this Introduction I concentrate on the main propositions about economics that so-called Austrians believe.

The science of economics

Proposition 1: Only individuals choose
Man, with his purposes and plans, is the beginning of all economic analysis. Only individuals make choices; collective entities do not choose. The primary task of economic analysis is to make economic phenomena intelligible by basing it on individual purposes and plans; the secondary task of economic analysis is to trace out the unintended consequences of individual choices.

Proposition 2: The study of the market order is fundamentally about exchange behavior and the institutions within which exchanges take place
The price system and the market economy are best understood as a "catallaxy," and thus the science that studies the market order falls under the domain of "catallactics." These terms derive from the original Greek meanings of the word *"katallaxy"* – exchange and bringing a stranger into friendship through exchange. Catallactics focuses analytical attention on the exchange relationships that emerge in the market, the bargaining that characterizes the exchange process, and the institutions within which exchange takes place.

Proposition 3: The "facts" of the social sciences are what people believe and think
Unlike the physical sciences, the human sciences begin with the purposes and plans of individuals. Where the purging of purposes and plans in the physical sciences led to advances by overcoming the problem of anthropomorphism, in the human sciences, the elimination of purposes and plans results in purging the science of human action of its subject matter. In the human sciences, the "facts" of the world are what the actors think and believe.

The meaning that individuals place on things, practices, places, and people determines how they will orient themselves in making decisions. The goal of the sciences of human action is intelligibility, not prediction. The human sciences can achieve this goal because we are what we study, or because we possess knowledge from within, whereas the natural sciences cannot pursue a goal of intelligibility because they rely on knowledge from without. We can understand purposes and plans of other human actors because we ourselves are human actors.

The classic thought experiment invoked to convey this essential difference between the sciences of human action and the physical sciences is a Martian observing the "data" at Grand Central Station in New York. Our Martian could observe that when the little hand on the clock points to eight, there is a bustle of movement as bodies leave these boxes, and that when the little hand hits five, there is a bustle of movement as bodies re-enter the boxes and leave. The Martian may even develop a prediction about the little hand and the movement of bodies and boxes. But unless the Martian comes to understand the purposes and plans (the commuting to and from work), his "scientific" understanding of the data from Grand Central Station would be limited. The sciences of human action are different from the natural sciences, and we impoverish the human sciences when we try to force them into the philosophical/scientific mold of the natural sciences.

Microeconomics

Proposition 4: Utility and costs are subjective
All economic phenomena are filtered through the human mind. Since the 1870s, economists have agreed that value is subjective, but; following Alfred Marshall, many argued that the cost side of the equation is determined by objective conditions. Marshall insisted that just as both blades of a pair of scissors cut a piece of paper, so subjective value and objective costs determine price. But Marshall failed to appreciate that costs are also subjective because they are themselves determined by the value of alternative uses of scarce resources. Both blades of the scissors do indeed cut the paper, but the blade of supply is determined by individuals' subjective valuations.

In deciding courses of action, one must choose; that is, one must pursue one path and not others. The focus on alternatives in choices leads to one of the defining concepts of the economic way of thinking: opportunity costs. The cost of any action is the value of the highest-valued alternative forgone in taking that action. Since the forgone action is, by definition, never taken, when one decides, one weighs the expected benefits of an activity against the expected benefits of alternative activities.

Proposition 5: The price system economizes on the information that people need to process in making their decisions
Prices summarize the terms of exchange on the market. The price system signals to market participants the relevant information, helping them realize mutual gains from exchange. In Hayek's famous example, when people notice that the price of tin has risen, they do not need to know whether the cause was an increase in demand for tin or a decrease in supply. Either way, the increase in the price of tin leads them to economize on its use. Market prices change quickly when underlying conditions change, which leads people to adjust quickly.

Proposition 6: Private property in the means of production is a necessary condition for rational economic calculation
Economists and social thinkers had long recognized that private ownership provides powerful incentives for the efficient allocation of scarce resources. But those sympathetic to socialism believed that socialism could transcend these incentive problems by changing human nature. Ludwig von Mises demonstrated that even if the assumed change in human nature took place, socialism would fail because of economic planners' inability to rationally calculate the alternative use of resources. Without private ownership in the means of production, Mises reasoned, there would be no market for the means of production, and therefore no money prices for the means of production. And without money prices reflecting the relative scarcities of the means of production, economic planners would be unable to rationally calculate the alternative use of the means of production.

Proposition 7: The competitive market is a process of entrepreneurial discovery
Many economists see competition as a state of affairs. But the term "competition" invokes an activity. If competition were a state of affairs, the entrepreneur would have no role. But because competition is an activity, the entrepreneur has a huge role as the agent of change who prods and pulls markets in new directions.

The entrepreneur is alert to unrecognized opportunities for mutual gain. By recognizing opportunities, the entrepreneur earns a profit. The mutual learning from the discovery of gains from exchange moves the market system to a more efficient allocation of resources. Entrepreneurial discovery ensures that a free market moves toward the most efficient use of resources. In addition, the lure of profit continually prods entrepreneurs to seek innovations that increase productive capacity. For the entrepreneur who recognizes the opportunity, today's imperfections represent tomorrow's profit.[1] The price system and the market economy are learning devices that guide individuals to discover mutual gains and use scarce resources efficiently.

Macroeconomics

Proposition 8:   Money is nonneutral

Money is defined as the commonly accepted medium of exchange. If government policy distorts the monetary unit, exchange is distorted as well. The goal of monetary policy should be to minimize these distortions. Any increase in the money supply not offset by an increase in money demand will lead to an increase in prices. But prices do not adjust instantaneously throughout the economy. Some price adjustments occur faster than others, which means that relative prices change. Each of these changes exerts its influence on the pattern of exchange and production. Money, by its nature, thus cannot be neutral.

This proposition's importance becomes evident in discussing the costs of inflation. The quantity theory of money stated, correctly, that printing money does not increase wealth. Thus, if the government doubles the money supply, money holders' apparent gain in ability to buy goods is prevented by the doubling of prices. But while the quantity theory of money represented an important advance in economic thinking, a mechanical interpretation of the quantity theory underestimated the costs of inflationary policy. If prices simply doubled when the government doubled the money supply, then economic actors would anticipate this price adjustment by closely following money supply figures and would adjust their behavior accordingly. The cost of inflation would thus be minimal.

But inflation is socially destructive on several levels. First, even anticipated inflation breaches a basic trust between the government and its citizens because government is using inflation to confiscate people's wealth. Second, unanticipated inflation is redistributive as debtors gain at the expense of creditors. Third, because people cannot perfectly anticipate inflation and because the money is added somewhere in the system – say, through government purchase of bonds – some prices (the price of bonds, for example) adjust before other prices, which means that inflation distorts the pattern of exchange and production.

Since money is the link for almost all transactions in a modern economy, monetary distortions affect those transactions. The goal of monetary policy, therefore, should be to minimize these monetary distortions, precisely because money is nonneutral.[2]

Proposition 9:   The capital structure consists of heterogeneous goods that have multispecific uses that must be aligned

Right now, people in Detroit, Stuttgart, and Tokyo City are designing cars that will not be purchased for a decade. How do they know how to allocate resources to meet that goal? Production is always for an uncertain future demand, and the production process requires different stages of investment ranging from the most remote (mining iron ore) to the most immediate (the car dealership). The values of all producer goods at every stage of production derive from the value consumers place on the product being produced. The production plan aligns various goods into a capital structure that produces the final goods in, ideally, the most efficient manner. If capital goods were homogeneous, they could be used in producing all the final products consumers desired. If mistakes were made, the resources would be reallocated quickly, and with minimal cost, toward producing the more desired final product. But capital goods are heterogeneous and multispecific; an auto plant can make cars, but not computer chips. The intricate alignment of capital to produce various consumer goods is governed by price signals and the careful economic calculations of investors. If the price system is distorted, investors will make mistakes in aligning their capital goods. Once the error is revealed, economic actors will reshuffle their investments, but in the meantime resources will be lost.[3]

Proposition 10:   Social institutions are often the result of human action, but not of human design

Many of the most important institutions and practices are not the result of direct design but are the by-product of actions taken to achieve other goals. A student in the Midwest in January trying to get to class quickly while avoiding the cold may cut across the quad rather than walk the long way around. Cutting across the quad in the snow leaves footprints; as other students follow these, they make the path bigger. Although their goal is merely to get to class quickly and avoid the cold weather, in the process they create a path in the snow that actually helps students who come later to achieve this goal more easily. The "path in the snow" story is a simple example of a "product of human action, but not of human design" (Hayek, 1948, p. 7).

The market economy and its price system are examples of a similar process. People do not intend to create the complex array of exchanges and price signals that constitute a market economy. Their intention is simply to improve their own lot in life, but their behavior results in the market system. Money, law, language, science, and so on are all social phenomena that can trace their origins not to human design, but rather to people striving to achieve their own betterment, and in the process producing an outcome that benefits the public.[4]

The implications of these ten propositions are rather radical. If they hold true, economic theory would be grounded in verbal logic and empirical work focused on historical narratives. With regard to public policy, severe doubt would be raised about the ability of government officials to intervene optimally within the economic system, let alone to rationally manage the economy.

Perhaps economists should adopt the doctors' creed: "First do no harm." The market economy develops out of people's natural inclination to better their situation and, in so doing, to discover the mutually beneficial exchanges that will accomplish that goal. Adam Smith first systematized this message in *The Wealth of Nations*. In the twentieth century, economists of the Austrian school of economics were the most uncompromising proponents of this message, not because of a prior ideological commitment, but because of the logic of their arguments.

Notes

*   This article originally appeared in the 2nd edition of *The Concise Encyclopedia of Economics*, edited by David Henderson. We gratefully acknowledge permission to reprint.

     I would also like to take the opportunity to acknowledge the continuing support of my research and educational endeavors by the J.M. Kaplan Fund, the Earhart Foundation, the Weaver family, and the Mercatus Center at George Mason University. In addition, the very able and cheerful assistance of Mr. Peter Lipsey is gratefully acknowledged.
1.   Entrepreneurship can be characterized by three distinct moments: serendipity (discovery), search (conscious deliberation), and seizing the opportunity for profit.
2.   The search for solutions to this elusive goal generated some of the most innovative work of the Austrian economists and led to the development in the 1970s and 1980s of the literature on free banking by F.A. Hayek, Lawrence White, George Selgin, Kevin Dowd. Kurt Schuler, and Steven Horwitz.
3.   Propositions 8 and 9 form the core of the Austrian theory of the business cycle, which explains how credit expansion by the government generates a malinvestment in the capital structure during the boom period that must be corrected in the bust phase. In contemporary economics, Roger Garrison is the leading expositor of this theory.
4.   Not all spontaneous orders are beneficial and, thus, this proposition should not be read as an example of a Panglossian fallacy. Whether individuals pursuing their own self-interest generate public benefits depends on the institutional conditions within which they pursue their interests. Both the invisible hand of market efficiency and the "tragedy of the commons" are results of individuals striving to pursue their individual interests; but in one social setting this generates social benefits, whereas in the other it generates losses. New institutional economics has refocused professional attention on how sensitive social outcomes are to the institutional setting within which individuals interact. It is important, however, to realize that classical political economists and the early neoclassical economists all recognized the basic point of new institutional economists, and that it was only the mid-twentieth-century fascination with formal proofs of general competitive equilibrium, on the one hand, and the Keynesian preoccupation with aggregate

variables, on the other, that tended to cloud the institutional preconditions required for social cooperation.

Further Reading

General reading

Boettke, P., ed. *The Elgar Companion to Austrian Economics*. Aldershot, UK and Brookfield, VT, USA: Edward Elgar, 1994.
Dolan, E., ed. *The Foundations of Modern Austrian Economics*. Mission, KS: Sheed and Ward, 1976.

Classic readings

Böhm-Bawerk, E. *Capital and Interest*. 3 vols. 1883. South Holland, ILL: Libertarian Press, 1956.
Hayek, F.A. *Individualism and Economic Order*. Chicago: University of Chicago Press, 1948.
Kirzner, I. *Competition and Entrepreneurship*. Chicago: University of Chicago Press, 1973.
Menger, C. *Principles of Economics*. 1871. New York: New York University Press, 1976.
Mises, L. von. *Human Action: A Treatise on Economics*. New Haven: Yale University Press, 1949.
O'Driscoll, G. and M. Rizzo. *The Economics of Time and Ignorance*. Oxford: Basil Blackwell, 1985.
Rothbard, M. *Man, Economy and State*. 2 vols. New York: Van Nostrand Press, 1962.
Vaughn, K. *Austrian Economics in America*. Cambridge: Cambridge University Press, 1994.

History of the Austrian school of economics

Boettke, P. and Peter Leeson. "The Austrian School of Economics: 1950–2000." In Jeff Biddle and Warren Samuels, eds., *The Blackwell Companion to the History of Economic Thought*. London: Blackwell, 2003.
Hayek, F.A. "Economic Thought VI: The Austrian School." In *International Encyclopedia of the Social Sciences*. New York: Macmillan, 1968.
Machlup, F. "Austrian Economics." In *Encyclopedia of Economics*. New York: McGraw-Hill, 1982.

PART I

THE SCIENCE OF ECONOMICS

1 Only individuals choose
*Anthony J. Evans**

1.1 Introduction

When Margaret Thatcher declared that, "there is no such thing as society", she seemed to exemplify a political philosophy that praised self-centred individualism ahead of collective solidarity. If ever a phrase became synonymous with a deeply contested economic doctrine, that was it. But intentionally or otherwise, she stumbled upon one of the most important philosophical discussions of the twentieth century. If only individuals choose, then the way to understand cultural concepts such as "society" is through an analysis of individual action. It might appear counterintuitive, but if we lose sight of individuals, "society" has no meaning.

The degree to which individuals are the products of their social environment is one of the perennial issues of the social sciences. To what extent should we place the individual at the centre of economic analysis? What causal role should we give to cultural factors? Was Adolphe Quetelet right to claim that, "society prepares the crime, and the guilty person is only the instrument"?[1] This debate lies at the heart of not only how social scientists should conduct research, but also our understanding of how free individuals conduct human action, and thus confronts our conception of the human condition.

Both the genesis and subsequent rise of methodological individualism are indelibly tied to the development of Austrian economics; however, the most common use has strayed from these routes. Rather than provide both a defence and yet another restatement of one particular interpretation of methodological individualism, I will acknowledge the inherent ambiguity of the term, and argue that one particular *form* of methodological individualism – Joseph Agassi's concept of *institutional individualism* (1975) – is not only a more consistent and accurate label for the traditional Austrian method, but also a more useful engine for future enquiry.

1.2 Individuals are the building blocks of the social sciences

"Methodological individualism" is the practice of viewing social entities as the products of individual action, and consequently putting individual choice at the centre of research technique. The term was first used by Joseph Schumpeter (in German in 1908 and in English in 1909) (Heath, 2005; Hodgson, 2007), although he was chiefly labelling a concept previously devised by his contemporary, Max Weber. Weber's interpretative sociology saw the singular individual as a basic unit, or "atom" of social research, and Schumpeter outlined how the premise of methodological individualism puts the individual at the starting point of an explanation for economic relationships. However, Carl Menger, the founder of the Austrian school of economics, had more involvement in the generation of the concept. Menger and Weber were influenced by each other and there's no reason to believe that the primary postulate of methodological individualism was any different. Although Menger never used this term, his "atomistic method" of pure theory clearly views individual choice as the building block of the (unified) social sciences. He tried to find the laws that built emergent economic phenomena from their "true elements" of individual action, and this approach became synonymous with Austrians, who deemed that, "we have here two tasks for economics. . .the tracing out of the unintended consequences of action. . .[and] the requirement that it [economics] make the world around us intelligible in terms of human action" (Kirzner, 1976a, p. 41). Ludwig Lachmann also stressed that explanations of social phenomena must ultimately lead to human plans, but it is important to make a distinction between whether this is true only in principle, and whether it should be followed literally. In other words aggregate statements such as "Romania has decided to join the EU" might be used as shorthand, or as provisional statements, but subsequent explanations should in principle be consistent with the expectations and actions of those individuals who brought it about.

Having said this, methodological individualism does not imply that we should favour the individual over the collective – it is primarily a position on what form of explanation should take place. Such is the breadth of this tenet it is shared with Analytic Marxists, who can accept the methodological position absent of any political (or ideological) connotation. Demonstrating this apolitical grounding, Jon Elster defines methodological individualism as "the doctrine that all social phenomena (their structure and their change) are in principle explicable only in terms of individuals – their properties, goals and beliefs" (Elster, 1982, p. 453).

This is in contrast to the methodological position of *holism*, which accounts for individual agency by appealing to larger wholes. This approach implies that societal phenomena determine individual preferences, and social facts exist above and beyond the constituent, individual parts. Indeed, society might even be seen as form of organic entity – an agent with its own rights, claims and interests. Karl Popper's concern was that a conflict between individual plans and "phantom" collective plans gives rise to totalitarianism; however, a more common form of holism is to view this organic entity in biological terms, as an evolutionary (or perhaps mimetic) phenomenon. But it is important to realize that methodological holism grew out of Emile Durkheim's endeavour to make sociology an autonomous science. Although this utilized a method consistent with the natural sciences, this required a distinct subject matter to avoid being reduced to psychology. The implication is that the subjective understanding of human action is possibly superfluous to an explanation of social activity, because it is the web of social relations in which they find themselves that ultimately determine the outcome.

The genesis of methodological individualism stems from the Austrian/ Weber school of interpretative sociology[2] and "through the Austrian trinity of Schumpeter, Hayek and von Mises, the term 'methodological individualism' was exported from economics into other disciplines" (Hodgson, 2007, p. 1). But before looking at the interdisciplinary evolution of the term, it is important that we first focus on the history within the domain of economics.

1.3 The rise and fall of *Homo economicus*

Neoclassical economics is built upon foundations of methodological individualism, where the economic system is assumed to be the aggregation of independent agents, and these agents constitute the basic unit of analysis. They are a-cultural beings that respond rationally, predictably and passively to changing prices. However, the peculiar characteristics of these agents (their tastes and expectations) are largely treated as givens, and the formation of these characteristics is explicitly ignored. Complex social phenomena are reduced to being merely the aggregated outcomes of individual optimization analysis. It follows the Robinson Crusoe method of abstracting from a social environment to concentrate on isolated choice, but instead of using this as a basis to contrast with the outcomes generated by complex interaction, it uses it as the basis of aggregation. This *atomistic* form of methodological individualism assumes that one can generate a conception of man that is pre-social, and use this for predicting the outcomes when such agents interact. However, "no significant explanation of social phenomena in terms of individuals alone has been advanced. In practice there is always a social and relational residual that is not reduced entirely to individual terms" (Hodgson, 2007, note 12., p. 8). This suggests that the social sciences cannot reduce social phenomena to psychological factors, and that psychology has an irreducibly social dimension (Heath, 2005).

In this regard, Mises' notion of purposeful human action and Robbins' notion of economizing man are both compatible with definitions of methodological individualism (since market phenomena are seen to be the outcome of the interaction of individuals), yet the *form* of methodological

individualism differs substantially (Kirzner, 1976b). Indeed it is remarkable how so many economists continue to falsely attribute the strong, neoclassical form of methodological individualism to Austrians, considering
that Austrians have explicitly demonstrated the differences (Hayek, 1948).
Mises referred to *Homo economicus* as a "fiction" (1949, p. 64), preferring
to view man as an active, creative force – warts and all:

> Economics deals with the real actions of real men. Its theorems refer neither to
> ideal nor to perfect men, neither to the phantom of a fabulous economic man
> (homo oeconomicus) nor to the statistical notion of an average man (homme
> moyen). Man with all his weaknesses and limitations, every man as he lives and
> acts, is the subject matter of catallactics. (Mises, 1949, p. 646)

Whilst methodological individualism does not automatically imply
epistemic positivism, there can be no doubt that the positivist hegemony – spurred by the allure of scientific authority – led to a distinction
between the neoclassicist "*Homo economicus*" and the Austrian "purposeful actor". Zwirn (2007) shows that atomistic individualism is compatible
with a methodological premise that individuals are independent of context
because in the natural sciences, laboratories can create such isolation.
But this assumes that the methods of the natural and social sciences can
be the same. The subsequent failings of positivism within economics
have generated an opportunity to move away from formal models, and
evidence of this occurring can be found across a broad range of trends:
the rise of micro foundations (which necessitates an end to free floating
aggregations); the expectations revolution (putting individual cognition at
the heart of research); and the rise of more qualitative methods (especially
those that permit interpretative access, such as ethnography). By stressing
individual action, interaction, and therefore strategic behaviour, the rise
of game theory in particular was seen by many to be the antidote to the
formal models that expunged acting man from economic analysis. And
finally the expansion of behaviouralism (particularly behavioural finance)
has concentrated on the nature of human choices and heterogeneous and
multifaceted nature of agency. Indeed the main lessons of experimental
research are that (1) *Homo economicus* does not improve our understanding of real world human action; (2) the institutional context of choice can
heavily influence the outcomes of interaction.

As we have seen, there has been a divergence in the use of methodological individualism within economics, and this chasm is one of the defining
characteristics of a unique paradigm of Austrian economics. It is also
important to realize that the development of economics has not been
uniform, and that a number of influential scholars have used a weaker
concept of methodological individualism than the dominant mainstream.

The likes of James Buchanan, Mancur Olson, Ronald Coase, Vernon Smith and Douglass North all pursue methodological individualism, but allow social institutions as core variables and a necessary part of the enquiry.

Many criticisms of methodological individualism are valid, but only in as much as they are targeted upon the "strong", or atomistic form. Neoclassical analysis has generated a rich "economics of life" but only by neglecting "the life of economics". I suggest that clarification needs to be made along two margins: first, to make the ontological position explicit; and second, to clarify the causal role of institutional forces. Although I will take material primarily from Austrian economists, it is important to reiterate that this is an issue that encompasses all social sciences. Whilst the discipline of economics might appear to be making a methodological U turn, I do not wish to imply that this is the entire story. Throughout this process other disciplines – sociology and political science especially – have developed and refined the notion of methodological individualism. In other words, an interdisciplinary debate has occurred outside the boundaries of economics that has demonstrated that the distinction between individualism and holism is too simplistic. There is actually an entire spectrum of methodological positions that fall within the label "methodological individualism", and the real debate is regarding what *form* one should pursue. The debate is actually a *trialogue* between atomists, institutionalists and holists.

1.4 Methodological individualism is indeed grounded in a conception of reality

Critics of methodological individualism have a valid point when they challenge the reasoning behind this foundational premise. Why is it that individual action is often seen as being the building block of social science? As mentioned previously, Schumpeter's definition of methodological individualism isn't free from ambiguity, and although Mises devotes a chapter in his magnum opus *Human Action* (1949) to the issue, he fails to clarify the point from a purely methodological position. The reason for this is that he entangles the methodological prescription that "social phenomena should be explained in terms of individual plans" with an ontological justification that "only individuals *have* plans". Udehn (2002) refers to this as the "ontological twist", but the key point is that Mises recognized that methodological individualism could only make sense within a corresponding ontological premise. Mises saw an "insurmountable obstacle" in taking collective units as the starting point due to the fact that at any point in time individuals belong to a number of different (and possibly conflicting) social groups. He views the postulate of individualism as a tool to deal with "the multiplicity of coexisting social units and their mutual antagonisms" (1949, p. 43). Far from denying the relevance of social wholes, Mises saw attention to individuals as the only way to study this because, "The life of a collective is lived in the actions of individuals constituting its body" (ibid., p. 42). Indeed:

> Individuals and their choice-making activity serves as the beginning of the Austrian analysis not because of a rejection of collective entities, but because *it is only by interpreting social entities as the composite outcome of individual activity that we can come to understand their meaning and significance.* (Boettke, 1995 p. 27; emphasis in original)[3]

Mises makes explicit mention of the ontological foundations of his conception of methodological individualism: "it is always single individuals who say *We*; even if they say it in chorus, it yet remains an utterance of single individuals" (1949, p. 44). To paraphrase Jon Elster, one cannot presuppose a purpose without identifying a person whose purpose we are presupposing! But what is the basis for this concept of reality?

As previously mentioned, both defences and critiques of methodological individualism have been based on an assumption of shared methods across scientific disciplines. Yet Frank Knight was just one of the broad stream of economists influenced by the Austrians to argue that the social sciences and the natural sciences are fundamentally distinct. We possess so-called "knowledge from within" about economic activity; not through observation, but through intuition – the intuition we possess as economic actors. Economic propositions are derived from our unique capacity for self-awareness, coupled with an empathy that can relate that knowledge to our fellow human beings. For Max Weber the concept of action was important because of our interpretative access that creates an ability to comprehend the underlying motives of other people. The fact that we can appreciate the intentions and plans of others (and thus "fuse horizons" with our subject matter) provides a source of knowledge entirely lacking within the natural sciences. In alignment with the likes of John Watkins, we – as individuals – have "direct access" to facts about individuals, whereas any knowledge we might possess about social wholes must merely be derivative (Udehn, 2002, p. 489).

According to Martin Hollis, rationalism provides an epistemological unity of mankind and thus the *possibility* of universal beliefs (1994). As Vincent Ostrom says, "We, as individuals, use our own resources as human beings to attempt to understand others, presuming as Hobbes did that there is a basic similitude of thoughts and passions characteristic of all mankind" (1997, p. 105). Therefore, Hodgson (2007) is quite correct to argue that methodological individualism isn't simply a neutral methodological device. It has an implicit assumption about the form of social reality, and this should be more explicitly acknowledged: it is a methodological premise based on an ontological truism that "all social phenomena are created, or caused, by individual human beings" (Udehn, 2002, p. 489). Mises and Hayek were clear that methods should correspond to realistic conceptions of reality, and this clearly distinguishes the Austrian use of methodological individualism from both atomism and holism.

1.5 There is an institutional form of methodological individualism

The second way in which Austrian economics provides a unique foundation for a clarified form of methodological individualism – the role of institutions – has been directly vindicated by the advances made by an array of methodologists over subsequent years. In short, it demonstrates that methodological individualism does *not* presuppose atomistic, autonomous agents, but allows for the causal role of social customs. It incorporates social constructs as both the products of, and shapers of individual choice. Early Austrians explicitly acknowledged the causal importance of social institutions, and reject the premise that the subject matters of economics are isolated agents:

> When he [man] is born, he does not enter the world in general as such, but a definite environment. . . Inheritance and environment direct a man's actions. . . He lives not simply as a man *in abstracto*; he lives as a son of his family, his race, his people, and his age; as a citizen of his country; as a member of a definite social group. . . His ideology is what his environment enjoins upon him. (Mises, 1949, p. 46)

But acknowledging the role of social institutions upon individual choice does not lead to inevitability of action, a lack of free will, or social determinism. On the contrary, the ubiquity of social groups means that a conscious desire over which to subscribe to and when is inevitable. Rather than institutions acting purely as constraints on human choice, they are also its manifestation. Routines, habits and customs are our guideposts, but of our own making since we consent to adopting them. Collective phenomena might well act as an autopilot for some of us, but the ego remains behind the wheel. Perhaps tacitly, perhaps by implicit consent; we choose to let institutions think for us.

Indeed this institutionally contingent application of methodological individualism has been the driving force of Austrian applied research. For Mises, social action should be understood as a special case of human action. Whether the focus has been on uncovering the evolution of money, prices, languages or law, such social institutions have provided the core objects of empirical enquiry.

The institutional form of methodological individualism is also impera-
tive if economists wish to generate theories of social change. The holist
position views institutions mainly as constraints or determinants to individual behaviour. The atomistic position views institutions as being little
more than shorthand for various forms of individual action. It should be
clear that a hybrid approach is required to mediate between these two
extremities, since it is the *interplay* between institutional analysis (assessments of the incentive structure) and institutional reform (creative action)
that generates social change.

Originating from Karl Popper, the term "institutional individualism"
was first used (with some degree of ambiguity) by Joseph Agassi (1960),
and he offered a fuller presentation in Agassi (1975). Although it has
often been presented as an alternative to methodological individualism,
I follow the likes of Ian C. Jarvie, who saw institutional individualism as
a particular form of methodological individualism; one that treats social
institutions as being as tangible as our physical surroundings.

Following Toboso (2001) I would like to present three key propositions:

- Purposes and interests can only be pursued by individuals.
- Institutions – the formal and informal rules that individuals face in
  a decision-making context – affect interactions and therefore must
  form part of the explanatory phenomenon.
- Institutional change is a consequence of individual interactions, and
  takes place within wider institutional frameworks.

What this implies is that "no impersonal active entity with apparent aims,
interests and driving forces of its own is included in the discourse as an
explanatory variable, nor is any other impersonal systemic factor that
possesses its own dynamics for which the responsibility may not, even
indirectly, be attributed to any person" (Toboso, 2001, p. 10). But this
differs substantially from strong (i.e., atomistic) methodological individualism because "besides the individual action. . . this institutional structure
must be taken into account" (ibid., p. 14; emphasis added). If material
conditions are not enough to determine behaviour, we must explicitly
include social institutions; social embeddedness must be at the vanguard
of research rather than an afterthought. To recap, this schema asserts the
following: only individuals are capable of choice; institutions affect our
choices; and institutions evolve through human action.[4]

Hodgson (2007) rejects the term "institutional individualism" because
"it gives one half of the story adjective status whilst the other half has
the prestige of being the noun" (p. 9). But the reason that individualism
should have explanatory priority is simply due to the primary position that

only individuals choose. Structures and individuals are both required facets of social explanation, but whilst social phenomena are *not* strictly reducible to the latter, social structures are always a product of, and directed by, individual purposes and plans.

1.6 Conclusion

The term "methodological individualism" is problematic for a number of reasons. As we have seen, its definition has evolved over time to the point where it has become compatible with a broad range of conflicting methodological techniques. The predominant usage suggests a purely *methodological* primacy for the individual over the collective, and implies that a proper application should/will actually reduce all social events to the individual level – despite this being both impossible and unnecessary. However, the "institutional individualism" form emphasizes how individual choice is neither isolated from, nor wholly determined by, our social environment. It clearly distinguishes rich, institutional approaches from the strong forms associated with both atomistic individualism and holistic individualism.

Austrians such as Menger, Mises, Hayek and Kirzner utilized a fundamentally different form of methodological individualism to neoclassical economists, and this chapter has argued that (1) their methodological position entailed an ontological justification that should be more explicit; (2) they gave room to causal explanations that stemmed from non-reducible institutional factors.[5] These two issues are separate sides of the same coin, since it is the very existence of social institutions that gives rise to intersubjective meaning (Boettke, 1995, p. 28). Indeed, a conception of individuals as purposeful actors permits the study of spontaneous orders, and provides the methodological techniques that *allow* us to marvel at how, through markets, resources are allocated without the need for central planning. Although there is no automatic link between methodological and political individualism, classical liberal political economy – and the social institutions of a decentralized market economy – can only be properly understood by recourse to methodological individualism. This primary proposition is a broad tenet united around the premise that only individuals have purposes, plans, or choice. When put this way it becomes clear why Jon Elster labelled it "trivially true". Although some criticize definitions that are "so broad that it would be difficult to find a social scientist who disagrees" (Hodgson, 2007, p. 5), there's no reason to reject consensus in favour of hullabaloo. The strength of the concept is its plainness, and whilst being trivially true, the implications of a consistent application are immense – both in terms of the procedures of social science but also the notion of individual agency. The bottom line of this starting point is that we can only attribute meaning to social phenomena through the lens of an institutionally contingent form of methodological individualism. Only individuals choose. . .and we do so through institutions.

Notes

*   I appreciate the constructive comments of Perri 6, Paul Dragos Aligica, Andre Azevedo Alves, Peter Boettke, Andy Denis, T. Clark Durant, Geoffrey Hodgson, John Meadowcroft, Ioana Negru and Nikolai Wenzel. All errors of content and delivery are my own.
1.   This quote is from Quetelet's most influential book, *Sur l'homme et le developpement de ses facultés, essai d'une physique sociale*, published in 1835.
2.   Note that Mises uses the term "praxeology" to mean what we understand as sociology.
3.   The myriad of cultural traditions, social relationships, legal rules, the norms of epistemic communities are what constitute "society". It is precisely to understand how these emerge and develop that the Austrians stress the primacy of the individual, since it is only at this level that *meaning* can be attributed to social phenomena. "Methodological individualism, far from contesting the significance of such collective wholes, considers it as one of its main tasks to describe and to analyze their becoming and their disappearing, their changing structure, and their operation. And it chooses the only method fitted to solve this problem satisfactorily" (Mises, 1949, p. 42).
4.   If this attention to institutions is pursued even further, we can investigate the role of social *structures*. This structural form of institutional individualism (stemming from the likes of Reinhard Wippler or James Coleman) is beyond the scope of this chapter, but note that a relaxation of the strict/atomistic form of methodological individualism is a prerequisite for a discussion concerning these issues.
5.   This chapter does not intend to delve into the subtleties (and possible conflictions) between these scholars. However, it is written with an attempt to be compatible with such discussions.

References

Agassi, Joseph. "Methodological Individualism". *The British Journal of Sociology* Vol. 11 No. 3 (1960): 244–720.
Agassi, Joseph. "Institutional Individualism". *The British Journal of Sociology* Vol. 26 No. 2 (1975): 144–55.
Boettke, Peter J. "Individuals and Institutions". In David L. Prychitko (ed.) *Individuals, Institutions and Interpretations: Hermeneutics Applied to Economics*, Aldershot: Avebury, 1995.
Elster, Jon. "Marxism, Functionalism and Game Theory". *Theory and Society* Vol. 11 No. 4 (1982): 453–82.
Hayek, Freidrich A. "Individualism: True and False". In *Individualism and Economic Order*, Chicago: University of Chicago Press, 1948.
Heath, Joseph. "Methodological Individualism". In *Stanford Encyclopaedia of Philosophy*, 2005, available at: http://plato.Stanford.edu/entries/methodological-individualism; accessed 18 January 2010.
Hodgson, Geoffrey M. "Meanings of Methodological Individualism". *Journal of Economic Methodology* Vol. 14 No. 2 (2007): 211–26, available at: http://www.geoffrey-hodgson. info/user/image/meanmethind-free.pdf, pp. 1–13; accessed 18 January 2010.
Hollis, Martin. *The Philosophy of the Social Sciences*. Cambridge, UK: Cambridge University Press, 1994.
Kirzner, Israel M. "On the Method of Austrian Economics". In E.G. Dolan (ed.) *The Foundations of Modern Austrian Economics*, Kansas City: Sheed and Ward, 1976a.
Kirzner, Israel M. "Equilibrium versus Market Process". In E.G. Dolan (ed.) *The Foundations of Modern Austrian Economics*, Kansas City: Sheed and Ward, 1976b.

Mises, Ludwig von. *Human Action*. London: William Hodge and Company Limited, 1949.

Ostrom, Vincent. *The Meaning of Democracy and the Vulnerability of Democracies*. Ann Arbor: University of Michigan Press, 1997.

Toboso, Fernando. "Institutional Individualism and Institutional Change: The Search for a *Middle Way* Mode of Explanation". *Cambridge Journal of Economics* Vol. 25 No. 6 (2001): 765–83, available at: http://www.uv.es/~ftoboso/ipe/toboso-cambri01.pdf, pp. 1–25; accessed 18 January 2010.

Udehn, Lars. "The Changing Face of Methodological Individualism". *Annual Review of Sociology* Vol. 28 No. 1 (2002): 479–507.

Zwirn, Gregor. "Methodological Individualism or Methodological Atomism: The Case of Friedrich Hayek". *History of Political Economy* Vol. 39 No. 1 (2007): 47–80.

2 Economics as the study of coordination and exchange
Christopher J. Coyne*

2.1 Introduction

In his 1963 presidential address to the Southern Economic Association, James Buchanan asked, "What Should Economists Do?" In doing so, Buchanan was challenging the prevailing orthodoxy that treated the economic problem of society as one of allocating scarce resources among competing ends. According to Buchanan, the allocation paradigm mis-construed the nature of the science of economics as well as the role of the economist. Instead of focusing on the issue of allocation, Buchanan argued that economists should focus on exchange relationships and the institutions within which exchange takes place.

According to Buchanan, the allure of scientism tends to pull economists away from the exchange paradigm and toward the allocation paradigm. The allocation paradigm focuses on the "problem" of how to allocate scarce resources, which in turn presupposes a solution to be found by economists. The result is that the study of economics becomes one of computation and maximization instead of focusing on purposeful human action and the process through which individuals interact and coordinate their often differing plans and goals. The allocation paradigm, Buchanan argued, drained the study of economics of purposeful individual action, as well as the process of learning and choice. Choice is fundamentally a human endeavor plagued with uncertainty instead of a mechanical pro-cedure performed by automatons. The study of economics is not one of maximization, but instead one of understanding the various institutional contexts within which imperfect humans must interact and exchange.

The message delivered by Buchanan in his presidential address was not new. Emphasis on coordination, interaction, and exchange was prominent in the work of David Hume and Adam Smith, in the writings of non-Ricardian English economists such as Bishop Whatley and Philip Wicksteed, and in the work of French economists such as A.R.J. Turgot and Jean-Baptiste Say. Further, these themes have always been a central focus for those writing in the Austrian tradition, including Carl Menger, Ludwig von Mises, F.A. Hayek, and Israel Kirzner.

The focus of this chapter is on the proposition that the study of economics

and the market order is fundamentally about exchange behavior and the institutions within which exchanges take place. This proposition frames the study of economics by focusing our attention on purposeful individual action, the conditions for interaction and exchange, and the process of discovery and learning. Specifically, the exchange paradigm draws attention to the process through which imperfect individuals, with differing interests and ends, enter into cooperative agreements with others. This paradigm forces economists to focus on the emergence and continual evolution of a complex array of relationships facilitating interaction, bargaining, agreements, and trades. This stands in stark contrast to the allocation paradigm that is void of any uncertainty, human error, or learning. Within this context, a solution to the allocation problem emerges through a set of exogenous variables instead of through an endogenous process.

This chapter proceeds as follows. The next section briefly discusses the main differences between the allocation paradigm and the exchange paradigm. Section 2.3 discusses the science of catallactics in relation to the study of economics. Section 2.4 considers two different notions of "coordination" used by economists. Section 2.5 considers the importance of institutions in the exchange paradigm. Section 2.6 concludes with a discussion of the continuing relevance of the exchange paradigm.

2.2   The allocation paradigm vs. the exchange paradigm

Meir Kohn (2004) traces the allocation paradigm to the work of Paul Samuelson and John Hicks.[1] Samuelson sought to restate economic theory in terms of mathematics in order to provide clarity and precision in economic arguments. Hicks sought to recast economics in terms of "value," which focuses on relative prices and the allocation of resources. The Walrasian framework, which attempts to analyze all markets simultaneously, is perhaps the best example of the theory of value. As Kohn points out, while the goals of Samuelson and Hicks were different, they complemented each other nicely. Hicks's focus on the theory of value fitted well with Samuelson's desire to mathematize economics. The ultimate result of this endeavor was that "adherents of the Hicks-Samuelson research program came to see the theory of value as *being* economics; they saw the two as identical and indistinguishable" (Kohn, 2004, p. 305; italics original). In other words, as the allocation paradigm took hold, the study of economics became synonymous with the notion of equilibrium with a central focus on the allocation of resources. The result was that the issues of exchange, institutions, and the process of coordination were pushed by the wayside.

For purposes of clarity, it makes sense to review the key similarity, as well as the main difference, between the allocation paradigm and the exchange paradigm. The main similarity is that both paradigms focus on the implications of the assumption that individuals act purposefully while realizing the central importance of gains from exchange. The main difference between the two paradigms is mainly due to the disparity in the assumptions regarding the outcomes of exchange (Kohn, 2004, p. 308).[2] The main assumption of the allocation paradigm is that the outcome of exchange is an equilibrium where all gains from exchange are exhausted. In other words, the result of exchange is a static equilibrium. The allocation paradigm assumes that trading takes place in an environment characterized by price taking, homogeneous goods, and perfect information. The main implication is that there are no informational issues associated with exchange and trade becomes costless. Further, the prereconciliation of plans means that there is no uncertainty and no need for the discovery of the unknown as individuals are aware of all possible states of the world. The core assumptions of the allocation paradigm allow its adherents to assume away the importance of institutions for exchange. Within a setting characterized by price taking, homogeneous goods, and perfect information there is no role for institutions. There is no role for such things as informal rules or norms (e.g., trust, social capital, the threat of ostracism, etc.) to facilitate trading relationships and no role for government to establish or enforce formal rules.

In contrast to the allocation paradigm, the exchange paradigm concludes that a static equilibrium is never achieved in real-world economies. Imperfect information, human error, and entrepreneurial discovery lead to constant changes in prices, goods, and services. Further, the exchange paradigm is characterized by the recognition of varying market structures, heterogeneous goods, and imperfect information. Instead of assuming that prices are given, the exchange paradigm focuses on the process through which prices emerge and change over time. Contrary to the price taker assumption of the allocation paradigm, the exchange paradigm emphasizes that prices emerge through the process of interaction, exchange, and competition (see Hayek, 2002). The implication is that prices are not exogenously given, but instead emerge endogenously through exchange.

In the exchange paradigm, an emphasis is placed on the entrepreneur as the central mechanism through which coordination takes place. Entrepreneurship entails an alertness to profit opportunities as well as a willingness to bet on perceived opportunities. Entrepreneurs drive economic change through arbitrage (i.e., buying low and selling high) and innovation (i.e., improvements in existing products or production techniques or the introduction of a new product or production technique).

A main implication of the exchange paradigm is that the tools of economics allow for pattern predictions, but not point predictions. In other words, economics provides the means to make general predictions regarding the pattern of relative prices and the economic process under differing conditions. However, economics does not provide the tools to predict specific outcomes or to discuss a unique static equilibrium.

A final characteristic of the exchange paradigm is the emphasis on imperfect information and dispersed knowledge. In reality, individuals are rarely aware of all of the relevant market participants and opportunities for exchange. Further, many interactions and exchanges are characterized by information asymmetries. Adherents of the exchange paradigm focus on understanding the mechanisms that allow individuals to overcome these imperfections and asymmetries. In other words, a central question asked by adherents of the exchange paradigm is: under what institutional arrangements can individuals best learn about exchange opportunities and overcome issues associated with asymmetric information and dispersed knowledge? As Section 2.5 will discuss in more detail, the role of institutions, as well as institutional change and evolution, is central to the exchange paradigm because institutions frame all interactions and exchanges.

2.3   Catallactics – the science of exchange

In considering why the allocation paradigm emerged as the dominant framework of orthodox economics, James Buchanan identified the use of the word "economics" as part of the problem (1964, pp. 215–16). According to Buchanan, focusing on economizing behavior leads economists to think in terms of maximization and allocation instead of in terms of coordination and exchange. In place of the word "economics," Buchanan suggested the use of "catallaxy" or "symbiotics" to draw attention to interaction, association, and exchange. The term catallaxy derives from the Greek verb *katallattein* (or *katallassein*) which means "to exchange," and "to admit into the community," as well as "to change from enemy into friend" (see Hayek, 1976, pp. 108–9).

In drawing attention to the role of rhetoric in framing the way economists approach their subject, Buchanan is one in a long line of thinkers to emphasize the relevance of the notion of catallaxy. Reverend Richard Whatley first suggested "catallactics" as a replacement for "economics" in 1831. Whatley's call for a shift in terminology was driven by his criticism of the narrow focus of the study of economics as the science of wealth (Rothbard, 1987). Whatley called for economists to move behind the study of wealth and to broaden their focus to the study of exchange.

Ludwig von Mises was the first economist to extensively integrate the notion of catallaxy into the study of economics. According to Mises, the price system and broader market economy are best understood as a catallaxy and the science that studies the market order falls under the domain of catallactics. Catallactics is part of the wider discipline of praxeology with a specific focus on "all market phenomena with their roots, ramifications, and consequences" (Mises [1949] 1996, p. 233). Catallaxy is grounded in purposeful human action and focuses on how market activity results in the emergence of exchange ratios and prices (ibid., p. 234).

Following Mises, Hayek (1976) also placed a central emphasis on the concept of catallaxy. Hayek was dissatisfied with the use of the term "economy" because "An economy, in the strict sense of the word in which a household, a farm, or an enterprise can be called economies, consists of a complex of activities by which a given set of means is allocated in accordance with a unitary plan among the competing ends according to their relative importance" (ibid., p. 107). For Hayek, the central issue is that the term "economy" is often used to refer not to a single enterprise, but rather to the array of networks and interactions between a wide variety of individual economies. However, the numerous networks and interactions of individual actors are not governed by a single hierarchy of ends like those of an individual economy. Instead, the array of economies consists of many individual actors each with a different hierarchy of interests and ends. Given this, Hayek preferred the term "catallaxy" to "economy" because the former refers to the order resulting from "the mutual adjustment of many individual economies in the market" (ibid., p. 109).

The use of "catallaxy" as an alternative to the use of "economy" is more than mere semantics. Words have meaning and those meanings are important in framing the analytical focus of economists. Catallactics focuses our analytical attention on exchange relationships, including the emergence and evolution of those relationships and the institutions within which exchange activity takes place.

2.4   Two types of coordination

A central tenet of Austrian economics is that the study of economics is fundamentally about exchange behavior. Exchange requires the coordination of the different plans and ends of individuals. Given this, a clear understanding of the concept of "coordination" is of central importance. As Klein (1997) notes, two notions of coordination have emerged in the economics literature. These two meanings have important implications for the way we frame and study economic issues.

The first use of the term coordination is best illustrated by the work of Nobel Laureate Thomas Schelling. In Schelling's use of the term, coordination entails "something we hope to achieve in our interaction with others" (Klein, 1997, p. 324). This type of coordination can be illustrated by a simple "coordination game" whereby individuals try to coordinate their actions with the actions of others. Common examples of such games include driving on the same side of the road or meeting at some focal location.

The second use of coordination is grounded in the notion of spontaneous order and can be found in the writings of Adam Smith, Carl Menger, F.A. Hayek, and Michael Polanyi. The notion of spontaneous order refers to an order that emerges from purposeful human action, but not from human design. Common examples of spontaneous orders include the emergence of money and language. These emergent orders facilitate coordination, interaction, and exchange.

Those focusing on the second type of coordination recognize that face-to-face interaction entails coordination between individuals as emphasized by the first type of coordination. Further, they recognize that individuals employ certain common norms and heuristics to achieve their ends. However, the second use of coordination is broader than the first because it focuses on the meta-order, as well as the fact that individuals must act based on context-specific knowledge of "time and place" (see Hayek, 1945).

The second use of coordination recognizes that in many cases individuals are not aware of the existence of other specific actors or their specific ends. For example, the entrepreneur produces a good or product while not necessarily knowing the specific individuals who will utilize the good or service in future periods. As Klein notes, in the context of the second use of coordination the individual "is responding to price signals and local opportunities; he is trying to gain lucrative insights. . . He does not perceive himself to be playing a coordination game with myriad distant people" (1997, p. 325). While the first use of coordination can be illustrated in a standard coordination game, the second use of coordination cannot be modeled using game theory because it refers to the broader meta-order consisting of numerous actors who aren't directly interacting with others.

According to Klein, the first (Schelling) type of coordination is evident from the actor's point of view while the second (Smith/Menger/Hayek/Polanyi) type of coordination is abstract from the actor's point of view (ibid., pp. 326–7). While the first type of coordination yields results that are agreeable to those interacting, the second type of coordination generates a form of general overarching order that is pleasing to an exogenous observer. The first type of coordination is focused on specific interactions (e.g., driving on the same side of the road) while the second type of coordination is concerned with the broader "meta-order" including the social rules that generate that order. From this standpoint, the second type of coordination goes beyond examining the recurring conventions that allow individuals to coordinate with others in specific situations (e.g., picking a focal meeting time and place). It is not that these conventions are unimportant, but rather that they offer limited insight into broader and more complex meta-order.

When economists do recognize the importance of coordination, they tend to focus on the first (Schelling) type of coordination while neglecting the second type (Smith/Menger/Hayek/Polanyi). One reason for this is the widespread use of game theory, which is more conducive to modeling Schelling type coordination situations. There is nothing inherently wrong with focusing on the first type of coordination, and it fits nicely with many insights from Austrian economics (see Langlois, 1994, pp. 537–8; Foss, 2000, pp. 49–51).

However, in addition to the first type of coordination, Austrians also emphasize the importance of the second type of coordination. Specifically, they focus on the importance of spontaneous order and the meta-rules within which interaction and exchange takes place. Recognizing the second type of coordination allows economists to consider the complexity of the overall system and to focus on the meta-institutions that allow, or prevent, coordination of the first type.

2.5 Institutions as the rules of the game for exchange

The two types of coordination discussed in the previous section take place within institutions. Institutions are the formal and informal rules governing human behavior, and the enforcement of these rules through the internalization of certain norms of behavior, the social pressure exerted on the individual by the group, or the power of third party enforcers who can use the threat of force on violators of the rules (North, 1990, 2005). Formal rules consist of codified rules such as constitutions, laws, regulations, bylaws, and so on, while informal rules consist of unwritten rules such as traditions, norms, and customs. Institutions create the "rules of the game" within which interaction and exchange take place. As such, they create incentives that influence human behavior for better or worse.

There is a clear connection between institutions and the two types of coordination discussed in the previous section. Solutions to the coordination "problem" associated with the first type of coordination (Schelling coordination) may be provided by certain formal and informal institutions. For example, informal norms and conventions may provide "focal points" allowing people to coordinate on a meeting time and place. Likewise, the meta-institutions of a society influence the second type of coordination (Smith/Menger/Hayek/Polanyi coordination) by creating general rules that facilitate or prevent social order. For example, Hayek (1960) argued for the importance of general meta-rules that allow individuals the freedom to engage in the discovery of what they do not already know. The foundation of Hayek's argument was the realization that knowledge of time and place was dispersed throughout society. In order for individuals to discover what they do not already know, they need the freedom to act and interact with others.

Those writing in the Austrian tradition have always placed an emphasis on the importance of institutions (see Garrouste, 2008). The same cannot be said for orthodox economics. Until the 1960s, the role of institutions was largely neglected by the mainstream of the economics profession. Ronald Coase's 1960 paper, "The Problem of Social Cost," was important in emphasizing the importance of institutions. Coase shifted the discussion of externalities from standard welfare economics to a consideration of comparative institutional arrangements. Harold Demsetz (1967) applied the insight of costs and benefits to the emergence and evolution of institutional arrangements. He argued that private property institutions would emerge where there was a net benefit to the existence of those institutions and where transaction costs were not prohibitively high.

The work of Douglass North in the 1970s (see North and Thomas, 1973) brought additional attention to the role of institutions in economic outcomes. In his work, North explored the connection between changes in institutions and such variables as population growth and political rents. During this time period, the work of Oliver Williamson (1975) on the economics of the firm also brought increasing attention to the importance of institutions. Indeed, the emergence of the subfield of "new institutional economics" is often linked to the work of Williamson. While there are many similarities between the new institutional approach and the Austrian approach to institutions, there are also some fundamental differences.

The Austrian theory of institutions focuses on the causal-genetic process through which institutions emerge and evolve. In other words, emphasis is placed on understanding the chain of events leading to the existence of institutions in their present form. Attempts to analyze institutions within the neoclassical framework tend to neglect this process and focus on the conditions necessary for equilibrium. This is because the neoclassical framework is static in nature, which prevents dynamic elements of change and evolution.

For example, while the transaction cost approach to institutions recognizes alternative institutional arrangements, those alternatives are often treated as discrete units with clear costs and benefits that are typically assumed to be known by the relevant actors. This approach tends to neglect the discovery and learning process through which institutions are discovered and adopted over time. In contrast, the Austrian approach to institutions emphasizes that the institutional process, much like the market process, consists of actors with limited knowledge who are engaged in continual discovery through trial and error.

Yet another characteristic of the Austrian theory of institutions is the central importance placed on informal institutions (e.g., culture, norms, traditions, values, belief systems etc.). Austrians emphasize that these informal institutions serve as a foundation for formal institutions. Where formal and informal institutions are aligned, the former will work in the desired manner. However, where there is a disconnect between formal and informal institutions, the former will tend to be dysfunctional (see Boettke, 2001).

For example, consider Hayek's discussion of the conditions necessary for an effective and sustainable constitutional democracy. He noted the importance of informal beliefs and dispositions, "which in more fortunate countries have made constitutions work which did not explicitly state all that they presupposed, or which did not even exist in written form" (1979, pp. 107–8). Hayek's point is that where the formal institutions are effective they codify the belief systems that are already part of a society's cultural endowment. There are numerous examples of failed efforts to establish or impose formal constitutions on societies (see Coyne, 2007). These efforts failed largely because the underlying informal institutions clashed with the formal institutions.

While highlighting these differences, it is important to note that those working in the field of new institutional economics have recently taken steps to address some of the issues raised by Austrians. For example, North (2005) has incorporated belief systems and cognitive elements into his analysis of institutional evolution and change. This includes a focus on institutional "path dependence," which recognizes that the way in which institutions and beliefs developed in past periods constrain the feasibility set of choices in the current period (see North, 1990; 2005).

The idea that "institutions matter" for economic outcomes received widespread recognition when Douglass North was awarded the Nobel Prize in 1993 for his work on institutions and institutional change. The result has been an increase in both the theoretical and empirical work on institutions. Empirical studies in this area have typically relied on two methods – detailed case studies and standard econometric techniques.

Perhaps the best illustration of the case study method is the work of Hernando de Soto. In *The Other Path* (1989), de Soto and his team of researchers compiled the list of procedures by actually going through the process of setting up a business in Peru. In doing so, de Soto was able to document how the existing formal institutional environment influenced entrepreneurial decision-making. The impetus behind the study was the recognition by de Soto that the informal sector comprised a significant portion of the Peruvian economy. He wanted to find out why Peru remained poor despite the fact that there was clearly entrepreneurial activity taking place. He concluded that the formal institutions clashed with the underlying informal institutions leading to perverse outcomes. Formal rules and regulations stifled productive entrepreneurship as entrepreneurs were forced into the underground economy. While informal institutions facilitated coordination and cooperation in the underground economy, development was limited due to constraints created by formal institutions.

There have been numerous quantitative studies exploring the role of institutions on economic outcomes. These studies typically analyze the connection between institutions (captured through some aggregate measure of institutions or institutional quality) and various outcomes. The seminal papers in this area are by Acemoglu et al. (2001; 2002) who consider the role of institutions in economic performance. After controlling for a variety of variables that could potentially explain development, the authors find that private property institutions are the main determinant for economic performance. Along similar lines, Rodrik et al. (2004) empirically analyze the role of institutions, geography, and trade on income. They find that institutions trump geography and trade in explaining differences in income across countries.

Building on this earlier work, Acemoglu and Johnson (2005) "unbundle" property institutions. They differentiate between "contracting institutions" (e.g., courts) that enforce agreements between private citizens and "property rights institutions" that protect citizens from government expropriation. They find that property rights institutions are more important than contracting institutions for economic performance. In other words, state expropriation through property rights violations are more harmful to economic performance than predation by private individuals against other private individuals. One explanation for this is that individuals can often avoid private predation through private mechanisms or by avoiding interaction with certain people. In contrast, when government engages in predation, it is difficult for citizens to avoid since the scope of government is typically broader than that of private individuals.

Empirical studies typically rely on aggregate measures of institutions or institutional quality. For example, the aforementioned studies by Acemoglu et al. utilize survey indicators of institutional quality from the International Country Risk Guide (ICRG), which provides a monthly analysis of economic, political, and financial risks for numerous countries. The ICRG places particular focus on the risk of expropriation of property. The Rodrik et al. study relies on the "Governance Matters" index, which attempts to measure the quality of public service provision, the quality of bureaucracy, the independence of civil service from political pressures, and the credibility of the government with regard to policy announcements. Other empirical studies of institutions rely on the Polity Index, which provides an overall measure of democracy or autocracy in a country. There are several concerns and issues with the use of these measures for the analysis of institutions.

For example, Glaeser et al. (2004) point out that these surveys and indices are poor measures of institutions. They contend that these measures are capturing institutional outcomes instead of providing a direct measure of actual institutions. For example, the threat of expropriation is an outcome of an array of other existing property rights institutions instead of a direct measure of those institutions. Further, they argue that the measures of political constraints do not reflect institutions, but rather the outcomes of recent elections or political events. As such, Glaeser et al. argue that the measures used in these studies fail to capture the essence of institutions that are characterized by durability and a sense of permanency.

Austrian economists would raise an additional issue with attempts at institutional aggregation. Specifically, Austrians would emphasize that efforts to provide an aggregate measure of institutions mask the underlying process through which institutions emerge and evolve. These measures abstract from purposeful action and the array of different plans that individuals pursue. Further, aggregation overlooks the discovery process through which institutions emerge and evolve. For example, the discovery of new technologies or the emergence of new norms changes the relative prices of institutional alternatives and hence their feasibility. The use of aggregate measures fails to capture the process of these relative price movements.

Recall the Austrian emphasis on catallaxy to describe the myriad associations, networks, and interactions occurring between individuals throughout society (see Section 2.3). Just as discussions of a "national economy" overlook the complex array of underlying relationships, so too do efforts to develop an aggregate measure of institutions. The social and economic phenomena underpinning informal and formal institutions are simply unobservable in statistical form.

Yet another issue with much of the empirical work on institutions is that it is largely atheoretical. In other words, many of these studies explore the correlations between various institutional measures and economic outcomes without specifying the precise causal mechanisms. For example, there is a literature that explores the role of legal and financial institutions for economic growth (see Demirgüç-Kunt and Levine, 2001; Glaeser and Shleifer, 2002). While this literature offers insight into the relationship between these variables, it offers little insight into why institutions emerged the way they did, or how they matter for economic outcomes.

In sum, the exchange paradigm leads one to focus on the institutional environment within which interaction takes place. Institutions create the rules of the game that facilitate or prevent exchange. In contrast to the exchange paradigm, the allocation paradigm tends to either exclude institutions altogether or treat them like any other choice variable. Working within the exchange paradigm, Austrian economics focuses on the underlying processes through which institutions emerge and evolve. This entails discovery and learning through continuous trial and error. Further, this approach emphasizes that the complex array of institutions that facilitate interaction and exchange is largely the result of spontaneous order. As Hayek notes:

> To understand our civilization, one must appreciate that the extended order resulted not from human design or intention but spontaneously: it arose from unintentionally conforming to certain traditional and largely moral practices, many of which men tend to dislike, whose significance they usually fail to understand, whose validity they cannot prove, and which have nonetheless fairly rapidly spread by means of an evolutionary selection. (Hayek, 1988, p. 6).

The implication is that no single mind can possibly comprehend the array of institutions that facilitate cooperation and exchange. From the standpoint of the exchange paradigm, the proper theory of institutions is causal-genetic and traces the process through which institutions emerge and evolve. It recognizes human limitations both in acting within a given set of institutions as well as in the design of those institutions.

2.6 The continuing relevance of the exchange paradigm

According to Kohn (2004), the economics research program grounded in the allocation paradigm is at an impasse. The stagnation of the research program is due to the inability of the allocation paradigm to provide "real-world" insights or to effectively inform economic policy. In its place, a new research program grounded in the exchange paradigm is emerging. Because those working in the Austrian tradition have always embraced the exchange paradigm, they are in a unique position to influence the direction of this emerging research program. Additionally, a review of recent trends in the economics profession should provide further reason for optimism among Austrians. Indeed, many of the interesting research themes and trends that have emerged over the past few decades have a distinct Austrian flavor. Consider the following examples.

In 1991, Ronald Coase won the Nobel Prize "for his discovery and clarification of the significance of transaction costs and property rights for the institutional structure and functioning of the economy." Likewise, in 1993, Douglass North won the Nobel Prize (along with Robert Fogel) "for having renewed research in economic history by applying economic theory and quantitative methods in order to explain economic and institutional change." Similarly, as discussed in the previous section, much of the more recent work by well-known economists such as Daron Acemoglu, Simon Johnson, James Robinson, Dan Rodrik, and Andrei Shleifer, among others, has focused on the role of institutions on economic outcomes. Of course not all of these economists have fully adopted the exchange paradigm, but they are addressing issues related to institutions and the context in which interaction and exchange take place.[3] These issues have been at the core of Austrian economics since its origins (see Garrouste, 2008).

Likewise, consider the renewed focus on "information economics" as evidenced by the 2001 Nobel Prize co-awarded to George Akerlof, Joseph Stiglitz, and Michael Spence, "for their analyses of markets with asymmetric information." Issues of information economics were addressed decades earlier in the work of F.A. Hayek and other Austrians who questioned the orthodox assumption of perfect information. Although many Austrians disagree with the conclusions of those working in the field of information economics (see, for instance, Boettke, 1996), the fact that these issues are being addressed and debated in the mainstream of the economics profession should be seen as a positive.

Austrian economics has often been marginalized by the broader economics profession. Part of this is due to the dominance of the value paradigm and part is due to the failure of those working in the Austrian tradition to effectively engage the profession. That said, with the emergence of a new research program grounded in the exchange paradigm, Austrian economics is as relevant as ever. There is much that Austrians can contribute to both the academic and policy discussions. Kohn (2004; 2007) provides several paths of research for those working within the exchange paradigm.

The first area of research focuses on the study of the history of economic thought. From this standpoint, the exchange paradigm provides a means of classifying past contributions (see Meijer, 2007; Wagner, 2007). It can also assist in resolving existing controversies within the economics discipline (see Marciano, 2007).

Work in economic theory is a second area where those working in the exchange paradigm can make a contribution. For example, Potts (2007) contends that the exchange paradigm should be developed into a clear and operational theory. He argues that the way this can be accomplished is by merging the exchange paradigm with evolutionary economics. Axtell (2007) argues that agent-based modeling offers the best means of clearly articulating the exchange paradigm.

A final area where adherents of the exchange paradigm can make a contribution is economic history. Research in this area relies on historical evidence to understand how various institutional arrangements influence interaction and exchange, as well as the resulting economic outcomes. The analytic narrative method, which blends the analytical tools of economics with the narrative form of exposition common in historical research, is conducive to this form of research (see Bates et al., 1998). This method fits well with the Austrian theory of institutions because it allows the researcher to trace the causal processes through which various institutional arrangements emerge and evolve.

Of all three strands of research, historically grounded research offers Austrian economists the best means of influencing the broader economics discipline. Unfortunately, within the current landscape of the economics discipline, most economists are not overly concerned with the history of economic thought.[4] Economic theory offers a better opportunity to influence other economists, but its reach is also limited because many economists are focused on empirical questions instead of on theoretical questions. Sound economic history offers the best potential for the effective demonstration of the interpretive power of the theoretical insights of Austrian economics. In addition to being of interest to those focused on empirical issues, work in this area can also contribute in a relevant way to current policy debates.

Ultimately, those working in the Austrian tradition should pursue their comparative advantage in research, no matter where it lies. However, no matter what they choose to pursue, Austrian economists must effectively engage other academics, as well as policy-makers and citizens. This is the only way to demonstrate the power and relevance of Austrian ideas and the exchange paradigm on which they are based.

Notes

* The author was the F.A. Hayek Fellow at the London School of Economic and Political Science at the time of this research and gratefully acknowledges the support of the Suntory and Toyota International Centres for Economics and Related Disciplines (STICERD) at the LSE.
1. Kohn differentiates between the "value paradigm" and the "exchange paradigm." Although I use the term "allocation paradigm" throughout to stay consistent with Buchanan's (1964) focus on allocation, the reader should note that this is the equivalent of Kohn's use of "value paradigm." Wagner (2007) traces the different visions of the value paradigm and the exchange paradigm back to Carl Menger and Leon Walras. A special issue of *The Review of Austrian Economics* (Volume 20, Number 2/3, 2007) was dedicated to a symposium on Kohn (2004).
2. Although I do not discuss them here, there are also differing normative implications of the two paradigms (see Kohn, 2004, pp. 320–30).
3. Kohn (2004, pp. 331–4) discusses the possibility of a "hybrid theory" that combines aspects of the allocation paradigm and the exchange paradigm. He rejects this possibility and provides a number of reasons why the two paradigms are incompatible.

4. This is not an indictment of the field of the history of economic thought, but rather a statement of fact about the current state of the economics discipline.

References

Acemoglu, Daron and Simon Johnson. 2005. "Unbundling Institutions," *Journal of Political Economy* **113**(5): 949–95.

Acemoglu, Daron, Simon Johnson, and James Robinson. 2001. "The Colonial Origins of Comparative Development: An Empirical Investigation," *American Economic Review* **91**(5): 1369–401.

Acemoglu, Daron, Simon Johnson, and James Robinson. 2002. "Reversal of Fortunes: Geography and Institutions in the Making of the Modern World Income Distribution," *Quarterly Journal of Economics* **117**(4): 1231–94.

Axtell, Robert L. 2007. "What Economic Agents Do: How Cognition and Interaction Lead to Emergence and Complexity," *The Review of Austrian Economics* **20**(2/3): 105–22.

Bates, Robert H., Avner Greif, Margaret Levi, Jean-Laurent Rosenthal, and Barry R. Weingast. 1998. *Analytic Narratives*. New Jersey: Princeton University Press.

Boettke, Peter J. 1996. "Review of Stiglitz's Whither Socialism?," *Journal of Economic Literature* **XXXIV**: 189–91.

Boettke, Peter J. 2001. "Why Culture Matters: Economics, Politics, and the Imprint of History," in Peter J. Boettke (ed.) *Calculation and Coordination*. New York: Routledge, pp. 248–65.

Buchanan, James M. 1964. "What Should Economists Do?," *Southern Economic Journal* **30**(3): 213–22.

Coase, Ronald. 1960. "The Problem of Social Cost," *Journal of Law and Economics* **1**(3): 1–44.

Coyne, Christopher J. 2007. *After War: The Political Economy of Exporting Democracy*. Stanford: Stanford University Press.

Demirgüç-Kunt, Asli and Ross Levine (eds). 2001. *Financial Structure and Economic Growth: A Cross-country Comparison of Banks, Markets, and Development*. Cambridge, MA: MIT Press.

Demsetz, Harold. 1967. "Toward a Theory of Property Rights," *American Economic Review* **57**(2): 347–59.

de Soto, Hernando. 1989. *The Other Path*. New York: Basic Books.

Foss, Nicolai. 2000. "Austrian Economics and Game Theory: A Stocktaking and an Evaluation," *The Review of Austrian Economics* **13**(1): 41–58.

Garrouste, Pierre. 2008. "The Austrian Roots of the Economic of Institutions," *The Review of Austrian Economics*, forthcoming.

Glaeser, Edward L. and Andrei Shleifer. 2002. "Legal Origins," *The Quarterly Journal of Economics* **107**(4): 1193–229.

Glaeser, Edward L., Rafael La Porta, Florencio Lopez-de-Silanes, and Andrei Shleifer. 2004. "Do Institutions Cause Growth?," *Journal of Economic Growth* **9**(3): 271–303.

Hayek, F.A. 1945. "The Use of Knowledge in Society," *American Economic Review* **XXXV**(4): 519–30f.

Hayek, F.A. 1960. *The Constitution of Liberty*. Chicago: The University of Chicago Press.

Hayek, F.A. 1976. *Law Legislation and Liberty, Volume 2: The Mirage of Social Justice*. Chicago: The University of Chicago Press.

Hayek, F.A. 1979. *Law, Legislation and Liberty, Volume 3: The Political Order of a Free People*. Chicago: The University of Chicago Press.

Hayek, F.A. 1988. *The Fatal Conceit: The Errors of Socialism*. Chicago: The University of Chicago Press.

Hayek, F.A. 2002. "Competition as a Discovery Procedure," *Quarterly Journal of Austrian Economics* **5**(3): 9–23.

Klein, Daniel B. 1997. "Convention, Social Order and Two Coordinations," *Constitutional Political Economy* **8**: 319–35.

Kohn, Meir. 2004. "Value and Exchange," *The Cato Journal* **24**(3): 303–39.

Kohn, Meir. 2007. "The Exchange Paradigm: Where to Now?," *The Review of Austrian Economics* **20**(2/3): 201–3.

Langlois, Richard. 1994. "The 'New' Institutional Economics," in Peter J. Boettke (ed.) *The Elgar Companion to Austrian Economics*, Aldershot, UK and Brookfield, VT, USA: Edward Elgar, pp. 535–40.

Marciano, Alain. 2007. "Value and Exchange in Law and Economics: Buchanan vs. Posner," *The Review of Austrian Economics* **20**(2/3): 187–200.

Meijer, Gerrit. 2007. "Value and Exchange in Economic Theorizing: The Contribution of the Freiburg School," *The Review of Austrian Economics* **20**(2/3): 171–86.

Mises, Ludwig von. [1949] 1996. *Human Action: A Treatise on Economics*, 4th edition. San Francisco: Fox and Wilkes.

North, Douglass C. 1990. *Institutions, Institutional Change and Economic Performance*. New York: Cambridge University Press.

North, Douglass C. 2005. *Understanding the Process of Economic Change*. New Jersey: Princeton University Press.

North, Douglass C. and Robert Paul Thomas. 1973. *The Rise of the Western World*. New York: Cambridge University Press.

Potts, Jason. 2007. "Exchange and Evolution," *The Review of Austrian Economics* **20**(2/3): 123–36.

Rodrik, Dani, Arvind Subramanian, and Francesco Trebbi. 2004. "Institutions Rule: The Primacy of Institutions Over Geography and Integration in Economic Development," *Journal of Economic Growth* **9**(2): 131–65.

Rothbard, Murray N. 1987. "Catallactics," in John Eatwell, Murray Milgate, and Peter Newman (eds) *The New Palgrave: A Dictionary of Economics*. New York: The Stockton Press, Volume 1, pp. 377–8.

Wagner, Richard. E. 2007. "Value and Exchange: Two Windows for Economic Theorizing," *The Review of Austrian Economics* **20**(2/3): 97–104.

Williamson, Oliver E. 1975. *Markets and Hierarchies*. New York: Free Press.

3 The facts of the social sciences are what people believe and think

*Virgil Henry Storr**

> [W]henever we interpret human action as in any sense purposive or meaningful, whether we do so in ordinary life or for the purposes of the social sciences, we have to define both the objects of human activity and the different kinds of actions themselves, not in physical terms but in terms of the opinions and intentions of the acting persons.
>
> (Hayek, 1948, p. 62)

3.1 Introduction

The aim of the social sciences is to explain and understand social phenomena. They are concerned with how the purposeful action of individuals operating on the basis of their own peculiar knowledge of their particular circumstances of time and place bring about orders that no single mind did or could deliberately design. Understanding purposeful human action and, so, the emergence of social phenomena, means understanding the opinions and beliefs that guide individual decision-making.

The facts of social sciences are, therefore, the meanings that individuals attach to their actions and their environments. The essential data of the social sciences are subjective in character. As Mises (1963, p. 26) argued in *Human Action*, "we cannot approach our subject if we disregard the meaning which acting man attaches to [his] situation." Similarly, as Hayek (1979, p. 53) argued in *The Counter-Revolution of Science*, "unless we can understand what the acting people mean by their actions any attempt to explain them. . .is bound to fail." The social sciences, if they are to explain social phenomena, must be concerned with what people think and feel, their assessments and valuations, the way they see the world and their place within it and the importance they place on particular relationships vis-à-vis others.

The opinions and beliefs that guide the actions of the individuals under study simply cannot be ignored, even if those beliefs are wrong, or irrational, or based on superstition rather than reason. The interactions between two individuals, for instance, are explainable only in terms of what they believe about the nature of their relationship (Hayek, 1948, p. 60). If Jack believes that Tom is his blood relative, whether Jack is in

30

fact mistaken or not is irrelevant to any explanation of Jack's behavior towards Tom. Similarly, if Jack and Tom were in fact blood relatives but neither of them knew it, a valid explanation of Jack's behavior toward Tom or Tom's toward Jack could not be based on their genetic connection to one another. The same is true, of course, for efforts to explain religious rituals. It is not the social scientists' "objective" assessments of the efficacy of prayer but individuals' "subjective" perceptions of the power of prayer that explains why some people pray and others do not.

If meanings matter, then, a central challenge for the social sciences is how to get at the meanings that individuals attach to their actions and their circumstances. Unlike actions, meanings cannot be directly observed. Moreover, stated opinions and beliefs can differ from the actual opinions and beliefs that informed an action. The facts of the social sciences, on first blush, seem irretrievably buried in the skulls of agents. Fortunately for the social scientist, however, subjective meanings are not simply locked away in the heads of people but are publicly available through cultural artifacts. Getting at meaning does not mean trying to gain access to individuals' private inner worlds but rendering intelligible the inter-subjective world of shared meanings, language, and culture.

This chapter explores the subjective character of the facts of the social sciences and the strategies that social scientists can use to unearth those facts. Section 3.2, will discuss why Mises, Hayek, and Schutz have stressed that the social sciences must be sciences of meaning. Section 3.3, then, explores the applied methods that are available to social scientists who are interested in the meanings that individuals attach to their actions and their circumstances. Section 3.4 offers concluding remarks.

3.2   Meanings as facts: from the subjective, to the inter-subjective, to culture

The defining characteristic of the Austrian school is, arguably, its commitment to subjectivism. As Hayek (1979, p. 52) famously wrote, "it is probably no exaggeration to say that every important advance in economic theory during that the last hundred years was a further step in the consistent application of subjectivism." The principle of subjectivism can be thought of as an acknowledgement that the facts of the social sciences are the opinions and beliefs that individuals attach to their actions and environments. It is a requirement that we reference the subjective purposes, perceptions, and plans of individuals, that is, their meanings, when attempting to explain and understand their behavior. Although Austrians have disagreed somewhat on how to interpret Hayek's dictum, differing on how radical the principle of subjectivism should be applied, there is no disagreement that the study of human action requires a focus on meanings. It is not controversial to assert that ours is a science of meaning. As Mises (1963, p. 51; emphasis added) wrote, "the task of the sciences of human action is the comprehension of *the meaning and relevance of human action*."

Alfred Schutz's work, perhaps more than any other Austrian's, has attempted to clarify exactly what we mean when we describe praxeology, the science of human action, as a science of meaning. As Schutz points out, "*meaning is a certain way of directing one's gaze at an item of one's own experience*" ([1932] 1967, p. 42; original emphasis). Saying that an individual's experience is meaningful, Schutz explains (ibid., p. 41), is to say that he, by selecting it out of his wealth of experiences and reflecting on it, has constituted it as such. Attaching meaning is an act of conscious will. We consciously direct our gaze to this or that event that has happened in the past, this or that opportunity that has presented itself in the present or this or that outcome that might occur in the future and, in so doing, we make that lived experience, current circumstance, or expected result meaningful. Subjective experiences, perceptions, and expectations do motivate actions, they can be what Schutz (ibid., p. 91) calls "genuine because motives" of actions, but they do not constitute the (sole) meaning of an action.

In which other way, then, are purposeful actions meaningful? What else, besides "genuine because motives," constitutes the meaning of a purposeful action? According to Schutz (ibid.), the "in-order-to motive" of that action also constitutes its meaning. As he writes (ibid., p. 61), "*the meaning of any action is its corresponding projected act*" (original emphasis). Before a person acts, she first chooses a goal. Next, she imagines the completed act. She then thinks of the intermediate goals that she must accomplish in order to complete the projected act. Her projection of the completed act is what motivates her action. Her actions and the intermediate actions that are required to complete the projected act are meaningless apart from the project that defines them (ibid., p. 63). She moves in order to bring about the act that she imagines. Think of a person's desire to read a book that is currently in her library down the hall. After deciding on the goal (retrieving and reading the book), she imagines the completed act (her reading the book at her desk in the bedroom) and the different actions she needs to perform in order to complete the act (getting up from her desk, opening the bedroom door, walking down the hall, entering the library, finding the book, walking back to her bedroom, sitting down at her desk, opening the book, and beginning to read). Her actions then are rightly understood as actions undertaken in order to complete the project (retrieving and reading the book at her desk). Her end goal, her in-order-to motive, is what constitutes the meaning of her actions.

According to Schutz (ibid., p. 31), "the scientific method of establishing subjective meaning is motivational understanding." It requires a consideration of an actor's motives not just his external behavior. Getting at the in-order-to motives, however, would seem to require that we heroically gain access to the internal worlds of their subjects. Indeed, observation alone is not likely to do the trick. Although observation may allow us to guess the ends and projected acts that give meaning to an action, even with simple acts, observation alone cannot reveal the meanings behind an individual's action. At the very least, the observer must possess some insight into the means-ends framework that the person is employing. Additionally, the observer would need some sense of which ends are within bounds and which the person being observed is likely to have ruled out. Absent these, the observer would be unable to determine whether an action was successful or not, whether the individual intended the outcome that occurred or was surprised by it, whether it was an intermediate step that was part of a more complex plan, or an independent act that should be considered on its own.

Kirzner (1976) makes a similar point using the simple example of a Martian doing research by looking at the earth through his telescope. If this Martian, Kirzner notes, were to train his telescope on any large US city he would eventually notice a fairly obvious pattern. First, he would notice rows of boxes. Next, he would observe that smaller boxes pass in front of these rows of boxes at regular intervals. He would additionally discover that once a day when the smaller boxes passed in front of the larger boxes bodies would emerge out of the larger boxes, move toward the smaller boxes and would then be swallowed by the smaller boxes. A Martian researcher observing this pattern may very well postulate "a definite law, the law of moving boxes and bodies" (Kirzner, 1976, p. 45). In developing this law, however, because the law does not give us any insight into the meanings behind the movements of these bodies and boxes, the Martian researcher "has not told us everything there is to be learned about this situation. A theory of moving bodies and boxes that does not draw attention to the dimension of purpose gives a truncated picture of the real world" (ibid.). Luckily, we are able to go further, to construct more meaningful social theories of human actions, than the researcher from Mars.

Lavoie (1991) has convincingly argued, however, that embracing subjectivism need not mean relying on introspection alone. That we have so much in common with one another is an important tool for social scientists, and a very real advantage that they have over natural scientists and Martian researchers studying human beings who cannot simply engage in introspection to gain insights about their subject matter. But, social scientists, Lavoie (ibid., p. 481) points out, have more at their disposal than introspection. Rather than having to penetrate into "the thought process of numerous other individuals," a feat that "sounds almost absurdly difficult," we can understand one another "because we all spent some substantial part of our lives being encultured into the [common] life-world" (ibid., p. 482).

Although we do not have direct access to the internal worlds of others and our knowledge of their interpretative schemas and their means-ends frameworks are necessarily incomplete, we can still make sense of their actions, we can still grasp an approximation of their intended meanings, because everyone belongs to an "intersubjective world common to us all" (ibid., p. 218). Stated another way, an individual's actions are intelligible because they are shaped by his subjective stock of knowledge that is largely composed of elements from the social stock of knowledge (Schutz and Luckmann, 1973, p. 262). As Schutz and Luckmann write (ibid., p. 100), when an individual encounters and experiences a novel or familiar situation in the life-world, it "is defined and mastered with the help of the stock of knowledge." When an event occurs, he "consults" his stock of knowledge to decide how to think about his situation and to decide what to do next. A person's subjective stock of knowledge contains everything that he has learned over the course of his life from how to walk and talk to the appropriate cultural rituals for a given situation. It would be a mistake, Schutz and Luckmann write (ibid., p. 254), to think of a person's stock of knowledge as being entirely "biologically modeled . . . [it is] to a large extent socially derived." As they insist (ibid., p. 243), "the everyday life-world is not private but rather intersubjective. . .because an individual is born into a historical social world, his biographical situation is, from the beginning, socially delimited and determined by social givens."

For Schutz and Luckmann (ibid., p. 262), then "the subjective stock of knowledge consists only in part of 'independent' results of experience and explication. It is predominantly derived from elements of the social stock of knowledge." The social stock of knowledge is the collective knowledge of a society. An individual's subjective stock of knowledge is socially conditioned and a society's social stock of knowledge is composed of subjective experiences intersubjectively communicated. Still, it is not simply, however, the sum of each individual's subjective stock of knowledge. It is both "more" and "less" than the sum of each person's subjective stock. "More" because no person could possess his community's entire social stock of knowledge and less because the social stock will not contain any number of novel experiences, recipes or insights that make up an individual's subjective stock of knowledge.

Arguably, the social stock of knowledge can be thought of as culture. Indeed, it is exactly what Geertz (1973, p. 5) has in mind when he refers to "webs of significance" in which man is suspended and which "he himself has spun." Like the social stock of knowledge, a people's culture contains interpretive schemes, relevance systems, skills, useful knowledge and recipes that members of the society can use to define and master situations. As Geertz writes (ibid., p. 89), by culture we mean "an historically transmitted pattern of meanings. . .a system of inherited conceptions. . .by means of which men communicate, perpetuate, and develop their knowledge about and attitudes toward life." Culture is a frame of reference, a backdrop, a way of seeing the world and an ethical system in which certain beliefs, actions, outcomes are possible and permissible and others are not.

To say that the facts of the social sciences are what people believe and think, is to concede that the social sciences must be preoccupied with culture. Although we cannot gain direct access to people's inner worlds, we can gain access to their cultural systems. As such, empirical work in the social sciences must resemble ethnographies and/or employ archival and oral history methods if social scientists are to learn the relevant facts.

3.3   Learning the facts: ethnography and thick descriptions

What applied methods should complement a science of meaning? If the facts of the social sciences are what people think and believe, then how are social scientists to go about learning the facts? Austrian economists have been reluctant to embrace quantitative empirical methods because they have doubts about the potential of statistical methods (alone) to accomplish this task.

Admittedly, there are some questions that can only be adequately explored by using quantitative measures and employing statistical methods. For instance, looking at whether or not there is a causal relationship between literacy and economic prosperity is a question that begs for a quantitative examination. If, say, literacy rates and indicators of economic well-being are correlated, then there is some reason, albeit not a definitive reason, to believe that a relationship does exist. If, on the other hand, these measures are not correlated, then there is some reason, again not a definitive reason, to believe that a relationship does not exist. The same rationale holds for utilizing more advanced statistical techniques like regression analysis, which reveals the relationship between one variable and the other variables that are believed to "explain" it.

There are several reasons why discovering a quantitative relationship of this sort can never (by itself) allow us to be certain of a relationship between two phenomena. Continuing with the example above, it is possible that the measures that we used for literacy and economic well-being are poor measures of the actual phenomena. If our measures are imperfect, then the meaning of any relationship between them is suspect. Moreover, even if our measures are perfect, the statistical relationship that we find can still be spurious. It is possible that higher literacy does not lead to more prosperity and that more prosperity does not lead to higher literacy, even though the two are correlated. A third, yet to be determined, variable might explain both. Although sophisticated statistical techniques have been developed to mitigate this danger, it can never be fully overcome. And, ultimately, recourse to a theoretical proposition that points to and argues for a particular causal relationship and interpreting his quantitative findings in the context of other relevant (quantitative and qualitative) information is unavoidable if the social scientist is to make sense of his results.

Specifically, then, it is not the use of quantitative methods that is worrisome to Austrian economists; to be sure, qualitative methods have their own pitfalls. Instead, they are particularly concerned about the privileging of quantitative over qualitative methods because they believe that the privileging of quantitative empirical methods over qualitative methods distorts empirical research in the social sciences. As Rizzo writes (1978, p. 53), "not all issues of interest are quantifiable. If we try to explain complex phenomena only by reference to quantifiable variables, then we are likely to be throwing away some information that we do, indeed, have." Privileging quantitative over qualitative approaches encourages social scientists to pursue certain questions and to disregard others. It also limits them to offering certain kinds of answers when they attempt to answer a question. And, in the worst cases, it pushes the social scientist to assign quantitative measures to phenomena that might not be measurable. Hayek ([1952] 1979, p. 89) has argued that this tendency to privilege quantitative over qualitative approaches in the social sciences:

> is probably responsible for the worst aberrations and absurdities produced by scientism in the social sciences. It not only leads frequently to the selection for study of the most irrelevant aspects of the phenomena because they happen to be measurable, but also to 'measurements' and assignments of numerical values which are absolutely meaningless.

If one approach had to be privileged over the other, it is likely that, for a science that recognizes people's thoughts and beliefs as the essential data, privileging qualitative over quantitative methods of apprehending history is more appropriate. Again, an empirical approach that hoped to illustrate and complement a social science that aims at recovering the meanings that individuals attach to their actions and environments must necessarily resemble ethnography and emphasize thick descriptions. Mises ([1957] 1985, p. 280) has argued that "thymological analysis," which tries to discover how and why people at specific times valued and acted in different circumstances, "is essential for the study of history." Similarly, Hayek

([1952] 1979, p. 88) has criticized "the common tendency to disregard all the 'merely' qualitative phenomena and to concentrate on the model of the natural sciences, on the quantitative aspects of what is measurable."

Although, as Hayek ([1952] 1979, p. 26) suggests, it might be appropriate to rely on introspection and then extrapolation to other minds when we are theorizing, we can do much better when we engage in empirical/ historical studies. Rather than making guesses based on introspection, people's beliefs and thoughts are arguably better accessed by observing what they do and asking them what they believe and think, by looking closely at their social, political, economic, and cultural environments, by examining their religious rituals and creeds, by listening to the stories that they tell one another, the poems that they recite, and the songs that they sing. The economist who wishes to understand economic life in a particular context, for instance, might very well have to pay attention to phenomena that might influence or be influenced by economic factors in addition to purely economic phenomena. As Weber (1949) noted, there are three relevant categories of phenomena for the economist who aims at understanding economic life: (1) pure "economic" phenomena (e.g., wages, prices, profits, etc.), (2) "economically relevant" phenomena (e.g., religious and cultural systems), and (3) "economically conditioned" phenomena (e.g., politics).

Geertz has described this process as attempting to "see things from the native's point of view." As he (1983, p. 57) explains, the aim is "to produce an interpretation of the way a people lives which is neither imprisoned within their mental horizons, an ethnography of witchcraft as written by the witch, nor systematically deaf to the distinctive tonalities of their existence, an ethnography of witchcraft as written by a geometer." The applied social scientist does not uncritically (re-)present what the native has expressed. Nor is his role to assume that his way of seeing is necessarily superior to the views of the individuals he is studying; he is not "endowed with a kind of supermind, with some sort of absolute knowledge, which makes it unnecessary for him to start from what is known by the people whose actions he studies" (Hayek [1952] 1979, p. 90). He does not merely voice their sentiments nor does he deign to speak on their behalf.

"Seeing things from the native's point of view" requires that we try to gain insight into how people see their own selves and situations by mining their archives, reading their literature, listening to their folklore and praise songs, conducting interviews, and living amongst them. But, it also means that we should attempt to situate and explain what Geertz calls "experience-near concepts" (what people believe and think) with the aid of "experience-distant concepts" (the theoretical tools we have at our disposal like rational choice economic theory). The ethnographer's task is not to put "oneself into someone else's skin" but "to grasp concepts that, for another people, are experience-near, and to do so well enough to place them in illuminating connection with experience-distant concepts theorists have fashioned to capture the general features of social life" (ibid., p. 58).

Additionally, representing "experience-near concepts" with the help of "experience-distant concepts" suggests that (in our empirical work) we should be developing thick over thin descriptions. Recall Ryle's (1971) now famous insight that we cannot figure out the meaning of an action without some knowledge of the context and the actor's motivations. In fact, we cannot tell the difference between an action and a reflex or a habitual response without knowing something about the context and specifically the intentions of the "actor." How, Ryle asks, can we distinguish between a wink (a conspiratorial gesture between compatriots) and an eye twitch (an involuntary response to an irritant) without knowing anything else about the context? Of course, we cannot. A thin description (e.g., Fred's left eye closed and opened rapidly) will not be adequate to distinguish between a wink and a twitch. We would need a thicker description of the scene (e.g., Pete and Fred are friends about to play a practical joke on the teacher) in order to conclude that it was one or the other. Since any worthwhile empirical exposition of the situation would be able to distinguish Fred's wink from a simple twitch, since the goal of empirical work is necessarily to make sense of the social world at a given time and place, then thick descriptions win out over thin ones.

It should be noted that to recognize that the facts of the social sciences are what people believe and think and so to privilege ethnography and thick descriptions in empirical/applied enterprises in no way suggests that we should abandon thin descriptions of the social world in our theoretical endeavors. On the contrary, thick descriptions are only possible if they are informed by thin descriptions. As Boettke writes (2001, p. 253):

> we need, in other words, both 'thin' and 'thick' description for our social theory to possess both meaning and relevance – coherence and correspondence so to speak.. . . The justification of the 'thin description' of economic theory is that it affords us more compelling 'thick descriptions' of the social experience of particular times and places.

Without a thin description of what distinguishes a twitch from a wink (i.e., one is an involuntary act and the other a conspiratorial gesture), thick descriptions of the situation would also fail to distinguish between the two. Stated another way, without theory/models that explain a phenomenon while abstracting away much of the social detail, without "experience-distant concepts" to use Geertz's formulation, the applied social scientist could not make sense of social life, he could not offer thick descriptions.

At best, he would be able to offer detailed accounts of social phenomena that offered little to aid our understanding. Though detail is necessary for an applied social science that tries to capture what people believe and think, it is not sufficient.

3.4 Conclusion

Social science disciplines are both theoretical and applied/historical. Whereas social theory aims at explaining the social world, applied social science and social history aims at understanding particular social phenomena. One relies on conception and the other on understanding. As Mises (1963, p. 51; emphasis added) wrote:

> the task of the sciences of human action is the *comprehension of the meaning and relevance of human action*. They apply for this purpose two different epistemological procedures: conception and understanding. Conception is the mental tool of praxeology [read social theory]; understanding is the specific mental tool of history [read applied social science].

While social theory and social history are distinct and can be divided conceptually, neither can get very far without the other. *Faith without works is dead and works without faith cannot lead to salvation.* As McCloskey (1991) notes, social theorists primarily construct models (they use metaphors) and applied social scientists write histories (they tell stories). "Metaphors and stories, models and histories," she writes (ibid., p. 61), "are two ways of answering 'why'. . . . the metaphorical and the analytical explanations answer to each other." As she continues (ibid., p. 63), "the point is that economists [and social scientists generally] are like other human beings in that they use metaphors and tell stories. They are concerned both to explain and to understand, *erklären* and *verstehen*." As McCloskey suggests, the best social science combines the two. "But wilt thou know, O vain man, that faith without works is dead? Was not Abraham our father justified by works, when he had offered Isaac his son upon the altar? Seest thou how faith wrought with his works, and by works was faith made perfect?" (James 2: 20–22).

Recognizing that the facts of the social sciences are what people believe and think has important implications for both *erklären* and *verstehen*. It suggests that social theorists, for instance, should articulate social theory that places the meanings that individuals attach to their actions and circumstances at the center (i.e., methodologically individualist approaches) but that also pays attention to how culture and context influence the meanings and so actions of individuals (i.e., social actors must be seen as tri-embedded in the society, polity, and economy). Similarly, it suggests that applied social scientists should utilize their theoretical tools to thickly describe and make sense of the social world (i.e., ethnographic and archival methods alongside if not over quantitative empirical methods).

Note

*   I would like to thank Dan Lavoie and Emily Chamlee-Wright for fruitful conversations on this topic. The standard disclaimer applies.

References

Boettke, Peter. 2001. *Calculation and Coordination: Essays on Socialism and Transitional Political Economy*. New York, NY: Routledge.
Geertz, Clifford.1973. *The Interpretation of Cultures: Selected Essays*. New York, NY: Basic Books.
Geertz, Clifford. 1983. *Local Knowledge: Further Essays in Interpretive Anthropology*. New York, NY: Basic Books.
Hayek, F.A. 1948. *Individualism and Economic Order*. Chicago, IL: The University of Chicago Press.
Hayek, F.A. [1952] 1979. *The Counter-Revolution of Science: Studies on the Abuse of Reason*. Indianapolis, IN: The Liberty Fund, Inc.
Kirzner, Israel. 1976. "On the Method of Austrian Economics," in Edwin G. Dolan (ed.) *Foundations of Modern Austrian Economics*. Kansas City, KS: Sheed and Ward, Inc.
Lavoie, Don. 1991. "The Progress of Subjectivism," in Mark Blaug and Neil de Marchi (eds) *Appraising Modern Economics: Studies in the Methodology of Scientific Research Programmes*. Aldershot, UK and Brookfield, VT, USA: Edward Elgar, pp. 470–86.
McCloskey, Deirdre. 1991. "Storytelling in Economics," in Don Lavoie (ed.) *Economics and Hermeneutics*. New York, NY: Routledge, pp. 61–75.
Mises, Ludwig von. [1957] 1985. *Theory and History: An Interpretation of Social and Economic Evolution*. Auburn, AL: The Ludwig von Mises Institute.
Mises, Ludwig von. 1963. *Human Action: A Treatise of Economics*. San Francisco, CA: Fox & Wilkes.
Rizzo, Mario. 1978. "Praxeology and Econometrics: A Critique of Positivist Economics," in L. Spadaro (ed.) *New Directions in Austrian Economics*. Kansas City: Sheed Andrews and McMeel, Inc.
Ryle, Gilbert. 1971. "The Thinking of Thoughts: What is 'Le Penseur' Doing?," *Collected Papers*, 2 vols, vol. 2. London: Hutchinson.
Schutz, Alfred. [1932] 1967. *The Phenomenology of the Social World*. Evanston: Northwestern University Press.
Schutz, Alfred and Thomas Luckmann. 1973. *The Structures of the Life-World*. Evanston, IL: Northwestern University Press.
Schutz, Alfred and Thomas Luckmann [1983] 1989. *The Structures of the Life-World: Volume II*. Evanston, IL: Northwestern University Press.
Weber, Max. 1949. *The Methodology of the Social Sciences*. New York, NY: The Free Press.

PART II

MICROECONOMICS

4 Economic value and costs are subjective
Edward P. Stringham*

4.1 Introduction

What makes goods valuable? Are objects intrinsically valuable, valuable based on how much labor they take to make, or are they simply valuable based on how much they satisfy people's subjective preferences? In a certain sense it might be accurate to exclaim, "We are all subjectivists now."[1] With a few exceptions, almost all modern economists believe that goods are valued based on how they satisfy individuals' subjective preferences. Yet there is disagreement about what it means to believe in economic subjectivism. George Mason University economist Bryan Caplan (1999) criticizes writers in the tradition of Austrian economics for portraying non-Austrians as non-subjectivists. He writes, "Innumerable Austrian essays and books use the word 'subjectivism' in the title. This leaves one with the impression that other economists fail to embrace subjectivism – an impression that is simply false." Caplan claims that although many of the Austrian views such as economic subjectivism are correct, he says they "are simply not distinctive enough to sustain a school of thought."

Caplan is undoubtedly correct that almost all modern economists believe in some type of economic subjectivism. Despite this truth, it would be odd to say that all economists believe in economic subjectivism in exactly the same way. Rather than using a dichotomous distinction to classify economists either as subjectivists or not, I will argue that we should recognize that economists can believe in economic subjectivism in several different ways. In this chapter I will present ten questions that explore the ways in which economists believe in economic subjectivism. These ten questions are certainly not exhaustive, many more could be written, but they are a first step towards recognizing that economists can be subjectivists in more ways than one. Using these ten questions as a guide, one could even create a "Subjectivism Purity Test" in much the same way that Bryan Caplan has created a "Libertarian Purity Test." Although almost all economists would be classified as subjectivists to some extent, some economists would be classified as more thoroughgoing subjectivists than others.

Making such distinctions is not just an interesting academic exercise. How much one believes in economic subjectivism has many important implications for how one practices positive economics and the normative recommendations one may or may not prescribe. For example, economists who believe that consumer utility is subjective but that producer costs are objective, can reach very different conclusions than economists who believe that consumer utility and producer costs are subjective. Similarly, economists who believe that outside observers can know what will satisfy an individual's subjective utility function will come to very different conclusions than the economist who believes that only individuals know what they like best. Or economists who believe that utility (which is subjectively determined based on individual preferences) can be observed, compared, and aggregated among many people will come to very different conclusions than economists who believe that people's utility levels are unobservable and incommensurable.

Question 1 begins by discussing an area of subjectivism where most economists agree: is economic value subjective? This area is what differentiates most modern economists from the classical economists and many non-economists. Question 2 discusses an area where many but not all economists agree: are costs subjective? This area is what differentiates many Austrians and certain neoclassical economists from orthodox neoclassical economists following Alfred Marshall's tradition. Questions 3, 4, 5, and 6 discuss areas where fewer still economists agree: can we survey people's subjective preference, can we measure an individual's utility, can we compare utility between individuals, and can we aggregate the utility of many people? For these questions one can find Austrians and neoclassical economists on both sides of the debate. Questions 7, 8, 9, and 10 look at alternative approaches to making welfare comparisons of a nation that do not purport to depend on measuring subjective utility such as looking at per capita income, migration patterns, societal wide cost–benefit with dollars as the unit of measurement, and a demonstrated preference Pareto rule. Where one stands on these issues depends on how far one is willing to extend the logic of economic subjectivism. And where one stands on questions of economic subjectivism has an important influence on how one analyzes and what one recommends for the world.

4.2   Question 1: What makes goods valuable?

There is widespread agreement in the economics profession that consumer goods are valuable based on how much consumers believe they will satisfy their preferences. This idea has revolutionized the way economics has been practiced over the past 130 years. This perspective is referred to as follows: "Marginal-utility economics is often called 'subjective-value' economics, and the doctrinal revolution also carries this name" (Buchanan, 1969, p. 9). Before the 1870s when Stanley Jevons, Carl Menger, and Leon Walras advanced the theory of marginal utility, many theorists believed in some form of a labor theory of value that said that the value of a good is determined by how long it takes to make. Economists pondered differences in "use value" and "exchange value" and they had a difficult time explaining many things such as why diamonds are more valuable than water.

Today, most economists rightfully reject the labor theory of value. Economists recognize that one hour of work from the average Joe does not produce the same value as an hour of work by Bill Gates. Certain people are smarter, work harder, or have different tools, so not everyone has the same productivity. Economists also point out that even if everyone had the same productivity the labor theory of value would still be flawed. A chef could spend one hour producing a delicious apple pie and a second hour producing an otherwise identical pie replacing the apples with dirt, and it takes no more than common sense to see that the value of the two pies will be different.

Most modern economists would accept that the value of the two pies would be determined by individuals' subjective perceptions about their marginal utility rather than some intrinsic value they may possess. The approaches of Jevons, Menger, and Walras had some important differences, but they reached similar conclusions.[2] In Carl Menger's explanation, for a good to be useful, a human want must exist, an object must have properties that can satisfy that want, and humans must know the object can satisfy their want. A good is valuable to the extent that a good can satisfy our wants, nothing more and nothing less. So goods are not objectively valuable; they are only valuable when people consider them useful. The same physical good may be useful at one point and not useful at another. As Buchanan explains (1969, p. 9), "Marginal utilities. . .were acknowledged to be dependent on quantities." This perspective allowed economists to explain the diamond and water paradox. Even though water is necessary for life and diamonds are not, the marginal utility of an additional unit of water (given that we have so much) is very low, whereas the marginal utility of an additional diamond is high. This simple approach changed the face of economics. Almost all modern economists accept a subjective theory of marginal utility so in this sense, "We are all subjectivists now."

4.3   Question 2: Are costs subjective?

Although most economists believe in a form of economic subjectivism when it comes to consumer goods, one way in which many economists are not fully on board with economic subjectivism is over their conception of costs. As James Buchanan explains:

> A distinction must be made between the orthodox neoclassical economics which incorporates the subjective-value or marginal-utility revolution in value

theory and the *subjectivist economics* of the latter-day Austrians, notably Mises and Hayek. The dependence of price (value) on marginal utility, subjectively determined, can be fully recognized, while essentially an *objective* theory of cost is retained. (1969, p. 23; original emphasis)

Neoclassical economists such as Alfred Marshall described demand and supply as a pair of scissors that cut paper to determine price. To Marshall the demand side was determined by subjective utility, but the supply side was determined by objective cost of production. In this view the price will be determined by where the subjectively determined demand curve intersected with the objective cost curve.

In contrast, Austrian economists such as Mises and many modern neoclassical economists view the supply curve as essentially the flipside of a demand curve. Just as a buyer's subjective preferences influence how much he is willing to pay to buy units of a good, a seller's subjective preferences influence how much he must be paid to sell units of a good. In the words of Mises: "Costs are a phenomenon of valuation. Costs are the value attached to the most valuable want-satisfaction which remains unsatisfied because the means required for its satisfaction are employed for that want-satisfaction the cost of which we are dealing with" ([1949] 1996, p. 396). When the seller gives up a unit of a good, he must consider what satisfaction he is forgoing. Each person will value the forgone opportunities differently so each person will have a different supply curve. For example, the individual attached to his childhood comic books will have a different supply curve than an otherwise similar individual with less attachment to his comics. One could pay the comic book owners different amounts to get them to sell because they have different subjective preferences for parting with their wares. According to this perspective, the supply curve is simply determined by sellers' evaluation of their opportunity cost or in other words what sellers foresee they are forgoing by making the sale. Just as buyers weigh the subjective marginal utility of gaining an additional unit of a good, sellers weigh the subjective marginal utility lost of having one fewer unit of a good. Referring to Marshall's analogy, Rothbard concludes (1962, p. 360), "costs are themselves subjective utilities, so that both 'blades of the scissors' are governed by the subjective utility of individuals."

So supply curves, like demand curves, are determined by subjective preferences rather than some objective cost of production. This perspective is explored in detail in James Buchanan's *Cost and Choice* (1969). Buchanan reaches the following conclusions about the subjectivist notion of cost:

1.   Most importantly, cost must be borne exclusively by the decision-maker; it is not possible for cost to be shifted to or imposed on others.

2. Cost is subjective; it exists in the mind of the decision-maker and nowhere else.
3. Cost is based on anticipations; it is necessarily a forward-looking or *ex ante* concept.
4. Cost can never be realized because of the fact of choice itself: that which is given up cannot be enjoyed.
5. Cost cannot be measured by someone other than the decision-maker because there is no way that subjective experience can be directly observed.
6. Finally, cost can be dated at the moment of decision or choice. (Buchanan, 1969, p. 43)

Costs are based on individual perceptions of utility forgone at the moment of choice. This utility forgone is not objective and not something that people can measure.

Whether one adopts a subjectivist notion of costs has some important implications for the way one practices economics. Many economists and many entire fields in economics rely on measuring costs for their analysis and normative conclusions. For example, the antitrust economists who accuse firms of charging above marginal cost (or below marginal cost in the case of accusations of predatory pricing) are assuming that costs can be measured from a positive point of view, and that divergence between price and cost is a problem from a normative point of view. In contrast, many economists who believe in economic subjectivism in this realm believe that these costs cannot be observed, and that it makes as much sense to worry about suppliers selling above marginal cost as it does to worry about buyers buying below their marginal benefit.[3]

Those who believe in subjectivism in the realm of costs say that both economic value and economic costs are subjective. Many neoclassical economists might be in full agreement with Buchanan on the above points. But whole fields in economics seem to rest on foundations that deny that costs are subjective, so not all economists should be classified as being economic subjectivists in the realm of costs.

4.4   Question 3: Can we survey people's subjective preferences?

Many economists accept some theory of subjective marginal utility and many also accept a theory of subjective marginal opportunity cost. Nevertheless, there is disagreement about how much external parties can know about individuals' subjective preferences. Many economists believe that outside parties can observe or survey individuals' utility functions with the goal of helping formulate future policies. Some of the more thoroughgoing economic subjectivists, however, argue that preferences are not constant and that it makes little sense to talk about someone's preferences independent of their specific time and place.

Economic thinking is thinking at the margin and the more thoroughgoing subjectivists argue that consistent marginal thinking means that it only makes sense to look at how people value goods in their specific situations. How much someone values a good at a given point in time will be influenced by a myriad of factors including how many goods they have recently consumed. Mapping all goods in a person's "subjective" utility function becomes less and less possible as one considers the number of things that influence people in a given day. Little things can put people in different moods, which will change how they value other goods, so it is unclear how economists could map a utility function to include all of the things that might influence a person's mood and propensity to consume something at a given time.

Economic subjectivism can be extended further if one rejects the idea of constancy of preferences. Murray Rothbard (1956, pp. 228–30) criticizes those who attempt to observe or ask people about their preferences and then think they can map those people's preferences for the future. Past choices do represent a person's preferences at the time they made the choice, but trying to create a map of someone's preferences will necessarily be limited to the past and just that time period in which one made the choices. For example, it would be a folly to observe a person make a choice as a young adult and infer that the person will make that same choice in her middle age. Even within short periods of times on two seemingly identical days people may make a different choice. Yes, some people eat the same item at every meal, but the fact that this is so rare should lead us to question any theory that encourages us to assume that past choices reveal future preferences.

Situations change and it seems impossible to know all of the factors that influence one's choice. Some people may even make a similar choice on a regular basis but that does not imply they will always make that choice. F.A. Hayek writes ([1968] 2002, p. 12), "We might be able to notice certain regularities ('empirical laws' in the specific sense in which Carl Menger contrasted them to theoretical laws) in the observed behavior of these variables. Often these regularities apply, but sometimes they do not." Austrian economists argue that economics differs from the natural sciences, because economics deals with humans who can always change how they react. So observing past choices demonstrates preferences when people made the choice, but that does not imply that those revealed preferences will be constant over time. From this perspective, it makes little sense to talk about what someone prefers independent of their specific situation.

One can also apply this logic to surveys that attempt to ask people about their preferences. For example, many cost–benefit analyses attempt to use surveys to attempt to figure out how much people value environmental amenities or public works projects. But much of the criticisms about inferring future demand based on observing past choices can be applied to surveys. Surveys are even more problematic because they require people to consider their demand in situations they have never been in. Boudreaux et al. (1999, p. 791) write:

> Asking people to reckon their demand curves for all goods, services, and amenities under a welter of different conditions is to ask the impossible. The impossibility of mapping a full schedule of preferences for every given survey respondent means that, by necessity, a certain number of alternatives must be excluded from the menu of options over which a person can hypothetically spend his or her money.

To these economists, it makes little sense to talk about how much people value something independent of them being in a specific situation where they have to make their choice. How much people value things will always be contingent on their time and place.

If one adopts this position, can economists say anything about people's preferences? Rothbard argues that economists cannot say that an individual values a good in all circumstances; the only thing economists can say is that an individual considered a good valuable in a specific situation. By observing someone making a choice, Rothbard says that economists can deduce that the person preferred his choice ex ante at that time. Rothbard (1956, p. 225) writes, "[A]ctual choice reveals, or demonstrates, a man's preference; that is, that his preferences are deducible from what he has chosen in action." When someone purchases a beer rather than a glass of wine we can say that the person preferred the beer to the wine at that time, but we cannot say that beer is always preferred to wine.

The implication of this aspect of economic subjectivism is that economists cannot go around telling governments what people really want. Preferences not only differ between individuals but people's preferences differ over time. When governments make choices for people rather than letting the individuals make their own choices, they are assuming that they can know what individuals really want independent of the market process. But according to Hayek, the outcome of the market process cannot be known ahead of time. Hayek ([1968] 2002, p. 9) says that we should "consider competition systematically as a procedure for discovering facts which, if the procedure did not exist, would remain unknown."

4.5 Question 4: Can we measure an individual's utility?
The next area of subjectivism where not all economists agree is whether subjective utility is measurable. Some economists believe that individuals value goods based on their subjective preferences, but also believe that how much they value goods can be measured by external parties. The idea is that just as doctors observe heart rates using stethoscopes,

economists can measure utility levels of individuals. More thoroughgoing economic subjectivists, on the other hand, argue against this perspective. Representing this point of view, James Buchanan (1969, p. 9) writes, "utility is a subjective phenomenon, and it is not something that can be externally or objectively measured."

The first question is, what would it take to measure utility levels? First, economists would need to create a unit they are going to measure and second, they would also need a way to measure that unit. Perhaps this could be done if economists could invent a utilometer to measure your number of utils. The problem, however, is that no such device exists, and according to economists such as Rothbard it never could. Rothbard (1956, p. 232; original emphasis) writes, "Psychological magnitudes cannot be measured since there is no objectively extensive unit – a necessary requisite of measurement. Further, actual choice obviously cannot demonstrate any form of *measurable* utility; it can only demonstrate one alternative being preferred to another." Since there is no such thing as a util, it is not possible to measure an individual's total level of utility.

To the economic subjectivist, economists can observe whether someone prefers something at the margin, but they cannot observe the magnitudes. Mises writes, "To prefer and to set aside and the choices and decisions in which they result are not acts of measurement. Action does not measure utility or value; it chooses between alternatives" ([1949] 1996, p. 122). Individuals rank goods as having more or less utility at the margin, but considering marginal utilities does not imply that total utility exists. As Rothbard (1956, p. 234; original emphasis) writes, "*there is no such thing as total utility*; all utilities are marginal." In the words of Mises ([1949] 1996, p. 122) "There is no abstract problem of total utility or total value."

Whereas some economists derive marginal utility mathematically as the first derivative of a person's total utility function, Austrian economists such as Mises talk about individuals' analysis of marginal utility as ordinal rankings of the relative value of additional units of a good. In the words of Mises (ibid., p. 703), "acting man does not measure utility. He arranges it in scales of gradation." When observing someone making a choice we can say that an individual preferred a glass of wine to a beer, but we cannot say how much more he preferred the wine. They cannot say how much more the choice was preferred because there is no a way of measuring magnitudes of utils. Rothbard ([1962] 2004, p. 258) writes, "Value scales of each individual are purely ordinal, and there is no way whatever of measuring the distance between the rankings; indeed, any concept of such distance is a fallacious one." In this perspective, utility is ordinal not cardinal. A good might provide marginal utility, but we cannot measure levels of total utility because there is no such thing as a "util."

4.6 Question 5: Can we compare utility between individuals?

The next way in which many economists believe in subjectivism less than others is in their belief that one can compare the utility between different people. One could believe that goods' utility is determined by subjective preferences, but also believe that one can compare the utility between the two people. Consider the classic example of taking one dollar from a rich person and giving it to a poor person. Economists such as Arthur Pigou argued that the principle of diminishing marginal utility implies a rich man does not value the dollar as much as a poor man, so redistributionist policies make society better off. A similar type of argument is often used for antitrust law saying that preventing monopoly practices will cause consumers to gain more than companies lose.[4]

Despite these arguments' popularity in policy debates, Lionel Robbins maintains that the arguments attempt to extend beyond what logic can prove. He says that the principle of decreasing marginal utility holds for individuals but that we cannot extend that argument between individuals. Robbins writes:

> [I]t is one thing to assume that scales can be drawn up showing the *order* in which an individual will prefer a series of alternatives, and to compare the arrangement of one such individual scale with another. It is quite a different thing to assume that behind such arrangements lie magnitudes which themselves can be compared as between individual scales. (1932, p. 122; original emphasis)

An individual can rank order how *he* values some choices in comparison to choices, but to Robbins economists cannot look at and compare how two different people value choices compared with each other. Any comparison between their relative levels of satisfaction would rest on interpersonal comparisons of utility, which Robbins and Rothbard argue are invalid. Rothbard ([1962] 2004, p. 258) writes, "there is no way of making interpersonal comparisons and measurements, and no basis for saying that one person subjectively benefits more than another."

Consider the example of taking a dollar from a rich man and giving it to a poor man. How can we say that the poor man will enjoy the dollar more? What if the rich person was a joyous soul and the poor person was miserable with everything he got? Rothbard (ibid., p. 302) writes, "It is certainly possible that a Rockefeller enjoys the services of each dollar more than a poor, but highly ascetic, individual does." The fact is we cannot make a judgment either way, because there is no way to compare the relative satisfactions between different people.

Robbins brings up an interesting question about the possibility of measuring people's utilities by examining their bloodstreams. But to Robbins even this would not allow us to measure their comparative levels of utility. Robbins (1932, p. 124; original emphasis) writes: *"There is no means of testing the magnitude of A's satisfaction as compared with B's. If we tested the state of their blood-streams, that would be a test of blood, not satisfaction."* Robbins adds, "Introspection does not enable A to discover what is going on in B's mind, nor B to discover what is going on in A's." Utility is a subjective phenomenon only in the mind of the person making a choice. One cannot make comparisons about two separate individuals who have different subjective assessments about the world.

Robbins and Rothbard maintain that the entire set of arguments about increasing social welfare by redistributing from rich to poor rests on invalid assumptions. To judge that redistribution makes society better off requires economists to measure the utility lost by the rich and compare it to the utility gained by the poor. But like it or not, no such measurement exists. Robbins writes:

> Hence the extension of the Law of Diminishing Marginal Utility, postulated in the propositions we are examining, is entirely illegitimate. And the arguments based upon it therefore are all lacking in scientific foundation.. . . The Law of Diminishing Marginal Utility does not justify the inference that transferences from the rich to the poor will increase total satisfaction. (1932, p. 125)

In this perspective, one cannot say that the poor will value something more than the rich. Following this logic to its extreme means that economists cannot say that any one person derives greater utility from something than someone else. We might observe that they might have different willingness to pay or willingness to be paid, but we cannot conclude that one person derived greater utility than the other. To the thoroughgoing economic subjectivist, there is no way to measure or compare utility between different people.

4.7 Question 6: Can we aggregate the utility of many people?
To the more thoroughgoing economic subjectivists utility is subjective, it is not cardinal, it is not comparable between people, and it cannot be measured. Nevertheless, some economists who have made important contributions to the theory of value subjectivism do not appear to be aware of the far-reaching implications of their theory. One issue where there is still disagreement is about whether the total number of utils of all people in society can be measured. Despite their arguments in favor of economic subjectivism elsewhere, some economists make surprisingly non-subjectivist arguments when defending their normative conclusions. From this perspective, many economists should not be classified as thoroughgoing subjectivists.

One of the more prominent examples of economists fitting this bill is Ludwig von Mises. After making many of the subjectivist arguments mentioned above, Mises makes a number of arguments at odds with important aspects of economic subjectivism. At various points in his writings Mises makes arguments using extremely non-subjectivist phrases such as the "well-being" of a nation, "commonweal," "social utility," and "social welfare" (Mises [1949] 1996, pp. 157, 174, 175, 271, 497, 721). In fact, Mises' whole defense of liberalism rests on his belief that policies should be judged against the yardstick of "human welfare" (ibid., p. 147). He writes:

> From this point of view one may describe the objective of social cooperation as the realization of the greatest happiness of the greatest number. Hardly anybody would venture to object to this definition of the most desirable state of affairs and to contend that it is *not* a good thing to see as many people as possible as happy as possible. All the attacks directed against the Bentham formula have centered around ambiguities or misunderstandings concerning the notion of happiness; they have not affected the postulate that the good, whatever it may be, should be imparted to the greatest number. (Ibid., p. 834; original emphasis)

Mises defends Bentham's notion that property is valued for its utility rather than for other reasons external to economics such as morality (ibid., p. 175). It is curious then, that Mises is often grouped with people much more subjectivist than him.

Besides the fact that "greatest happiness of the greatest number" aims at two conflicting goals (should we aim for the maximum happiness of a lesser number of people or should we aim for a slightly less than maximum happiness for a higher number of people?) the concept is completely undefined. Nowhere does Mises specify what he means by "social utility", "social welfare," or the "well-being" of a nation. Mises' notions, if they are to mean anything at all, seem to have much more in common with Harvard and MIT economists Abram Bergson and Paul Samuelson who believed that one could examine society's social welfare function and that one should formulate policy based on it.

It seems that Mises, Bergson, and Samuelson were all followers of Bentham, but the main difference between Mises and his Massachusetts counterparts is that the latter were more explicit about what they meant. Whereas Mises did not talk about social indifference curves, for policy to be judged based on how much "a policy is beneficial to the commonweal" (something he supports; [1949] 1996, p. 175), Mises had to believe this could be measured in some way, otherwise his standard is useless. But if one accepts the economic subjectivism of later writers, one must conclude precisely that. Rothbard (1956, p. 255) writes:

> It is not possible, however, for an observer scientifically to compare the social utilities of results on the free market from one period of time to the next. As

we have seen above, we cannot determine a man's value-scales over a period of time. How much more impossible for all individuals!

To Rothbard, an individual can decide whether he likes Choice A versus Choice B at any given time, but he is not in a position to rank Choice A versus Choice B at different points in time. When trying to investigate how a policy affects "social utility" one would need to come up with a way of ranking the preferred state of the world according to the well-being of the "commonweal."

But if one accepts that utilities are ordinal rather than cardinal, one is led into a conundrum. Kenneth Arrow looked into deriving a social welfare function based on individuals' ordinal preferences, and found that under certain plausible conditions, the most socially preferable state of the world is undefined. One cannot say that social utility is higher in State of the World 1 compared with State of the World 2. A dictator could say *he* prefers State of the World 1 according to his subjective preferences, but an economist could not say that either state of the world has higher social utility. From this perspective the famous mathematical economist Kenneth Arrow is more of an economic subjectivist than Mises!

4.8   Question 7: Is monetary income a proxy for national utility?

Up until now we have been discussing ways in which many economists attempt to measure and aggregate individuals' subjective utility, things that cannot be done according to the more thoroughgoing economic subjectivists. Many economists agree that there is no such thing as a util, yet they do not want to abandon welfare comparisons completely. Instead they rely on other measures to try to approximate well-being of people. One of the more talked about proxies for well-being of a nation is per capita income. Much of the literature on economic growth relies on per capita income statistics as the benchmark to compare nations.

Money enables people to purchase other things, and since more is preferred to less, many economists assume that maximizing monetary income should be the normative goal of society. This standard does not rely on interpersonal comparisons of utility; instead it relies on something that can actually be measured, namely dollars. Is this standard in accordance with economic subjectivism? Rothbard ([1962] 2004, p. 300) writes, "We can – at least, theoretically – measure monetary incomes by adding the amount of money income each person obtains, but this is by no means a measure of psychic income." To Rothbard, individuals are concerned with utility or psychic income, not just monetary income: "it is *psychic* and not *monetary* income that is being maximized" (ibid.; original emphasis).

This position can be explained using simple economics from either a neoclassical or a Misesian approach. As Mises points out, monetary income is a positive, but having to work to get monetary income is a negative (what Mises [1949] 1996, p. 65 calls the disutility of labor). When someone is free to make his own choice, he will choose his most preferred mix of labor and leisure. In his ideal combination an individual will want to work no more or no less. If, however, an individual is forced to work less and consume more leisure than he would have preferred, he is worse off because he had to work less and will have less money. Likewise, if an individual is forced to work more than he would have preferred, then he is also worse off because although he has more money, he has less leisure than he would have preferred. In addition to the obvious examples of forced labor, basic microeconomics shows that there are many ways to make people work more than they would have liked. A lump sum tax, for example, makes a person poorer without reducing the marginal monetary payoffs of working that can induce someone to consume less leisure (that is, work more) than he would have preferred (Rothbard [1962] 2004, p. 915). In this case, monetary income in the society has gone up even though a person is made worse off. Or in the case of forced labor, monetary income might go up even if those forced to work are obviously worse off.

This means that policies to maximize monetary income alone (without regard to all of the non-pecuniary benefits or psychic income individuals enjoy) will not make people happier. When individuals are free to maximize their psychic income, they will choose their optimal mix of labor and leisure, which for some includes working more in high-paying professions. But others will choose a different combination, which could include non-monetary forms of psychic income such as living the life of contemplation. Can we say that one person has a higher psychic income than the other? Rothbard writes: "psychic income, being purely subjective, cannot be measured. Further, from the standpoint of praxeology, we cannot even ordinally compare the psychic income or utility of one person with that of another. We cannot say that A's income or "utility" is greater than B's" ([1962] 2004, p. 300). Outside observers can measure monetary income, but they cannot measure psychic income, which is what matters (Block, 1977, p. 115). Because psychic income is immeasurable one cannot compare two individuals and say that one is better off.

An implication of this point of view is that one cannot look at monetary incomes in different regions and conclude that one group is better off. The average person in Alaska has a higher monetary income than the average person in Hawaii, but we cannot say the average Alaskan is happier than the average Hawaiian, because we have no way to observe their psychic income. The same goes for the average person in Mexico compared with the average person in the United States.[5] Looking at monetary incomes might have some use, because a place with low monetary income might indicate that government has interfered more in the area of exchangeable goods, but it is entirely possible for a country to have high monetary income and government that interferes more in choices relating to leisure.[6] More monetary income may be a good thing, but to the economic subjectivist it is not the only thing.

4.9   Question 8: Are migration patterns a proxy for national utility?
Another way in which economists talk about getting a proxy for well-being is by looking at migration patterns between countries. Following the Tiebout model to its extreme, Dinesh D'Souza (1999) says, "There is one pretty objective measure of what countries work well, and that is do people want to come there?" The examples most commonly given are net migrations from East Berlin to West Berlin or from Mexico to the United States. This proxy does not fall prey to the same problem of looking at monetary income, because when people choose where to reside they take into account not just monetary income but also total psychic income of the two places. If we observe an individual choosing to migrate from country A to country B, we can say that the individual viewed the total package in country B as preferable to that in country A. We can say that the people demonstrated their preference of what country they preferred. It does not require economists to observe psychic income or compare utility levels; all it requires is for economists to observe people's choices.

Despite the simple graces of this theory, one can question how usable the standard is. While we certainly can say that the 10 million Mexicans who migrated to the United States demonstrated that they preferred current day United States to current day Mexico, can we say that total or average utility is higher in the United States than Mexico? Mexico still has 100 million people who have not demonstrated that they prefer the United States to Mexico, so one interpretation of their actions is that those 100 million people actually prefer living in Mexico to the United States. Does that demonstrate that Mexico is more preferred than the United States?

One could argue that in a zero transaction cost world without immigration restrictions, more than 10 million Mexicans would migrate to the United States and this might be true.[7] But if we observed 50 million people migrating and 60 million people staying could we say that the United States is preferable to Mexico? If one just counted numbers, more Mexicans are demonstrating that they prefer to live in Mexico than are demonstrating they want to live in the United States. And even if the number migrating were 70 million compared with 40 million staying, unless economists had a way of measuring and comparing the total psychic income of those leaving to those staying it is not clear what measuring the number of people making a choice even tells. The migrants' consumer surplus or psychic income associated with migrating might be very small compared with the extremely large consumer surplus or psychic income of those staying. Economics is not just about adding up the numbers of people who make a choice. Following such a standard would imply that relative values of goods could be determined by voting, a view that is at odds with our most basic principles of economic subjectivism.

Another way that migration patterns might be used would be to look beyond the number of Mexicans leaving versus staying, and instead compare the number of Mexicans migrating to the United States to the number of Americans migrating to Mexico. This eliminates the problem stemming from the fact that most Mexicans and most Americans stay in their native country. But this standard also has problems. Although an estimated 10 million Mexicans live in the United States, an estimated 1 million Americans live in Mexico. Many of these 1 million Americans are very rich expatriates who could have chosen to live anywhere in the world, whereas many of the 10 million Mexicans living in the United States have much more limited means. Which group of migrants benefits from their move more? Although the actual number of Americans preferring to move to Mexico is less than the number of Mexicans preferring to move to the United States, unless one can measure the marginal utility gained by the 10 million Mexicans moving to the United States and compare that with the marginal utility gained by the 1 million Americans moving to Mexico, the net migration patterns say little about total utility in a country. Coming to such a conclusion would be akin to saying that the 3 million Ford consumers derive more utility from their purchase then the 300 000 Mercedes consumers. We can deduce that the 3 million Ford consumers preferred their choice to all others, and we can deduce that the 300 000 Mercedes consumers preferred their choice to all others, but we cannot say that the Ford consumers preferred their choice more than the Mercedes buyers preferred their choice. And it would be entirely erroneous to try to infer from the data that Ford is better that Mercedes.[8]

4.10   Question 9: Can cost–benefit efficiency be a proxy for utility?

Measuring monetary income or observing migration patterns cannot be used to make comparisons about national well-being because they do not capture important aspects of utility such as psychic income or consumer and producer surplus. The most popular way of taking consumer and producer surplus into account is by looking at societal-wide cost–benefit analysis. This construct, known as Kaldor-Hicks efficiency, cost–benefit efficiency, or simply economic efficiency, takes into account a measure of consumer surplus and producer surplus calculated in dollar terms. By looking at net willingness to pay associated with different potential outcomes, economists have quantitative figures they can rely on to compare different policies. Bryan Caplan (1999, p. 835) writes, "this criterion of efficiency has many advantages over Rothbard's approach. In particular, it actually allows one to make efficiency judgments about the real world – to judge, for example, that Communism was inefficient, or rent control is inefficient, or piracy was inefficient."

Not only is economic efficiency held up as useful for positive analysis, many economists also hold up Kaldor-Hicks efficiency as their normative ideal. Policies, legal cases, and property rights should be determined based on how well they maximize economic efficiency. Supporters say it is the best usable proxy for well-being because it not only takes into account factors like monetary income, but also factors like consumer and producer surplus. This construct has advantages over traditional social welfare functions, because it does not attempt to sum up imaginary utils, it attempts to sum up an objective and cardinal unit: dollars. Different states of the world can be compared by measuring all people's consumer and producer surplus for all goods and then seeing which state of the world has the highest willingness to pay associated with it.

But to certain economic subjectivists, comparing net willingness to pay associated with all different states of the world is much easier said than done. To the thoroughgoing economic subjectivist, Kaldor-Hicks efficiency requires outside observers to know more about individuals' utility functions than outside observers possibly can know. It is one thing to observe a transaction and market price, but how can one observe consumer and producer surplus for all goods, and how can one compare net consumer and producer surpluses in all possible states of the world?

We know that at the current margin of choice, most Americans are willing to spend an additional one-fifth of one cent to consume their 80th gallon of water in a given day, and we also know that the marginal utility of the 80th gallon exceeds the marginal utility of the one-fifth of one cent forgone. But what is my consumer surplus for all 80 gallons? What is your hypothetical maximum willingness to pay for your 70th gallon, your 10th gallon, or your 5th gallon? If someone had four gallons and was contemplating purchasing his fifth, we might be able to observe his willingness to pay for the fifth gallon. But given that we are so far from that situation, it is difficult for most people to think about what they would do with only five gallons or how much they would be willing to pay for each of them.

If calculating the consumer surplus for one person were not difficult enough, cost–benefit efficiency requires the calculation of consumer surplus of water for *everyone*. And once one has calculated the consumer surplus for water, the economist then has to calculate the consumer surplus for all other goods.[9] Once one is done calculating total consumer and producer surplus for all goods for everyone in society one then has to compare the net surplus associated with that state of the world, with the net surplus of every other imaginable state of the world.[10]

To the most thoroughgoing subjectivist, not only is economic efficiency incalculable for simple positive analysis, it is especially meaningless for normative issues. To those whose normative ideal is maximizing economic efficiency, property rights and all other policies must be formulated in a way that maximizes wealth, but to the economic subjectivist there is a problem of infinite regress. When property rights are yet to be defined, willingness to pay is indeterminate, and when willingness to pay is indeterminate, there is no unique assignment of property rights that maximizes wealth. Gerald O'Driscoll (1980, p. 357) writes, "Maximization makes sense if we know who has what rights, and what rules govern the choice process. The suggestion that the maximization principle be used to determine the rights distribution and the legal rules is almost incoherent." How can willingness to pay determine property rights when willingness to pay is determined by property rights?[11]

Since willingness to pay is only meaningful within a system of defined property rights, we have a circularity problem of using economics to render policy. Economists would need to know who owns the property to solve these maximization problems. Unless economists assume that all people are exactly the same and would spend their money exactly the same way, then the assignment of property rights will matter for evaluating economic outcomes. This means that economists cannot say that a certain outcome is socially preferable even if the standard is willingness to pay. The problem relates to the Scitovsky Reversal Paradox, which shows the potential incommensurability of efficiency levels. This is the case when the willingness to pay attached to one outcome exceeds another under the current assignment of property rights, but once property rights are rearranged the ranking is the opposite. This problem can surface if preferences vary across individuals or if individuals' preferences vary over time. Since changes in property rights can alter the production possibilities frontier, even in a simple two-person world we can have a situation where Person 1's preferred bundle is only attainable in State of the World A and Person 2's preferred bundle is only attainable in State of the World B. Which state of the world is more socially efficient (i.e., which state of the world will have the most willingness to pay associated with it)? The answer will depend on the distribution of property rights. When the first person is assigned a large portion of the property rights, the net willingness to see State of the World A will be higher than to see State of the World B, but when the second person is assigned a large portion of the property rights the results will be the opposite.

Consider an example of a neighbor who wishes to play his stereo at night when a neighbor wishes to sleep in perfect quiet. If the person wishing to sleep is a rich old man and the person wishing to play the stereo is a poor young man, chances are the rich man is willing to pay a lot more money for quiet than the young man is willing to pay to play. In this case, a quiet neighborhood is Kaldor-Hicks efficient. But if property rights were reassigned so that the old man becomes a poor miser and the young man becomes a rich bachelor, the willingness to pay associated with quiet will decrease and the willingness to pay associated with music will increase. Is the society with the music richer than the quiet society? Since the two have different preferences, the willingness to pay associated with the two outcomes will differ according to the assignment of property rights.

Not being able to determine the efficient outcome is an issue whenever property rights are up in the air. Consider someone who accidentally damages a Stalin statue outside the residence of a government official. Is this action efficient or inefficient? If the net willingness to pay attached to having the statue in place is positive, then damaging the statue is inefficient, and if the net willingness is negative (assuming the transaction costs of negotiating to remove the statue are prohibitive), then damaging the statue is efficient. But the evaluation will clearly be contingent on the existing assignment of property rights. In societies where dictators own a large portion of resources we see high prices associated with Stalin statues (either in terms of willingness to pay or willingness to be paid to remove the statues), but when property rights are rearranged away from dictators these statues become worthless, and historically are often destroyed. When a Stalin-loving dictator owns most of the property, the state of the world with the Stalin statue in place is more efficient (the willingness to pay attached to that outcome is higher), but when individuals own most of the property, the state of the world without the Stalin statue is more efficient. Is the society with numerous statues of government officials richer than a world without? We cannot answer the question unless we know the distribution of property rights. Rizzo (1980, p. 646) writes, "There is no way, then, to stand outside the law and see how it measures up against an external standard."

If making comparisons about what state of the world is richer for one society is not difficult enough, these issues are even more problematic when making income comparisons between different societies. One must consider not just how one society would rank two social outcomes, but how two societies with different sets of preferences would compare outcomes. When price vectors, preferences, and population size in two societies differ, comparisons about which society is better off become even more awkward (Sen, 1976).

It makes sense to examine how much people value things at the margin *in their existing situations*, and speculators might also guess about how people will react in slightly different situations. But how much people are willing to pay for goods is influenced by each individual's time and place. As Hayek has argued, it is precisely because nobody knows that outcome of markets that we need markets. An outside observer cannot peer into the minds of all individuals and calculate market prices, or the entire consumer surplus for all goods for possible states of the world. Without being able to compare net surplus between different states of the world, economists cannot make comparisons about which societies are more economically efficient.

4.11   Question 10: Can a demonstrated preference approach to the Pareto principle allow us to make relative comparisons about social utility?

If one rejects all of the above ways of making welfare comparisons between different states of the world, what is one left with? In *The Elgar Companion to Austrian Economics* entry on "Austrian Welfare Economics," Tyler Cowen (1994, p. 304) writes, "Welfare economics has received only sporadic attention from those economists usually classified as Austrian. In some cases, the Austrians argue explicitly that welfare economics is an empty box." One set of arguments that Cowen mentions is Rothbard's "Toward a Reconstruction of Utility and Welfare Economics" (1956) where Rothbard critiques existing conceptions of welfare economics, and then at the end presents a different point of view.

Rothbard's proposal can be seen as a twist on Pareto's concept of efficiency. The mainstream conception of Pareto efficiency says that something is an improvement if it makes at least one person better off without anyone worse off, and it says that the world is efficient if no remaining Pareto improvements exist. While many economists pay lip service to this conception of efficiency, few economists use it for real-world policy prescriptions, because as long as at least one person does not like to see others gain, then nothing can be a Pareto improvement. With Rothbard's proposal (1956, p. 250; original emphasis), on the other hand, "we are not interested in his opinions about the exchanges made by *others*, since his preferences are not demonstrated through action and are therefore irrelevant," so he concludes that all one can say is that trade makes parties better off while making no one worse off. Government intervention, in contrast, may benefit the intervener, but we know that it necessarily makes at least one person worse off. Following the premises of the Paretian economists, Rothbard goes on to state:

> Generally, even the most rigorously Wertfrei economists have been willing to allow themselves one ethical judgment: they feel free to recommend any change or process that increases social utility under the Unanimity Rule. Any economist who pursues this method would have to (a) uphold the free market as always beneficial, and (b) refrain from advocating any governmental action. In other words, he would have to become an advocate of "ultra" laissez-faire. (Ibid., p. 253)

Since government action makes at least one person worse off, whereas markets allow all people to maximize (subject to the constraints of the market) their individual utility, Rothbard then states we can say "that the free market maximizes social utility."

This argument has received a lot of attention, some of it positive and much of it negative. Authors such as Laurence Moss and David Prychitko have all criticized Rothbard's discussion of social utility. Others argue that Rothbard is illegitimately attempting to blend positive economics with libertarian policy conclusions, and others argue that Rothbard is illegitimately making claims about society's cardinal utility. Might it be that Rothbard is not as thoroughgoing a subjectivist as many people believe?

Despite the controversy of those pages, an interesting and little known fact is that Rothbard himself did not take them too seriously: On a tape recorded lecture series with little circulation, "A Short Course on Free Market Economics," Murray Rothbard actually says,[12] "I had a lot of fun with this myself. . .in my first article that ever came out." He describes how trade increases the utility of both parties involved and then he says, "If we want to use the term society, which I do not really like anyway, then we can say that social utility is increased." He then says, "When the government enters the picture whatever the government does is decrease someone's social utility, usually of course it's the taxpayer." Rothbard then states:

> Unfortunately I have been accused, or I won't say accused, it has been maintained that my whole basis for laissez faire rests on this whole *social utility nonsense* [emphasis added]. *Of course* it really doesn't. It's all *really a gimmick* [emphasis added] to show that if you really go along with this whole Pareto-optimality-social-utility then you have to confine yourself to laissez faire. It's not my major argument for laissez faire. Any rate, the trouble with those people who think it's my major argument are so inamorate that that's all they can focus on. (Rothbard, Tape 6, "Cost of the Firm" Side B, 35:57 to 37:44)

So while some economists have chided Rothbard's alleged formalism in welfare economics as a pretense of knowledge and others have defended it, they all seem to be reading too much into his writing. Rothbard did not claim to be able to compare the levels of social utility in the free market to other systems. And ultimately Rothbard was explicit that his defense of the free-market depends not on utility comparisons but on rights.

4.12   Conclusion

The principles of economic subjectivism underlie much of modern economics and their importance cannot be overstated. But although almost all economists believe that goods are valued based on how much they satisfy a person's subjective preferences, some economists believe in economic subjectivism in more ways than others. Rather than classifying economists as subjectivists or non-subjectivists, this chapter has discussed some of the ways that economists may or may not be subjectivists. If given a test on economic subjectivism, certain neoclassical economists will score higher than others. Bryan Caplan, for example, might be in agreement with the most thoroughgoing subjectivist on Questions 1–8. In that sense an economist like Caplan would score higher on an economic subjectivism test than someone who believes in social utility such as Ludwig von Mises. But when it comes to Question 9 about cost–benefit efficiency, Caplan scores lower on the economic subjectivism test than a Lionel Robbins or a Murray Rothbard. The more thoroughgoing subjectivists would say that outside observers cannot know how much an individual would be willing to pay for all units of a good under different circumstances, so they cannot calculate and compare consumer surpluses of different states of the world. Yes, Caplan is correct that almost all economists can be classified as believing in some type of economic subjectivism, but many can only be classified as believing in economic subjectivism in the weakest sense. Economists will disagree over what they consider the optimal realm of economic subjectivism, but they should agree that not all economists embrace economic subjectivism to the same degree.

Economic subjectivism has many implications from a positive and normative point of view. From a positive point of view, economic subjectivism rules out many of what might be considered unscientific endeavors of economists. Robbins (1932, p. 125) writes, "Indeed, all that part of the theory of Public Finance which deals with 'Social Utility' goes by the board." Positive economics would still have a lot to say about the world, it just would not attempt to do things like claiming to compare total levels of utility. From a normative point of view, although economic subjectivism is completely value free, embracing it means one is more likely to actually rule out whole classes of normative prescriptions. For example, the person who rejects interpersonal comparisons of utility is less likely to support schemes that forcibly make some worse off for the betterment of the commonweal. Nothing is stopping the economic subjectivist from supporting a specific policy for other normative reasons, but it would be illogical for him to reject adding up utility and then support a policy because it increases total utility.

Exactly how much one embraces economic subjectivism is likely to influence the types of policies one is willing to support. Let us consider some examples. Economists who embrace even moderate subjectivism are much less likely to favor laws mandating that goods be priced according to the number of hours they take to make.[13] This might be one of the reasons why full-fledged socialists are rarer among economists compared with other groups. For those economists who delve deeper into economic subjectivism, there are further implications still. Economists who embrace subjectivism of costs are less likely to favor laws that mandate how much firms charge. Economists who recognize that preferences differ among individuals, are not constant, and are not readily apparent independent of actual choice will be likely to favor government schemes to provide "goods" to benefit all people.

Many justifications for government use utilitarian arguments, which assume that subjective utility is cardinal and commensurable between different people. But the most thoroughgoing economic subjectivists reject these premises. How can we maximize the sum of utils in society when we have no way of adding up or even measuring imaginary utils?[14] In addition to rejecting utilitarianism, the most thoroughgoing subjectivists reject other attempts to create proxies for societal well-being such as monetary income, migration patterns, or cost–benefit analysis. Each of these policies measures something but none measure psychic utility. If consequentialist theories such as utilitarianism or economic efficiency norm are meaningless then what are we left with? For one economic subjectivism does not rule out deontological or rights-based theories. Economic subjectivism does not provide any arguments for rights, but it rules out a substantial number of consequentialist schemes. Perhaps this is why many thoroughgoing economic subjectivists happen to judge policy based on rights. And they also happen to be libertarian.

Notes

*   Thanks to Nick Snow and Thurman Wayne Pugh for helpful research assistance, and to Peter Boettke and Benjamin Powell for helpful comments and suggestions.
1.   Here we are referring to economic subjectivism, which says that that what people consider valuable is subjective. It has nothing to do with ethical subjectivism or metaphysical subjectivism.
2.   For a discussion of some of the differences see Rothbard ([1962] 2004, p. 315).
3.   This is only a subset of arguments in the area of antitrust. The antitrust arguments based on Kaldor-Hicks efficiency differ.
4.   Again I should emphasize that this is only a subset of arguments in the area of antitrust. The antitrust arguments based on Kaldor-Hicks efficiency differ.
5.   Matters get even more complicated when prices and available goods differ between countries, not to mention preferences of individuals (Rothbard [1962] 2004, p. 301).
6.   Restrictions on alcohol, drugs, or gambling can fit this bill.

7. On the other hand, it might not actually turn out that way. In a zero transaction cost world, it might be the case that all migrant workers would be hired from lower wage countries such as Vietnam rather than from relatively higher wage countries such as Mexico. Mexicans might only be coming to the United States as much as they are because of the high transaction costs of Americans hiring other migrant workers.
8. It is even more problematic to use migration patterns to show the superiority of free-markets. Although many migrants flee to come to a nation with more economic opportunity, economic research also shows that higher welfare benefits are another motivating factor at the margin. Simply observing the net number of migrants does not enable one to disentangle these two factors.
9. Once while I was in graduate school at a social event, a University of Chicago educated professor was pondering, "How do we calculate the consumer surplus for air?" I responded, "Simple, we just take the integral with respect to air."
10. The advocate of economic efficiency might argue that efficiency comparisons do not require calculating the consumer and producer surplus for all goods in all states of the world; it just requires calculating the marginal changes in consumer and producer surpluses between two states of the world. Although comparisons between two close states of the world might be easier, if that was all economists could do, they could not ensure they were at all global, as opposed to a local, optimum of economic efficiency.
11. The following four paragraphs are based on White and Stringham (2004, pp. 378–80).
12. I am grateful to Bryan Caplan for him spending $200 when these tapes were available and for him letting me listen to his copy.
13. Nothing would stop an economic subjectivist from advocating such a policy since economic subjectivism is only about positive economics, but most people would probably find that position questionable.
14. Such criticisms apply equally to act utilitarianism and rule utilitarianism since even though the theories have differences, both of them attempt to maximize utils in society.

References

Block, Walter (1977). "Coase and Demsetz on Private Property Rights," *Journal of Libertarian Studies* **1**(2): 111–15.
Boudreaux, Donald, Roger Meiners, and Todd Zywicki (1999). "Talk is Cheap: The Existence Value Fallacy," *Environmental Law* **29**(4): 765–809.
Buchanan, James M. (1969). *Cost and Choice: An Inquiry in Economic Theory*. Chicago: University of Chicago Press.
Caplan, Bryan (1999). "Why I Am Not an Austrian Economist. . .and Why You Shouldn't be Either," *Southern Economic Journal* **65**(4): 823–38.
Cowen, Tyler (1994). "Austrian Welfare Economics," in Peter J. Boettke (ed.), *The Elgar Companion to Austrian Economics*, Aldershot, UK and Brookfield, VT, USA: Edward Elgar, pp. 304–12.
D'Souza, Dinesh (1999). "Transcript of Interview with John Stossel," in *Is American Number One*, available at: http://tinyurl.com/is-america-number-one; accessed 10 February 2010.
Hayek, F.A. [1968] (2002). "Competition as a Discovery Procedure," reprinted in *Quarterly Journal of Austrian Economics* **5**(3): 9–23.
Mises, L.V. [1949] (1996). *Human Action: A Treatise on Economics* (4th edition). San Francisco: Fox and Wilkes.
O'Driscoll, Gerald (1980). "Justice, Efficiency, and the Economic Analysis of Law: A Comment on Fried," *Journal of Legal Studies* **9**(2): 355–66.
Rizzo, Mario (1980). "The Mirage of Efficiency," *Hofstra Law Review* **8**(3): 641–58.
Robbins, Lionel (1932). *An Essay on the Nature and Significance of Economic Science*. London: Macmillan.
Rothbard, Murray (1956). "Toward a Reconstruction of Utility and Welfare Economics," in Mary Sennholz (ed.), *On Freedom and Free Enterprise: Essays in Honor of Ludwig von Mises*, Princeton: Van Nostrand Company, pp. 224–62.

Rothbard, Murray [1962] (2004). *Man, Economy, and State*. Auburn, AL: Mises Institute.
Sen, Amartya (1976). "Real National Income," *Review of Economic Studies* **43**(1): 19–39.
White, M. and E. Stringham (2004). "Economic Analysis of Tort Law: Austrian and Kantian Perspectives," in M. Oppenheimer and N. Mercuro (eds), *Law and Economics: Alternative Economic Approaches to Legal and Regulatory Issues*, New York: M.E. Sharpe, pp. 374–92.

5 Price: the ultimate heuristic
Stephen C. Miller

5.1 Introduction

The primary difference between the two 2002 Nobel Laureates in Economic Science, Daniel Kahneman and Vernon Smith, revolves around the following proposition: the price system economizes on the information that economic actors have to process in making their own decisions. While both researchers focus on individual decision-making in a world of incomplete information, they arrive at essentially opposite conclusions. One emphasizes the limitations of human cognition while the other emphasizes how *in market settings* people seem capable of overcoming those cognitive limitations. The truth is that people do not "overcome" their cognitive limitations where market prices and incentives are present, but they do discard their counterproductive biases and mental shortcuts. Instead, they rely primarily on price signals. According to current behavioral researchers, in market settings individuals tend to be less biased and stubborn; that is, they more closely resemble *Homo economicus*. It follows that the price system spurs rational behavior.

When the subjects of an economic experiment exhibit some sort of "irrationality," they don't appear to make decisions based on unbiased expected value calculations. Instead the subjects are observed using mental shortcuts, called heuristics, to make decisions. For example, these decisions can include: whether to accept a bid in an auction, or whether to sell a good at less than its known purchase price. The behavioral observation is that subjects guess at expected values rather than calculate. They make guesses about the seller's and buyer's surpluses, about transactions costs, and so on. Kahneman's research program is to essentially test how and where these guesses tend to be wrong, and Smith's research program tests how and where these guesses tend to be right. When looked at side-by-side, the finding in behavioral economics research is that when the cost of mistakes rises, the tendency to make those mistakes falls. In a sense, subjects in experiments exhibit rationality at the highest level – when making decisions, they economize on thinking itself.

Market actors are not perfect calculators of costs and benefits. Bias exists, and it is often costly. Bargaining can fail, viable profit opportunities are sometimes abandoned, and consumers often experience remorse. Behavioral economics provides a valuable approach for understanding these events, and can be a useful tool for identifying ways to improve on the status quo.

But behavioral economics does not necessarily support government intervention in markets. One obvious criticism of that view is that presumably political actors are just as prone to bias and other cognitive failures as market actors. Further, markets have a profit-and-loss mechanism that is not present in the political sphere. The profit-and-loss mechanism relies on market prices, and ultimately it is because of market prices that markets can overcome the hurdles of limited information and imperfect cognition.

5.2   Heuristic versus bias

Heuristics only appear "irrational" where individuals misapply them. A heuristic, by definition, is imperfect – it will be inapplicable in certain situations. If an individual wishes to minimize cognitive costs, then there exists the possibility of "wrong" decisions – that is, the possibility that an otherwise effective heuristic can fail in certain settings. Shortcuts have limited usefulness, but are adopted by rational individuals so long as they tend to succeed more often than they fail. Sometimes the terms "heuristic" and "bias" are used interchangeably,[1] but there is an important distinction between the two: the use of heuristics is a way to reduce the costs of decision-making, from seeking information to the conscious weighing of costs and benefits; but many definitions of bias include some concept of *partiality* or *prejudice*. Truth is complex, perhaps unknowable. Heuristics are a tool for approximating truth, while bias is a tool for avoiding truth. It is certainly possible that an individual can cling to a mental shortcut to the point that it becomes bias. But the use of mental shortcuts is not necessarily (or even especially) related to bias. An appropriate, efficient heuristic will even tend to reduce bias.

The human mind evolved in a non-market setting – prior to the emergence of complex market activity and the multitude of choices it brings. Many heuristics and other decision-making tools are appropriate for survival in small, homogeneous groups near subsistence. The behavioral/experimental economics findings of cognitive bias, from availability bias to loss aversion, suggest that many evolved heuristics can inhibit exchange and the mutual gains from trade. However, the pressures of supply and demand have a tendency to punish those who hold onto ineffective heuristics. Bias can be reduced as the cost of bias increases, and in market settings, prices play an important role in that process.

Both as consumers and producers, market actors use a variety of mental shortcuts, that is, heuristics, when making decisions. The market price of an input or final good is the most important, and the one heuristic that characterizes market settings. Prices provide information of a unique kind: information entangled with incentives. They convey relative scarcities for goods and services, but also provide a clear incentive to buy more or buy less. Individuals have severe cognitive limitations; they are simply unable to account for all market conditions at once. But in market economies, decisions in the face of incomplete information are aided by price signals. Prices are the primary heuristic that allows market actors to overcome their cognitive limitations. Without market prices, the cognitive limitations that Austrians and behavioral economists emphasize prevent rational economic calculation.

5.3 Heuristics and rationality

One view of behavioral economics is that its conclusions generally support government intervention in markets, because of its emphasis on the intersection of irrationality and ignorance – traditionally a blind spot in neoclassical economics. Ignorance is best defined as a lack of knowledge, but the definition of "irrationality" is in dispute among economists: some adopt a *substantive* definition while others use a *procedural* notion of rationality. In this chapter, irrationality refers to the tendency of human beings to be hampered by bias in their decision-making. Irrationality is often about how people deal with their lack of knowledge; standard neoclassical search theory presumes that ignorance forces individuals to make guesses. A typical version of this view is that guesses are normally distributed around some mean "truth." So long as there are enough guessers, the average guess will tend to be correct (Caplan, 2002). People have imperfect knowledge, but they make their best-informed guesses about the probabilities of events in the face of uncertainty.

Both irrationality and ignorance are hurdles that must be overcome in markets, but simply identifying those hurdles does not necessarily imply that those hurdles are insurmountable. If there were no hurdles to overcome, there would be very few profit opportunities for entrepreneurs to find. For example, it is because of asymmetric information in used car markets that manufacturer-certified used cars are profitable. Reputation ends up being a very important asset in markets, and to build a positive reputation sellers will tend to share their surpluses with consumers, even when asymmetric information may allow them to extract more in the short term.

Often the "Ultimatum Game" is used as an example of how people are not always economically rational. The Ultimatum Game is an experiment where one subject must make a take-it-or-leave-it offer, that is, an ultimatum, to another. Player 1 is given a sum of money, for example $10, and must divide it between herself and someone else, a Player 2 unknown to her. Suppose Player 1 offers $3 to Player 2, leaving $7 for herself. If Player

2 accepts the offer, then Player 1 receives $7 and Player 2 receives $3. But if Player 2 rejects the offer, neither player receives any payment. A perfectly "rational" person in the position of Player 2 will accept any positive offer, since even if Player 1 offers one cent, one cent is still preferable to nothing.

The experiments show that many people in Player 2's position will reject very low offers (presumably out of spite). Further, Player 1 antici- pates such a reaction to lowball offers, and usually makes an offer closer to 50 percent of the total than to zero (Thaler, 1992, p. 22). Behavioral researchers often recognize that rejecting a positive offer can be rational, if fairness is more important than a small sum of money (ibid., pp. 23–4). Given fairness as a value, an alternative test of rationality would be to see if people in the Player 2 position accept smaller and smaller shares as the absolute sum of money to be divided increases. For a given individual, the minimum acceptable percentage is surely lower for a $100 000 version of the Ultimatum Game than it is for a $10 version. In fact, in higher-stakes Ultimatum Games, more experienced players do tend to make very low offers (List and Cherry, 2000).

Some behavioral researchers believe the overall tendency to reject offers out of spite is relevant in markets where one party has strong market power, that is, where sellers (or buyers) have significant monopoly (or monopsony) power. Thaler (1992, p. 31) says: "Just as the recipient in an ultimatum game may reject a small but positive offer, a buyer may refrain from purchasing at a price that leaves a small bit of consumer surplus but is viewed as dividing the surplus in an unfair manner." The extension of an interesting behavioral finding into market activity is deeply flawed. Thaler offers a mistaken notion of consumer surplus. If consumer surplus is the difference between the maximum that a consumer is willing to pay for a good and the price paid, then there can be no forgone consumer surplus in a situation where the buyer is *unwilling* to pay the seller's price. The consumer's unwillingness to buy may be based on a notion of fairness or a multitude of other factors. But when a consumer is unwilling, that person *by definition* has no consumer surplus. The buyer's demand price is funda- mentally subjective, based on subjective values and beliefs; it is therefore nonsensical to presume that one of those values (fairness) is somehow exogenous or apart from consumer demand.

The behavioral experiments do show that most human beings have a notion of fairness that affects their valuation of goods and services. But the experiments also show that fairness has its limits – higher stakes lead to more narrowly "rational" behavior.[2] It is not that notions of fair- ness hinder rational economic action, but that notions of fairness are yet another subjective value that rational sellers (and buyers) take into account when engaged in exchange.

5.4 Calculation and the role of market prices

Basic microeconomic theory is fundamentally a story of market prices. Mainstream micro theorists define equilibrium as the point where the market price is stable, and price is stable only when quantity supplied equals quantity demanded. If price is above the equilibrium, quantity supplied exceeds quantity demanded, which is a surplus, and that prompts sellers to lower their prices. If price is below the equilibrium, then quantity demanded is greater than quantity supplied, and a shortage results. The shortage prompts sellers to raise their prices. It is only in equilibrium that there is no pressure on price to rise or fall. Even though conditions, that is, the supply and demand schedules themselves, are constantly shifting, these pressures will continually push price *toward* equilibrium. This understanding of prices coincides with the explanations given in most modern textbooks, and even seems to be understood by the editors of the *Washington Post*, who wrote in response to calls for regulation of gas prices:

> When oil prices spike, it is because of scarcity – for example, scarcity caused by hurricane damage to petroleum infrastructure on the Gulf Coast. The best way to manage that scarcity is for producers to make a special effort to get oil to the market and for consumers to make a special effort to cut back. Higher prices encourage both of those responses; rather than complain of price gouging, Congress should celebrate price signals. By contrast, controlled prices create no pressure for extra production or conservation. They just create gas lines: Witness the 1970s. (11 November 2005, p. A24).

The standard depiction of prices appears passive; prices are moved when sellers observe a surplus or shortage. The insight is that when prices rise or fall, the change transmits an important bit of relevant information. Buyers are alerted to the scarcity, and, in response to the incentive of a higher price, buy less. That information is a *price signal*. Price signals, in the Austrian view, suggest a two-sided relationship between changes in relative scarcities and market prices: increased scarcity relative to alternatives will push prices up, but the movement of price transmits that information – that the good in question has become relatively scarce – throughout the market. This role of price signals is so important that, Ludwig von Mises famously said, in the absence of price signals rational economic calculation is *impossible*.

In his classic critique of socialism, Mises ([1920] 1990) argued that only market settings can generate useful prices. In behavioral jargon, Mises argued that by removing market prices, you rob producers at all levels of their best available heuristic. Joseph Salerno (1990, p. 36) explained: "Mises's. . .central insight is that monetary calculation is the indispensable tool for choosing the optimum among the vast array of intricately-related production plans that are available for employing the factors of production within the framework of the social division of labor." Salerno's elucidation of Mises is, in essence, that in markets prices are the ultimate heuristic device – they make rational economic activity possible. Socialism, a system without private property, is fundamentally a non-market setting. Some authority may assign prices, but outside of a market setting, those prices are simply not an effective guide for making decisions. Profit-and-loss accounting becomes guesswork, and thus decisions about what and how much to produce lose their meaning.

Without market prices, for example, producers can only with great difficulty decide which inputs to use. F.A. Hayek (1945) buttressed that case with his argument that, over an entire economy with essentially infinite combinations of inputs to create thousands (millions?) of final products, those decisions are too difficult to make because the knowledge of what can be done, how it can be done, is not held by any one person. This holds for the knowledge required to produce even a simple consumer good. The market prices of various substitute inputs do not provide producers with all of the information about their appropriateness for production. But those input prices do tell them how much they can afford to sell. Market prices allow alternative inputs to be weighed against each other through the mechanism of profit-and-loss accounting.

5.5   Is behavioral economics compatible with Austrian economics?

What makes "Austrian" the claim that prices both provide incentives and send signals? Surely the prototypical neoclassical economist would not disagree that, for example, rising gasoline prices will induce consumers to change their behavior accordingly. Veltheus (2004, p. 373) summarizes the difference between the neoclassical and Austrian views:

> Whereas according to the Austrian view prices play an active role in the discovery process by spreading information yet unknown to actors on the market in a disequilibrium situation, they merely "summarize" knowledge already known in an equilibrium situation according to neoclassical economics.

In disequilibrium, standard neoclassical price theory appears to only tell a story of incentives. If quantity supplied exceeds quantity demanded in a particular market, a surplus exists. The neoclassical story is that the surplus creates downward pressure on price, and the falling market price induces consumers to purchase more and sellers to supply less. Price provides an incentive to act, but does not appear to inform actors.

But in a sense, this example of a rapidly falling price can itself be indicative of a surplus, in other words sellers and buyers *are* receiving an important signal. This is a point emphasized by F.A. Hayek (1945, p. 525), when he explains that the "man on the spot" needs to know "*how much more or less* difficult to procure [resources] have become compared with other things with which he is also concerned, or how much more or less urgently wanted" those resources are (emphasis original). In the neoclassical paradigm if people want something more urgently, then that is an increase in demand that, ceteris paribus, leads to a higher price. The difference between the schools is one of emphasis: the standard neoclassical story emphasizes the mechanism by which price moves toward a new equilibrium. The Austrian emphasis is on the mechanism by which demanders of a good respond to the movement in price.

For Hayek's "man on the spot," information is necessary. But clearly what that individual needs most is relevant information. Hayek (ibid.; emphasis original) argued that for such an individual a great deal of information is irrelevant:

> There is hardly anything that happens anywhere in the world that *might* not have an effect on the decision he ought to make. But he need not know of these events as such, nor of *all* their effects. It does not matter for him *why* at the particular moment more screws of one size than of another are wanted, *why* paper bags are more readily available than canvas bags, or *why* skilled labor, or particular machine tools, have for the moment become more difficult to acquire.

Much information is irrelevant, though. Further, much of the information for Hayek's man on the spot could potentially be a waste of his time, or even misleading. Hayek's view stands in stark contrast to the neoclassical treatment of information in search theory. Search theory does not really discuss the heterogeneity of information, nor does it emphasize the fact that some information is not just irrelevant, but can be misleading. Individuals lacking information, in the search-theoretic world, seek out more – and their search bears a cost. The presumption, above all, is that information is a direct (though not necessarily linear) function of search time. This approach only makes sense if information is fundamentally non-neutral, that is, objective. In a world where "information" includes not just facts, but rules of thumb, "common sense," and other kinds of heuristic devices, it is possible for a continued search to be counterproductive and hinder decision-making. In such cases, a graphical representation of the relationship between search time and information may not pass a "vertical line test" and thus not be a mathematically tractable function.

In essence, this criticism is another way of voicing Austrian concerns about how people actually make decisions in the face of imperfect information. Bryan Caplan (2002) has pointed out how bias presents a problem for the neoclassical approach of treating error as being randomly distributed around some mean "truth":

> I grant that there is one big defect in the neoclassical approach to imperfect knowledge. But it is a defect that Austrians almost never mention! The problem: Do the probabilities that people assign fit the facts? At least as researchers, most economists assume that beliefs about the world are on average correct. But empirically, this is often not so. Flying is much safer statistically than driving, but many people refuse to accept the fact. A large field known as behavioral economics documents such biases.
>   . . .Now what is Prof. Boettke going to tell you? I suspect that he is going to say that merely focusing on people's erroneous beliefs "makes me an Austrian."[3]

Caplan's emphasis on systematic bias in his research may not make him an "Austrian," but it certainly separates him from the neoclassical orthodoxy. Further, Caplan and Stringham (2005) established the importance of systematic bias in the political economy of both Mises and Bastiat. Whether the insights from behavioral economics, including Caplan's research, are considered Austrian or not, they have Austrian roots and are important issues for Austrian economists to keep in mind; in many ways those insights (along with empirical inquiry) can serve to strengthen Austrian critiques of the neoclassical view of imperfect information.

Viewed through the lens of systematic bias, it is possible to consider Austrian economics and behavioral economics to be complements rather than substitutes. Where some behavioral economists part ways with the Austrian view is in their failure to recognize the difference between market interaction and other social settings. Just as Mises and Hayek emphasized the importance of market-generated prices more than 80 years ago in the Socialist Calculation Debate, current generations of Austrian economists must do the same in current debates over behavioral anomalies and cognitive bias. To borrow John List's phrase, behavioral economists need to "meet the market," to understand that people change their behavior when market-generated prices and the incentives behind them are present. The new generation of Austrian-influenced economists are well-equipped to make the introduction.

5.6 Conclusion

Seemingly half of the movies made in the 1980s contained at least one scene of a Wall Street brokerage office with a price ticker streaming in the background. Invariably, someone gets a phone call or sees a newspaper headline that gives some vital information that affects the trading for a particular stock. By the time the protagonist jumps up to look at the ticker, the price of that stock is already plummeting (or rocketing up) in reaction to the news. Most of the people watching the ticker do not know why the price is changing so quickly, but the change prompts them to get on their phones and get busy buying or selling. Those people, like Hayek's man on the spot, do not need to know *why* the price has changed, the price change itself is sufficient – they know when they must act, and what to do. The ticker is a purely heuristic device; it cannot convey all of the potentially relevant information. But it provides a shortcut, a quick and simple guide for individual decision-makers. In a very simple, direct way, the characters in the movie are responding to market prices the way anyone else does. In the time it takes them to recognize what is going on, they shed any cognitive biases they may have, and take the new price signals at face value.

Only where price signals are unavailable or substantially distorted by intervention will other heuristic devices take over. It is important not to overstate this – notions of fairness, loss aversion, and so on, do not disappear in market settings. They merely diminish; behavioral research confirms that higher stakes and market experience cause drastic changes in how people interact, and in general the change is always toward reduced bias. It is not that price necessarily trumps all other information, but it forces individuals to examine how relevant their other information is, and how useful their current mental tools are.

It is precisely because of the Austrian emphasis on imperfect knowledge that they view prices as so important to rational economic calculation. The Mises-Hayek insight about the role of prices in calculation is the key reason for the difference between Vernon Smith and Daniel Kahneman in their approaches to their study of markets. If human beings did not have cognitive limitations, if they did not fail to make systematic errors in their reasoning, then prices would be unnecessary. Prices allow people to avoid the difficult, perhaps impossible, task of determining the objective truth behind market conditions.

Notes

1. For example, in behavioral literature "availability bias" is also called the "availability heuristic."
2. The difference between "lab" and market settings can be quite pronounced, as demonstrated in several articles by John List and various co-authors. A good example of such work can be found in List (2006).
3. Caplan goes on from here to offer his "Hayek said the sky is blue" objection, that is, simply agreeing with Hayek or Mises on a particular point (the sky is blue, systematic error is a feature of politics, etc.) does not make one an Austrian economist.

References

"A Call to Inaction," Editorial. *Washington Post*, 11 November, 2005: A24.
Caplan, Bryan. 2002. "Why I Am Not an Austrian Economist. . .and Why You Shouldn't Be Either," Opening statement to the Boettke-Caplan Debate at George Mason University (21 November 2002) available at: http://www.gmu.edu/departments/economics/bcaplan/capdebate.htm; accessed 21 January 2010.
Caplan, Bryan and Edward Stringham. 2005. "Mises, Bastiat, Public Opinion, and Public Choice: What's Wrong With Democracy," *Review of Political Economy* **17**(1): 79–105.

Hayek, F.A. 1945. "The Use of Knowledge in Society," *American Economic Review* **35**(4): 519–30.

List, John A. 2006. "The Behavioralist Meets the Market: Measuring Social Preferences and Reputation Effects in Actual Transactions," *Journal of Political Economy* **114**(1): 1–37.

List, John A. and Todd L. Cherry. 2000. "Learning to Accept in Ultimatum Games: Evidence from an Experimental Design that Generates Low Offers," *Experimental Economics* **3**(1): 11–29.

Mises, L.V. [1920] 1990. *Economic Calculation in the Socialist Commonwealth*. Auburn: Ludwig von Mises Institute.

Salerno, J. 1990. "Why a Socialist Economy is 'Impossible'," in *Economic Calculation in the Socialist Commonwealth*. Auburn: Ludwig von Mises Institute.

Thaler, R. 1992. *The Winner's Curse*. Princeton: Princeton University Press.

Veltheus, Olav. 2004. "An Interpretive Approach to Meanings of Prices," *Review of Austrian Economics* **17**(4): 371–86.

6 Without private property, there can be no rational economic calculation
Scott A. Beaulier

It would hardly be unjust to say that the rationalistic approach is here opposed to almost all that is the distinct product of liberty and that gives liberty its value. Those who believe that all useful institutions are deliberate contrivances and who cannot conceive of anything serving a human purpose that has not been consciously designed are almost of necessity enemies of freedom. For them freedom means chaos.

(F.A. Hayek, *Constitution of Liberty*, 1960, p. 61)

6.1 Introduction

Economists generally focus on the positive incentives that property rights create. Perhaps the most widely recognized positive result of clearly defined property rights is a prevention of the "tragedy of the commons" (Hardin, 1968). When people are left alone to pursue their own self-interests in an environment lacking property rights, undesirable social outcomes – also known as the tragedy of the commons – often result. For example, when there were no regulations on buffalo hunting in the 1800s, overharvesting occurred, driving buffalo in the United States to near extinction.

On the other hand, we know that when property rights are well-defined and protected, people have a strong incentive to be good stewards of resources. In fact, if resources are valuable enough and property rights are well-defined, people will engage in or encourage the production of goods that might have at one time been thought of as endangered or vanishing. For example, buffalo populations have increased in the West now that property rights in buffalo have been created, meaning that buffalo can be privately owned and sold at a profit.

Giving people the proper incentives to care for resources is only one beneficial aspect of property rights, however. An equally important, but less tangible, benefit of clearly defined property rights is that such rights enable the communication of market values and the relative scarcity of particular products. For example, when water rights are individually owned, and individuals must buy their water from private owners, the price of the water reflects the true scarcity and value of the resource. By contrast, this information is often obscured by government subsidies and price controls, meaning that the market is unable to accurately convey the value of water.

Economists have long focused on the role that property rights play in making markets work, largely due to the information created and communicated when individuals and firms freely exchange their privately owned goods and services. Adam Smith emphasized the importance of private property rights when he wrote:

> Commerce and manufactures can seldom flourish long in any state which does not enjoy a regular administration of justice, in which the people do not feel themselves secure in the possession of their property, in which the faith of contracts is not supported by law, and in which the authority of the state is not supposed to be regularly employed in enforcing the payment of debts from all those who are able to pay. ([1776] 1981, p. 910)

Ludwig von Mises, F.A. Hayek, and other Austrian economists built on Smith's work in this area. For Austrian economists, markets can only send proper signals about relative scarcity when a certain set of institutions, namely private property and the rule of law, are in place. Mises ([1927] 1996, p. 184) was quite explicit about the importance of private property when he argued that "interventionism," which aims at regulating and restricting property rights, "cannot attain the ends that its advocates intend it to attain." According to Mises ([1932] 1981, p. 102; emphasis added):

> To suppose that a socialist community could substitute calculations in kind for calculations in terms of money is an illusion. In a community that does not practice exchange, calculations in kind can never cover more than consumption goods. They break down completely where goods of higher order are concerned. Once society abandons free pricing of production goods rational production becomes *impossible*. Every step that leads away from private ownership of the means of production and the use of money is a step away from rational economic activity.

For Mises, interventions into the marketplace are self-defeating, and they distort the information created by property rights. At the limit, the complete abolition of property rights would make rational economic calculation impossible.

The Austrian "impossibility" argument is well known and nicely summarized by Peter Boettke ([1998] 2001, p. 31):

1. Without private property in the means of production, there will be no market for the means of production;
2. Without a market for the means of production, there will be no monetary prices established for the means of production;

3. Without monetary prices, reflecting the relative scarcity of capital goods, economic decision makers will be unable to rationally calculate the alternative use of capital goods.

In other words, when the capitalist institution of private property is abolished, rational economic calculation is no longer possible.

Austrians often discuss property rights as they would exist in a purely capitalist or purely socialist society. However, property rights in the real world are complex and often poorly defined. Since property rights are crucial for the coordination of economic activities, the central question for economists and policy-makers becomes the question of how to gather accurate information about the scarcity of resources in a world with imperfect property rights. The collection of information is greatly complicated by the fact that the market is a large, complex, and rapidly changing social institution; no individual could possibly hope to acquire the information necessary to control or exploit the market. As Hayek ([1945] 1980, p. 78) notes:

> [The knowledge problem] is rather a problem of how to secure the best use of resources known to any of the members of society, for ends whose relative importance only these individuals know. Or, to put it briefly, it is a problem of the utilization of knowledge which is not given to anyone in its totality.

The knowledge of "the particular circumstances of time and place" in the market (ibid., p. 80) is inextricably linked to property rights. Therefore, changes in property rights, such as privatization programs, can affect the dispersal of knowledge within an economy, which ultimately affects individual behavior and overall economic performance.

6.2 Neoclassical privatization

In standard economic theory, property rights are said to reduce uncertainty, internalize externalities, and provide people with the much-needed incentive to take care of the things they own. Thus, it would seem that the best way to deal with any problems resulting from common-pool resource ownership would be to "privatize, privatize, privatize" (Friedman, 1991). Nevertheless, state-led privatization efforts in practice have produced uneven distributional consequences and sometimes make bad situations even worse.

The reason many efforts to privatize resources have failed is because the policy-makers in charge of the privatization misunderstand the role property rights play in communicating market information. The policy-makers in charge of privatization efforts, who are usually trained in neoclassical economics, act as Adam Smith's ([1759] 1982, pp. 233–4) "man of system";

they try to stand outside of the economic system and act as though they have full information about all relevant prices, costs, and consequences of their reform proposals. In an ideal world, these planners would be fortunate enough to have full and complete information, and thus the neoclassical approach to economic reform could be defended because it would engineer a unique solution in which society's overall well-being is maximized.

Real-world economic planning, however, takes place in an environment of uncertainty in which cultures and expectations vary. In such an environment, our knowledge about the economic system is not even probabilistic. To be able to form a useful probabilistic model, there needs to be some general idea of possible outcomes and a confidence that the possible outcomes are exhaustive. In complex economic systems, however, knowledge is fragmented and dispersed. As a result, the most planners can hope for is to form highly imprecise, imperfect estimates of possible outcomes.

Perhaps the easiest way to understand the economic problems involved in centralized reform efforts is to look at recent experiments with privatization. Throughout Eastern Europe and the former Soviet Union, extremely intelligent economists, such as Anders Aslund, Jeffrey Sachs, and Andrei Shleifer, were put in charge of post-communist reform and privatization programs. When the experts came onto the scene, a number of key industries, which were previously nationalized, were ready to be privatized. They tried to come up with comprehensive reform plans in which "waves" of privatization were introduced. The initial values of industries undergoing privatization were based on cost-plus estimates of asset values. Once established, the privatizations were carried out through auctions, management-employee buyouts (MEBOs), and voucher privatization schemes.

While the idea of privatizing state-owned industries was a noble one, the actual outcomes of post-communist privatizations have been generally viewed as disappointing. The predicted post-privatization "take-offs" in economic growth did not occur. Many Eastern European countries are struggling to find their way in the post-communist period. The Russian economy, where reforms were heavily influenced by Aslund, Sachs, and Shleifer, has enjoyed an overall rate of growth near zero since the collapse of communism (Leeson and Trumbull, 2006).

Corruption problems surfaced in many of the privatization schemes. The benefits of many privatization programs flowed primarily to political insiders and people loyal to the new governments. Many of the previous de facto owners viewed the privatization programs as illegitimate and engaged in destructive behaviors against the new class of property owners, such as rioting and stealing capital before the new property owners took over; such behaviors increased the enforcement costs of privatization and lowered overall welfare for the reforming economies.

The new governments' desires to create equity among their citizens often overrode concerns with economic efficiency. Since the main objectives of privatization programs were to disperse the benefits of privatization to all citizens, create a middle class, and "buy" the public's support for privatization, many governments attempted to "democratize" ownership by giving all citizens stakes in the old state-owned resources. Privatization in practice, however, did not usually produce the ideal results for which the reformers hoped; the programs proved cumbersome, and the resources were difficult to value initially. As a result, voucher programs with well-intentioned aims ended up benefiting a small minority of influential shareholders.

These unexpectedly poor outcomes were often due to the fact that many of the assets being privatized were not worth nearly as much as the reformers thought they were worth. For example, some state-run firms had little positive value and should have been shut down instead of privatized. The mixed track record of post-communist privatization is largely a result of economists basing policies on a flawed neoclassical model of economic behavior. The reformers lacked the necessary information to properly value and sell off property that was formerly controlled by the state, so their privatization schemes failed to attain the level of success the reformers hoped for. Peter Boettke ([1994] 2001, p. 192) explains the problem as follows:

> The problem with the conventional privatization package, however, is that one cannot value assets without a market, but a reliable market cannot exist without private property. The whole point of the privatization schemes of vouchers or public auction is to create private ownership. But how is the value of assets to be determined without a market in the first place? In other words, a voucher program is predicated on the ability to value assets, even though the whole point of the exercise is to create markets that will enable participants to assess the value of assets. If valuation could take place independent of the private property context, then privatization would be redundant and unnecessary.

6.3   Spontaneous privatization

The Austrian approach to privatization, in contrast to the neoclassical model, emphasizes the subjective and contextual nature of property rights. Austrian economists want the government removed from the reform process. When the government takes a laissez faire approach to privatization, each industry can find its own way towards the market, free from central direction. In many industries, the de facto owners become the new stakeholders. While spontaneous privatization might create inherent biases, it does a better job of putting local knowledge to work because the de facto owners have a firm understanding of relevant resource values and existing property rights. When spontaneous privatizations occur, a government's role in economic reforms is limited; this mode of privatization is preferable to government-controlled privatization because the knowledge necessary for reform can only emerge from decentralized markets.

The neoclassical, top-down approach and the spontaneous approach to privatization differ in many other important ways. A centralized approach to privatization involves an attempt to coordinate the actions of different people within a set of clearly defined instructions, which will ideally produce efficient economic results. Laissez faire or spontaneous privatization, by contrast, makes no assumptions about the rules necessary for efficient results. Instead, abstract, general rules will emerge from the decentralized market. Successful privatization and coordination will come about as people take account of other people's behavior. If, for example, many different people are bargaining over rights to one resource, spontaneous privatization will allow such rights to increase in value, which will cause some potential owners to lose interest in the expensive right and look elsewhere for opportunities. By keeping asset values fixed, the neoclassical approach to privatization, by contrast, sends a false signal to potential owners about the relative scarcity of rights.

Clearly, the neoclassical and Austrian approaches to privatization differ in the ways in which they make use of knowledge. In the neoclassical approach, the parameters that guide privatization are not flexible. The feedback received by planners in control of privatization must be consolidated, so changes to the privatization programs are made only gradually. Spontaneous privatization, by contrast, incorporates every piece of relevant information. The value of resources can adjust immediately to changes in opinion, and the nature of rights can evolve without any commands from a central authority.

Ultimately, neoclassical privatization programs are problematic because they represent an attempt to centrally design economic institutions. The reformers specify certain objectives, such as increased economic efficiency or greater equality among a nation's citizens, and they hope privatization programs can help achieve some of the stated goals. Once the goals are clearly defined, resources are then allocated according to some centralized view of objectives and opportunities. When a thorough dose of real, or "robust," political economy is introduced into their privatization schemes, however, the reforming countries' growth prospects become bleaker.

Austrian economists generally reject the traditional, or neoclassical, approach to privatization because it works on the assumption that the privatization problem is simply an engineering problem. As Austrian economists recognize, the design of a property rights system cannot be reduced to a formulaic problem with a readily available solution. The more appropriate attitude for policy-makers who want to avoid the errors of rational constructivism is to view themselves as gardeners, not engineers. Vernon Smith (2003, p. 502), among others, makes a distinction between evolved rules and constructivist rules when he writes:

> Rules emerge as a spontaneous order – they are found – not deliberately designed by one calculating mind. Initially constructivist institutions undergo evolutionary change adapting beyond the circumstances that gave them birth. What emerges is a "social mind" that solves complex organization problems without conscious cognition.

For Smith and Austrian economists, policy-makers face an insurmountable epistemic constraint if they try to control the privatization process. Rather than try to control the process, the act of privatization itself should be turned over to the market so that local knowledge is able to surface.

Even though neoclassical privatization might be flawed in both theory and practice, the alternative is not a system of central planning in which property rights are abolished but, rather, laissez faire or spontaneous privatization. Spontaneous privatization can be understood as "all privatization efforts that occur outside the initiative and central direction of the state" (Hill and Karner, 1996, p. 81). In other words, spontaneous privatization comes from the bottom up. Spontaneous property rights emerge slowly, and the definition and enforcement of the emerging rights do not come all at once but, rather, develop as the rights become more legitimate and valuable. Hernando de Soto (2000, pp. 164–71) offers a nice summary of extralegal rights and spontaneous privatization. According to de Soto (p. 165), "the right of universal access to property is now recognized by nearly every constitution in the world and by many international conventions." However, as de Soto notes, though property rights are needed for economic development and poverty alleviation, privatizations have often failed because:

> most legal procedures to create formal property are not geared to process extralegal proofs of ownership that lack any visible chain of title. . .

> What the government had not taken into account was that when people finally acquire property, they have their own ideas about how to use and exchange it. If the legal system does not facilitate the needs and ambitions, they will move out of the system in droves. (Ibid., pp. 166–7)

According to some legal scholars, such as Holmes and Sunstein (1999), the extralegal rights we are discussing are meaningless because property rights cannot exist without the state. However, though legal scholars may dispute the status of extralegal rights, they are meaningful and must be examined because people give meaning to extralegal rights. The basic problem with state-led privatization, and the main reason Austrian economists view spontaneous privatization favorably, is that officials guiding state-led privatization lack the incentives and information to correctly privatize scarce resources. When top-down, formal privatization efforts are initiated, these reforms often fail to acknowledge the rights of the de facto owners in control of the resources. As a result, the de facto owners face perverse incentives to resist reform, deplete a resource's value, or do both.

Critics of the argument for spontaneous privatization often interpret the argument as a defense of anarchy and chaos, instead of order and rationality. These critics point to the hierarchical, and often successful, decision-making of entrepreneurs within firms as examples of how gradual and rational approaches to a muddled business world can produce desirable results. Further, critics of spontaneous privatization argue that, in an environment in which transaction costs are high, centralization and planning are often superior to decentralization (Coase, 1937); since high transaction costs seem to be symptomatic of reforming and transition economies, a more centralized approach to reform might be justified.

Laissez faire privatization is not an argument against planning or rationality, however. The argument for spontaneous privatization is one in which the rationality of individuals in control of resources is embraced. Defenders of spontaneous privatization want to allow the de facto owners of resources to take advantage of local knowledge, arguing that this approach is more effective than highly centralized, bureaucratic privatization programs. De facto owners have a better idea about which assets are valuable enough to privatize and which are not. Moreover, de facto owners have a better sense of how problems of simultaneity and sequencing of privatization should be dealt with; when one resource is privatized, it sometimes creates a pressing need for others to be privatized.

Though Austrian economists generally favor spontaneous privatization when compared with top-down privatization, spontaneous privatization is not free from problems. First, spontaneous privatization cannot occur in a society that does not value or respect private property rights. The prevailing cultural norms in a given country act as a hard constraint on privatization efforts. Without the right cultural environment, property rights systems will not be robust. As Peter Boettke ([1996] 2001, p. 257) puts it, "Rules are only RULES if customary practice dictates." But, cultural problems are not unique to spontaneous privatization programs; in fact, they act as a constraint against any kind of reform, whether it be top-down or spontaneous. Moreover, it is unclear to what extent culture is malleable and how quickly it can be changed.

When we talk seriously about spontaneous privatization, enforcement problems are also an obvious cause for concern. Since spontaneous privatization is extralegal, what are the mechanisms for resolving disputes? Formal sources of authority, such as courts and regulators, are inadequate for dealing with such disputes because these sources of authority run contrary to the nature of extralegal rights. Without formal enforcement, titling and transferring of rights is more costly. On the other hand, informal rights evolve and become sophisticated during the course of spontaneous privatization. Over time, some of the rights that emerge from the informal sector gain recognition and acceptance by formal legal systems, making it possible for the formal systems to enforce the property rights that have emerged through an organic and legitimate process.

Finally, capital flows and foreign direct investment opportunities may not be realized when property rights are decentralized. The "dead capital" problem described by de Soto (2000) arises because banks require clear, formal property rights systems for lending. Because of their extralegal status, informal rights may not be effective in promoting capital investment and widespread economic growth. Though it may be more difficult for entrepreneurs operating outside of the formal property rights system to obtain capital, it is not impossible. Microfinance programs and collective efforts that pool savings together are bottom-up approaches that have surfaced to deal with this challenge.

6.4   Conclusion

Property rights play a central role in disseminating knowledge and information throughout an economic system. Austrian economists favor laissez faire, or spontaneous, privatization because this approach to privatization recognizes the important and sensitive information available to de facto owners. De facto owners have a strong incentive to get the institutions "right" when privatizing; by contrast, when economic experts make mistakes while privatizing, they are not residual claimants. De facto owners lose wealth when things go wrong; policy-makers, such as Jeffrey Sachs, who are in charge of privatizations occasionally lose consulting contracts when things go badly but are, for the most part, unaffected. Thus, spontaneous privatization encourages efficient privatization by minimizing the role of the state and its central planners.

Top-down privatizations persist nonetheless. This type of reform continues to be supported by policy-makers who think a certain amount of control and hierarchy is necessary. Despite the popularity of top-down privatization, the value of spontaneous privatizations may soon be realized in parts of the world desperately in need of bottom-up privatization, such as sub-Saharan Africa, since the mixed results of neoclassical privatization have caused many to rethink their conventional understanding of property rights. As frustrations with the neoclassical approach to privatization continue to mount, Austrian economists may have an important role to play in making the case for spontaneous privatization.

References

Boettke, Peter. [1994] (2001). "The Reform Trap in Economics and Politics in the Former Communist Economies," in Peter Boettke (ed.) *Calculation and Coordination.* London: Routledge, pp. 191–12.
Boettke, Peter. [1996] (2001). "Why Culture Matters," in Peter Boettke (ed.) *Calculation and Coordination.* London: Routledge, pp. 248–65.
Boettke, Peter. [1998] (2001). "Economic Calculation: The Austrian Contribution to Political Economy," in Peter Boettke (ed.) *Calculation and Coordination.* London: Routledge, pp. 29–46.
Boettke, Peter and Peter Leeson. (2004). "Liberalism, Socialism, and Robust Political Economy," *Journal of Markets and Morality* **7**(1): 99–111.
Coase, Ronald. (1937). "The Nature of the Firm," *Economica* **4**(16): 386–405.
de Soto, Hernando. (2000). *The Mystery of Capital.* New York: Basic Books.
Friedman, M. (1991). "Economic Freedom, Human Freedom, Political Freedom," California: Public Lecture at the University of CSU-East Bay, available at: http://www.cbe.csueastbay.edu/~sbesc/frlect.html; accessed 10 February 2010.
Hardin, Garrett. (1968). "The Tragedy of the Commons," *Science* **162** (Dec.): 1243–8.
Hayek, F.A. [1945] (1980). "The Use of Knowledge in Society," in F.A. Hayek (ed.) *Individualism and Economic Order.* Chicago: University of Chicago Press, pp. 77–91.
Hayek, F.A. (1960). *The Constitution of Liberty.* Chicago: University of Chicago Press.
Hill, Peter J. and Marge Karner. (1996). "Spontaneous Privatization in Transition Economies," in Terry Anderson and Peter J. Hill (eds) *The Privatization Process.* London: Rowman & Littlefield, pp. 81–96.
Holmes, Stephen and Cass Sunstein. (1999). *The Cost of Rights.* New York: W.W. Norton.
Leeson, Peter and J. Robert Subrick. (2006). "Robust Political Economy," *Review of Austrian Economics* **19**(2–3): 107–11.
Leeson, Peter and William Trumbull. (2006). "Comparing Apples: Normalcy, Russia, and the Remaining Post-Socialist World," *Post-Soviet Affairs* **22**(3): 225–48.
Mises, Ludwig von. [1927] (1996). *Liberalism.* Irvington-on-Hudson, NY: Foundation for Economic Education.
Mises, Ludwig von. [1932] (1981). *Socialism.* Indianapolis, IN: Liberty Fund.
Olson, Mancur. (1965). *The Logic of Collective Action.* Cambridge, MA: Harvard University Press.
Smith, Adam. [1759] (1982). *The Theory of Moral Sentiments.* Indianapolis, IN: Liberty Fund.
Smith, Adam. [1776] (1981). *An Inquiry into the Nature and Causes of the Wealth of Nations.* Indianapolis, IN: Liberty Fund.
Smith, Vernon. (2003). "Constructivist and Ecological Rationality in Economics," *American Economic Review* **93**(3): 465–508.

7 The competitive market is a process of entrepreneurial discovery
Frederic Sautet*

7.1 Introduction

Throughout most of the last century, the Austrian school of economics has held a different view of the market and competition than its more mainstream counterparts. A strict adherence to certain methodological principles (detailed in the other chapters of this book) resulted in a thoroughly subjectivist approach to the main concepts that today define the Austrian view of markets. At the core of this approach is the idea of entrepreneurship, which has been among its central theoretical constructs since the writings of Carl Menger (and others before him if we consider economists such as Richard Cantillon and Jean-Baptiste Say as proto-Austrians).

Introducing the entrepreneurial function in economic analysis has far-ranging implications in terms of the way one understands and appreciates the functioning of the market economy. The main difference (with an economic analysis that does not take the entrepreneurial function into account) resides in the idea of the market as a *process*. The idea of process does not refer to a mysterious property of markets. Rather, it makes explicit the way markets constantly reallocate resources over time so as to satisfy consumers as much as possible. It refers to the idea that the market economy is a system that engenders the incentives and the information necessary to discover and correct its own maladjustments in the allocation of resources. This may sound paradoxical to some but while markets have been omnipresent in the discourse of economists, they also have often been simply seen as a metaphor where supply equates demand in equilibrium. Actual markets, however, are more than just a metaphor, and they are more than just a space over which people exchange goods and services. The market is a process driven by entrepreneurial discovery (i.e., entrepreneurship). Entrepreneurship can roughly be understood as the human propensity to discover hitherto unknown gains from trade. An important distinction discussed in this chapter is between the notions of entrepreneurial discovery on the one hand and the entrepreneurial (market) process on the other. In the Austrian approach, the entrepreneurial market process is what competition is about: to compete means to be entrepreneurial. Understanding markets as an entrepreneurial process enriches our understanding of the market economy and helps us appreciate better the way the social order comes into existence.

The idea that competitive markets are a process of entrepreneurial discovery is one of the most forceful propositions in the social sciences. This proposition contains three distinct concepts: market, competition, and entrepreneurship. In order to understand the meaning of the entire proposition, I proceed to examine, in the next three sections of the chapter, each of these concepts in turn. In the fifth section, I pull all the ideas together and I attempt to provide a full picture of the market as an entrepreneurially driven discovery process.

7.2   The market

From its beginning economics has been concerned with the notion of exchange of goods against other goods. Trade is at the center of Adam Smith's *Wealth of Nations* ([1776] 1981), which begins with the exposition of the principles of the division of labor and the extent of the market. While for a long time, the focus of the discipline was on wealth and its generation (with many errors along the way; chief among them were the mercantile view and the labor theory of value), the key elements through which wealth was generated were trade and capital. As Smith famously explained, there is a "certain propensity in human nature. . . to truck, barter, and exchange one thing for another" (ibid., p. 14). Because it is at the center of economic life, trade is also Smith's departure point to explain the division of labor and its consequences. This led to the first notion of the "market" concept in economic theory, which was developed by classical economists: the market as a *space for exchanges*. This notion itself gave birth to two different views of the market: on the one hand, a notion of the market as a *metaphor* (or an ideal type) and, on the other hand, a view of the market as a *process* (see Figure 7.1).

Classical economists defined trade the way the common man would understand it. It was an act of exchange of goods against other goods. This act of exchange would take place in "markets," which were nothing more than the places where people would meet to trade. This goes back to the medieval towns where buyers and sellers would get together in specific locations (e.g., fairs) at certain times to haggle over the prices of the goods on offer. In this view, markets are primarily a space where exchanges take place (see Figure 7.1).

Many nineteenth-century economists followed this view. In Alfred Marshall's *Principles of Economics* ([1890] 1936), the market is in the background as the space where supply and demand schedules exist and meet, but the focus is on utility, value, and prices. In time, this focus was reinforced by the rise of Walrasian general equilibrium theory and, following

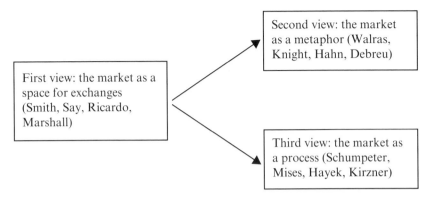

Figure 7.1   Three different views of the "market" in economic theory

upon the ideas of Frank Knight, the theory of perfect competition in the 1920s. In Léon Walras's work the market has been disembodied and is not a physical space anymore. Buyers and sellers do not haggle over prices, as they are individually too small to affect them. Prices are determined outside the market itself by the auctioneer who finds the market equilibrium through a groping process. Walras assumed the pre-reconciliation of individual plans. There is no market as such in the theory, and there is no need for it. In most theories that stemmed from Walras's work markets are redundant; they are not the means through which the prices of goods are determined. They are simply a metaphor where supply equates demand in equilibrium (see the second view of the market in Figure 7.1).

Note that the concept of equilibrium per se is not the problem. Indeed, the concept of equilibrium can be useful. As a method of contrast, it enables the economist to understand the complexity of a changing world by isolating the change under study. This is the way many economists such as Marshall would use the concept. This is also the way Ludwig von Mises would use equilibrium or a variation on the idea (i.e., the evenly rotating economy). A problem arose in economics, however, when equilibrium analysis came to be used as a metaphor or an ideal type (which supposedly describes reality) and, eventually, as an indictment of what actually happens in markets.[1]

While the notion of market has been present in contemporary economics, the focus has been more on the end state (equilibrium) than on the actual process by which prices and quantities emerge. Since the 1930s, economics has found itself in a strange situation. While markets are omnipresent in the discourse of economists, they also are rarely explained. This is why sociologists such as John Lie find it strange that economists insist so much on the function of markets while never describing their actual role. As Lie (1997, p. 342) puts it: "The market is a central category of economics. . . It is then curious that the market receives virtually no extended discussion in most works of economic theory or history. . . The market, it turns out, is the hollow core at the heart of economics." Paradoxically the market has become a black box, which, under certain conditions, guarantees a specific outcome. Even with the advent of the economics of information and the influence of the neo-institutionalist approach, the market remains somewhat of a mystery.

This comes in sharp contrast to the Austrian view – especially in the works of Friedrich Hayek, Ludwig von Mises, and Israel Kirzner – which sees the market at the core of economics. Markets are at the core of the Austrian approach because they are the means by which the social order comes to exist in harmony. In Mises' view the market is neither a place nor a hollow conceptual core; it is a *process*. It goes beyond the first view of markets as described above and which relates to the fair or the bazaar. Austrian economists avoided the confusion that one can sometimes find in economics between the notion of trade on the one hand and that of the market on the other. Trade and market are two distinct analytical subjects, and confusing the two is one of the reasons why in contemporary economics, the market is not understood as a process. In a two-individual economy model, trade can take place without having any market. The two individuals can bargain over the exchange ratio between two goods. This bargaining process is directed by their own preferences over the goods in their possession and alternative goods they can produce. This is a trade, but it is not part of a market. While the market is made up of individual trades, its nature goes beyond the sum of individual trades.

For Mises, the market is more than just a series of simultaneous trades between parties. It is the process by which social harmony, through the use of monetary prices and private property rights, comes into existence. Social harmony is the result of a market process through which prices are determined and resources are allocated. While the second view impoverished the first one by considering the market merely as a metaphor, the third view enriched the first notion by going beyond the space for exchanges and by considering the market as a process (see Figure 7.1).

Israel Kirzner often comments on hearing Mises explaining that the market is a process.[2] At first, Kirzner did not understand the meaning of Mises' claim. Mises meant that the market is not only a space where people may haggle over prices; it is also a process by which knowledge is generated, information comes to be known, and prices are determined throughout society (e.g., the law of one price is the result of the market process at work). The Misesian emphasis over the notion of market as a process (which encompasses the market as a physical space where trades take place) is what separates traditional market theory from the Austrian view. The market is central in the Austrian approach because it is a process. Understanding the market as competitive is to understand the market as a process.

7.3 Competition

The second important concept of the proposition under study is that of competition. The evolution of the concept of competition has followed the move from the first view of market to the second one. There are fundamentally two meanings behind the concept of competition in economics. The first meaning refers to competition as a state of affairs as developed by Frank Knight in the 1920s. The second meaning refers to competition as a process of entrepreneurial discovery as developed by Mises, Hayek, and Kirzner.[3] It is important here to mention that I am not arguing about the definition of competition. As in the case of the concept of market, economists of various schools are free to define competition as they please. My goal here is to emphasize the existence of the market process as a key aspect of competition that should not be ignored.

The meaning of competition among nineteenth-century economists was pretty clear. Competition meant *rivalry* among people for the attainment of certain ends. To compete is what people did when they haggled over prices in fairs or when they offered cheaper and better products to their customers. This view changed in the twentieth century, as the meaning of competition evolved, following upon the ideas of Knight, from "rivalry" to "a (static) state of affairs" (Machovec, 1995).[4] In the state of affairs approach, a competitive situation exists when neither producers nor consumers can individually influence the final result of the market. Market actors have little or no capacity to choose how to compete. The outcome of the market is not the result of choices that individuals make with regard to price and quantity. In other words, the competitive order that emerges is independent of the choices (in terms of prices and quantities) actors make.[5] Individual actors are too "small" to influence the market outcome.

There is something very powerful in this view of competition, as it depicts the interconnectedness of every actor in the market. However, it rests on an ideal understanding of the market, as it relates only to an already attained equilibrium where competition (as market process) is absent.[6] The interconnectedness of every actor in the market is in fact illusory because the pre-reconciliation of plans assumes it from the outset (instead of explaining it). Instead, Austrian economists have argued that it is, paradoxically enough, thanks to the introduction of the creative, unpredictable entrepreneurial element that many features of actual markets, such as the reconciliation of plans can be understood. The apparent social orderliness of actual markets can best be explained through the introduction of the entrepreneurial element in human action.[7]

In the actual marketplace, the order that emerges is the result of the *actions* and *decisions* of many individuals who are all interconnected via the price system. It is precisely because individuals choose prices and quantities that the market generates an order in which there exists a tendency for prices to be driven towards the marginal and average cost of production. It is because of rivalry that meaningful prices indicating the relative scarcities of all the goods emerge. These prices are essential to rational economic calculation. The actual competitive order is the result of individual decision-making with regard to prices and quantities. More specifically, it is the result of the choices individuals make in their capacity as entrepreneurs. In the Austrian approach, "to compete" is to act as an entrepreneur; it means to be entrepreneurial (see below).

Rivalry is at the heart of the market process. The layperson's use of the notion of competition illustrates a scientific reality that is captured by paying attention to the notion of market process. Austrian economists see competition as an activity (of trying to outbid rivals) that generates the *process* that is the market itself. The market process is really a process of competition whereby individuals make choices regarding what they want to achieve and how they want to achieve it.

To be fair, neoclassical economists have come to view, over time, some aspects of competition that have long been emphasized by Austrian economists. This is the case for instance of William Baumol's notion of market contestability and his attempt to reintroduce the entrepreneur in competition models.[8] Moreover, many neoclassical economists have now distanced themselves from the approach Henry Simon and George Stigler took on competition (and anti-trust) in the 1940s and 1950s.

This being said, what distinguishes Austrian economists from their neoclassical colleagues is the elaborate understanding of the role of the entrepreneurial function and how it gives rise to the market process. The traditional understanding of competition is limited because it rests on a "closed" framework, which cannot account for novelty.[9] Austrian economists have drawn attention to the open-ended environment in which "relevant opportunities may exist without their having, at the outset of the analysis, already been recognized."[10] As Kirzner explains, in an open-ended framework "there are no known limits to the possible. An economics which seeks to grapple with the real-world circumstance of open-endedness must transcend an analytical framework which cannot accommodate genuine surprise. Austrian economics has sought to accomplish this goal by focusing attention on the nature and

function of pure entrepreneurial discovery."[11] We now turn to the notion
of entrepreneurship and entrepreneurial discovery.

7.4 Entrepreneurship

We have stipulated above that the market is a process and that competition is a rivalrous activity. The key element that explains the nature of
the market and of competition is the entrepreneurial function – which
can roughly be understood as the human propensity to discover hitherto unknown gains from trade. With the domination of the idea of the
market as metaphor, traditional economics has come to assume that the
exploitation of gains from trade takes place automatically. In the second
view, markets are always in a state of perfect coordination: individuals
do not need to grasp gains from trade, as they have already been automatically grasped and exploited. In other words, individual plans are fully
coordinated from the outset, and there is no scope for the entrepreneur.

7.4.1 *The notion of entrepreneurial discovery*

Austrian economists – and this started as far back as Carl Menger – have
always maintained that there is no reason to assume that gains from
trade are known and exploited from the outset. This means that one must
present a mechanism by which gains from trade come to be perceived and
exploited. This mechanism is *entrepreneurial discovery*.

The concept of entrepreneurship is a notoriously difficult one to pin
down. Entrepreneurship is mostly understood in two ways. Many, if not
most, economists understand the entrepreneurial role as that of starting a
business or "industry captain." This can be referred to as the *behavioral
view* of entrepreneurship. In this view, the entrepreneur is a businessper-
son who carries out a plan to start or develop a commercial venture by
gathering the necessary factors together. While this is an important role in
a market economy, the theory remains within the confines of optimizing
behavior and equilibrium.[12]

Mises and Kirzner developed another approach to entrepreneurship.
In this view, the entrepreneur *discovers* gains from trade that were hitherto unknown to market participants. This is not to say that the one who
opens up a business could not also be an entrepreneur (in the Kirznerian
sense) – in the real world, the two generally go together. It is simply
that the key element in entrepreneurship is *discovery*, which is manifest
in all sorts of situations, and not only in the case of business start-ups.
The discovery approach can also be referred to as the *cognitive view* of
entrepreneurship. It does not regard entrepreneurship as an optimization
problem or an ideal type (as in the case of the behavioral approach) but
rather as a universal function in human action. A non-market example

can easily clarify the reason why discovery is the essential function of entrepreneurship.[13]

Let us imagine that Robinson Crusoe, alone on his island, goes fishing every morning with a line that he has kept with him after the wreckage of his ship. This fishing method is not very productive as he spends on average two hours before he gets a fish. As he ponders his plight, Crusoe has what may be a bright idea. He has noticed that there are a considerable number of vines around the island. Some of them are very big, but others are thin and very sturdy. He realizes that, by carefully arranging a number of well-chosen vines, he might be able to make a net and use it to improve his productivity while fishing. Implementing this idea takes a good deal of work and time. He has to find the right vines, and put them together in a way that enables him to catch the size of fish he wants. Also, he is not sure how long the vines will last in the water. They may just dissolve and prove to be inadequate for net building. However, we can assume that after a few experiments, he is in possession of a fully functioning net that enables him to catch five fish an hour on average. In other words, his productivity has gone up tenfold.

To achieve this feat, Crusoe has deployed available resources (the vines as well as his own time and energy). As he reflects on the number of fish he can now catch in an hour, he may be tempted to ascribe this result entirely to the resources used in constructing the net. Without these resources he could not have had his net. Yet, in a deeper sense, the use of the net can be attributed entirely, not to those resources, but rather to the "bright idea" that Crusoe had at the beginning. Without the idea of building a net, the vines on the island, and Crusoe's time and energy would not have been seen as resources (i.e., capital goods) to use in the course of action. It was because of the initial idea that his entire fishing production methods and productivity changed. The bright idea is an entrepreneurial discovery and thus it is the entrepreneurial element in Crusoe's new fishing activity. Crusoe is an entrepreneur not because he was able to build the net (which could be seen as the equivalent of starting a business) but because he had the *idea* of building a net and realized that he could do so with the vines on the island (hence, the importance of the *cognitive* view of entrepreneurship).

Crusoe's situation inspired his new idea. It is because he was spending too much time fishing that he came to realize that he needed to improve his production capabilities. This is where the notion of alertness, as Kirzner explains it, comes into the picture. Crusoe's change of situation was not automatic; he had to *realize* that there were gains to be captured by changing his method of production. As part of this process, he had to *realize* that vines could be used to make a net. It is because of his alertness to new "profitable" solutions that he came to see the vines as inputs into his net-building idea. Until then, vines were just plants without any usefulness to Crusoe. He recognized the potential role of the vines into his production process because he came to realize how unsatisfying his fishing productivity was. His alertness to the new use of vines stemmed from his unsatisfying fishing situation, but was not caused by it.

The Crusoe example illustrates the idea that entrepreneurial discovery can be present in all sorts of contexts, including non-market ones. This is to be distinguished from the notion of entrepreneurial (market) process, which consists of continual and simultaneous entrepreneurial discoveries creating a systematic process of adjustment of resource allocation in society (see below).

7.4.2   Contemporary issues in the Austrian theory of entrepreneurship

Alertness is central to the Kirznerian view of entrepreneurial discovery. In Kirzner's work, entrepreneurship *is* the alertness necessary for the discovery of opportunities.[14] Alertness is not a form of human capital and thus one cannot intentionally invest in it. Rather, it is the human propensity to notice what was not known before and that is in one's own interest to know. Kirzner has often been criticized for putting too much emphasis on alertness as opposed to other characteristics that one may find necessary to entrepreneurship, such as judgment and imagination. But Kirzner's insistence on the idea of alertness does not mean that he is blind to the role of creativity, imagination, and judgment in entrepreneurship. It simply means that before one unleashes one's own creativity, imagination, and judgment, one has to come to recognize one's own creativity, imagination, and judgment. A "eureka" moment is always necessary for the realization that a new vision is possible – imagining what that vision is about can only come once one is aware of that new vision.[15] This means that in order for an entrepreneur to apply his entrepreneurial judgment, he has first to be aware of what it is that he has to apply his judgment to.[16] Alertness enables economists to theorize about the emergence of novelty in a way that is impossible within the close-ended framework of traditional economic models. It accounts for the human experience of realization (i.e., discovery) of new ends and new means. In other words, it enables an open-ended view of economic phenomena.

This is why the claim that alertness is the ability to react *only* to existing opportunities (and not to the creation of new opportunities) is misleading.[17] Alertness is the propensity that enables the discovery of what is possible to create *within* the current state of the world and with regard to what one can imagine for the future. In other words, entrepreneurial creation is constrained by the present state of the world, but is not limited in the way one can apply one's own imagination to the future. In this sense sheer creation is entirely part of what alertness enables. The concept of alertness grounds entrepreneurial discovery within the possible and the actual (i.e., the current reality of the world) and, at the same time, enables human imagination (considering the present state of the world) to create the future. This is especially crucial in the context of market transactions where human creativity is bound by factor prices on the one hand and by individual preferences on the other.[18] However, within these boundaries, entrepreneurial imagination can roam free. In the non-market context, while Crusoe is free to imagine all sorts of ways to go fishing (including using dynamite, for instance), he is constrained by the reality of his world. In this sense, alertness is the propensity to introduce new information in the world (i.e., being creative) while being constrained by the state of reality (vines, and not dynamite, are available on the island).[19]

Alertness does not operate in a void. As Don Lavoie (1991) emphasized, being alert to an opportunity may be interpretative. Why some people are more alert than others to profit opportunities is difficult to know. The way individuals may direct their gaze may be influenced by cultural attitudes and other factors such as personal experience.[20]

In the Crusoe non-market scenario, monetary profit has no role to play in entrepreneurial discovery. However, the scenario is still one in which gains have inspired the discovery. It is because Crusoe realized that a new production process could improve his lot that he was alert to the potential new use of the vines. His discovery was (1) motivated ex ante by a pure gain (perhaps in terms of the activities he could engage in with the time he could save from fishing), even though this gain was not monetary, and (2) generated ex post a pure gain (Crusoe is better off in a world where he has spent the time and energy to build a net that increased his productivity tenfold than in the initial situation). Crusoe's bright idea was a "profitable" one.

When entrepreneurship is manifested in markets, a bright idea takes the form of an entrepreneur realizing that inputs can be acquired for a certain sum of money and used in a production process to make an output that can be sold. No process of physical production in the market economy occurs without someone first having noticed its possibility. The profitable idea consists in perceiving a positive price differential between the input prices and the prices at which the output can be sold (accounting for the opportunity cost of capital). In other words, in the market context, entrepreneurial discovery is (1) driven ex ante by the potential pure monetary profit that can be realized and (2) sanctioned ex post by the monetary profit (or loss if the idea was mistaken) that is incurred as a result of the activity. Under the right institutional conditions, the profit and loss mechanism ultimately determines whether the entrepreneurial discovery was socially beneficial, that is, if buying the resources and turning them into an output made sense from the perspective of the alternatives available for those resources.

Monetary profit exists because market prices do not reflect entirely the information available in the market about consumers' preferences, technology, and resource availabilities. When an opportunity for making a pure profit is discovered by an entrepreneur, it reflects the fact that a gap (in knowledge) exists in the market between what is known and what could be known. Entrepreneurial discovery consists in the discovery of a knowledge gap. At the societal level, the entrepreneurial process tends to address the "knowledge problem" (as identified by Hayek) existing in society (Hayek, 1945; Kirzner, 1973, 1984; O'Driscoll, 1977). Profit opportunities and knowledge gaps in the market are one and the same thing.[21]

One must insist on the idea that monetary profit is not a return on alertness or on entrepreneurship. Entrepreneurship and alertness are not productive factors for the reason that they are *necessary* to the deployment of productive factors. The element of entrepreneurship is itself not a resource (in the sense in which land, lumber, steel, labor, and machinery are resources).[22] As a result, monetary profit is not a return, but a residual, which exists due to the conditions of radical uncertainty in the market.

The issue of pure profit and monetary calculation also relates to another debate among Austrian economists. Murray Rothbard (1985) and Joseph Salerno (1990, 1993) hold the view that the Misesian position on entrepreneurship is not about alertness and discovery, but about economic calculation and price coordination. They are right to emphasize this aspect of entrepreneurship, but it constitutes only part of the theory. Meaningful economic calculation can be effected only once the object over which the calculation will take place is known (i.e., discovered). One cannot calculate (i.e., appraise and compare alternatives) if one has not first become aware of the existence of those alternatives. In other words, one needs to have an idea before making any monetary calculation (e.g., one needs to have the idea that a restaurant could be built at a certain location before making any calculation as to what resource to use to build the restaurant). Unless the entrepreneur knows which opportunity and which potential inputs could be part of his opportunity, he cannot make any monetary calculation.

At the same time, any discovery of a profit opportunity is driven by current resource prices, which in themselves determine whether a pure profit opportunity could be seized. This means that a discovery is only made possible (in the market context) because of monetary calculation based on current market prices. Therefore, being alert to a pure profit opportunity necessarily also involves monetary calculation (to calculate whether a potential pure profit exists). Entrepreneurial activity in the market is thus dependent on monetary calculation in order to (1) discover what resources need to be reallocated and (2) once the reallocation is done, whether it was desirable from a societal perspective.

It follows that monetary calculation goes hand in hand with discovery: they are two sides of the same coin. Rothbard and Salerno are right to insist on the calculation aspect emphasized by Mises. However, by introducing the concept of alertness, Kirzner has brought to bear the importance of discovery in the monetary calculation that entrepreneurs may engage in. Monetary calculation without discovery is not enough to describe entrepreneurship per se (it may simply be a case of "Robbinsian maximizing" as Kirzner would put it[23]): entrepreneurship primarily consists of discovery.

Another issue that has been discussed among Austrian economists in the last two decades has to do with whether one can conceive of a "propertyless" entrepreneur.[24] In his work, Kirzner isolates the entrepreneurial function: the entrepreneur is pure and propertyless (something that other economists such as John Bates Clark and Mises have done before him). Isolating the entrepreneurial function not only has the merit of clarifying the imputation of the different factor incomes (as Clark showed), but it also enables economists to establish the very nature of that function. The entrepreneurial function is about introducing novelty into the economic system. This is what the discovery of new means and ends is all about. This role is unthinkable in the closed universe of neoclassical equilibrium. For this reason, all factors (capitalist, laborer, and land-owner) are present in the neoclassical world except the entrepreneurial function. Similarly, all the neoclassical factors are linked to ownership (of capital goods, labor and land) except the entrepreneurial function.

It has been argued that the notion of entrepreneurial losses shows that propertyless entrepreneurs cannot exist in the real world.[25] Surely entrepreneurial losses fall on a resource owner (exercising his capitalist function), but he may not be the one who made the initial discovery. The capitalist function may consist in taking (already recognized) risks while lending resources, which is analytically separated from the entrepreneurial function (i.e., discovering new opportunities). Indeed, one can imagine a case where the entrepreneur presents the already-recognized (risky) opportunity to the capitalist. In such a case, the capitalist will act as a "Robbinsian maximizer" in choosing whether to pursue it. Losses reflect the uncertainty of the future, not the impossibility of isolating the entrepreneurial function. It is true that in reality the individual exercising his entrepreneurial function always possesses at least one factor: his own labor. But the fact that the entrepreneurial and capitalist functions are, in reality, often found in the same individuals does not mean that entrepreneurship must be analytically connected to the ownership of factors.

Finally, another important debate has revolved around the role of entrepreneurship in equilibration. In Joseph Schumpeter's work (1942, 1982), the entrepreneur, through an act of creative destruction, famously takes the economy away from its former equilibrium path before it reaches a new equilibrium.[26] This contrasts with Mises and Kirzner who see the role of the entrepreneurial function as bringing the induced variables more in line with the underlying ones, thereby performing, at some level, an equilibrating role.[27] But whether equilibrium tendencies dominate has been hotly debated. Everyone now acknowledges that, after two decades of debate over equilibration, it is difficult to make a definitive statement about the ultimate impact of entrepreneurial activity regarding the path to equilibrium.[28]

It is true that "equilibrium" is an elusive concept in the "living economy." In the market context, however, the role of entrepreneurship can only be understood with references to "false prices," that is, prices that do not reflect entirely the information contained in the underlying variables of the market.[29] In this context, Mises (1966, pp. 337–8) states that:

> the essential fact is that it is the competition of profit-seeking entrepreneurs that does not tolerate the preservation of *false* prices of the factors of production. The activities of the entrepreneurs are the element that would bring about the unrealizable state of the evenly rotating economy if no further changes were to occur.

Thus, when Mises (and Kirzner) talk about the equilibrating role of the entrepreneurial function, it is in the context where all the underlying variables are frozen. In this context only, entrepreneurial activity would bring about equilibrium.[30] In the living economy, entrepreneurial activity can be seen as *corrective* of earlier market decisions and *adaptive* to new market conditions, but this does not imply that the attainment of any equilibrium is possible (and even meaningful). It is only absent further unanticipated change that entrepreneurial discoveries would bring a perfect pattern of coordination in place. The insight about the corrective nature of entrepreneurship is important because it shows that the market process is not a random series of changes but rather a systematic, self-adjusting process. The entrepreneurial market process consists of continual and simultaneous entrepreneurial discoveries of maladjustments in the price structure. The source of these maladjustments can be found in (not yet revealed) changes in the underlying variables of the market (consumer preferences, resource supply conditions, etc.).

Having established the nature and role of entrepreneurship in markets, let us now turn to the complete picture, explaining how the competitive market is an entrepreneurially driven process.

7.5   The competitive market as an entrepreneurially driven process

In the sections above, I argued that the market is a process, competition is a rivalrous activity among producers for the consumer's dollar, and entrepreneurial discovery is the driving force of the social order. "What distinguishes the Austrian School and will lend it immortal fame," wrote Mises (1978, p. 36), "is precisely the fact that it created a theory of economic action and not of economic equilibrium or non-action." In the Mises-Kirzner system, human action is ever present and is the key explanation behind market phenomena. What is strange from the perspective of Austrian economics is that neoclassical economists never denied the unrealistic aspect of their view of markets and competition, but they nonetheless found it acceptable enough to indict reality whenever the latter deviated from the model.

Mises saw the market as a relentless, entrepreneurially driven process. This is the subject of Part IV of *Human Action*, which details the functioning of the great society based on market exchanges – Mises uses the term "catallactics." Mises (1966, p. 255) writes that "the driving force of the market, the element tending toward unceasing innovation and improvement, is provided by the restlessness of the promoter and his eagerness to make profits as large as possible." In another passage (ibid., p. 331), he states: "The operation of the market is actuated and kept in motion by the exertion of the promoting entrepreneurs, eager to profit from the differences in the market prices of the factors of production and the expected prices of the products." It is clear that in Mises' mind the market *is* an entrepreneurially driven process.

I argued above that the idea of the market as a process of entrepreneurial discovery entails more than the notion of the market as a space for exchanges. The difference between the two views is the idea of *interconnectedness* among human activities (i.e., "connexity" as Mises puts it). The connexity of the market can only be explained if one views the market as a process. This is an important point because this interconnectedness is assumed in equilibrium theory (i.e., in the second view of the market that we saw above), while it is established in the Austrian approach. The mechanism that creates the connexity of human activities is entrepreneurial monetary calculations. This mechanism rests on the existence of a medium of exchange and also on the non-specificity of labor as a factor of production.

As money is present in all exchanges and thus links together the decisions of everyone by virtue of being a *medium of exchange*, entrepreneurs are able to discover opportunities that may require, for their exploitation, a large division of labor and knowledge. The simultaneous exploitation of numerous entrepreneurial discoveries creates a concatenation of affairs among the various economic actors simply because entrepreneurs bid resources away from their alternative uses. This bidding process (based on entrepreneurial monetary calculation) creates interconnectedness among human activities. Prices are not isolated elements in the marketplace; they result from the complex relationships that prevail at any moment in society.[31]

Imagine that all factors were purely specific and could be only used for producing one commodity and nothing else. Each factor would have only one use. In such a world, entrepreneurs would never bid resources away from alternative uses. As a consequence, there would be no connection between one type of production and another type. In a world of purely specific factors, the connexity of human activities would be absent, and entrepreneurs would not calculate how to reallocate resource factors to new uses. In such a world, the allocative problem disappears.

There is a market process because as entrepreneurs make discoveries, they calculate (through the use of money prices) how to reallocate resource factors that are non-purely specific to new lines of production. This creates a general interconnectedness among human activities because most factors can be used in more than one production process. While many factors may be non-specific, Mises saw labor as a particularly crucial resource factor in creating this connexity. "Each entrepreneur is eager to buy all the kinds of specific labor he needs for the realization of his plans at the cheapest price," explains Mises. "But the wages must be high enough to take the workers away from competing entrepreneurs" (1966, p. 594). It is the entrepreneurs competing for hiring the services of labor that create interconnectedness among human activities. If labor were absolutely specific, entrepreneurs could only use the type of labor compatible with their production and nothing else – this would impede the ability to compare the different alternatives available to entrepreneurs and to individuals supplying their labor. But the "fact that *one* factor, labor, is on the one hand required for every kind of production and on the other hand is, within the limits defined, nonspecific, brings about the general connexity of all human activities. It integrates the pricing process into a whole in which all gears work on one another. It makes the market a concatenation of mutually interdependent phenomena" (ibid., p. 392; emphasis in original). The market is an entrepreneurial process of discovery because it rests on the monetary calculations that entrepreneurs make while competing for the use of different factors, especially that of labor. This process creates a general connexity of human activities, which not "only determines the price structure but no less the social structure, the assignment of definite tasks to the various individuals" (ibid., p. 311). In other words, the market process creates human social cooperation under the division of labor.

This is why Mises understood that in the market every product competes against every other product. It is the reason why the (free and open) market is always competitive. In so far as entry in any market is available, the relentless entrepreneurial market process does not stop, and is not dependent on the number of producers or consumers. The sheer possibility of entry to anyone interested in competing with the incumbents (even if the costs of entry are non-trivial) defines a competitive outcome (i.e., competitive prices). In this sense, markets are always competitive as long as entry is permitted.[32]

The issue of competition brings to bear the institutional question. For the entrepreneurial market process to be fully at work, three conditions are jointly necessary (but perhaps not sufficient): (1) property rights must be (formally or informally) defined, enforced, and freely transferable,[33] (2) a (reliable) medium of exchange must be used to establish relative (money) prices, and (3) entry in markets must be open (i.e., no restriction of entry by the use of legislation). When at least these three conditions are present, entrepreneurs set in motion the market process. Attenuation of property rights (e.g., zoning), various market regulations (e.g., minimum wage laws), or the existence of privileges in a few markets may affect the well functioning of the entrepreneurial process, but it does not necessarily destroy it. These conditions are jointly necessary because if one (or more) of them is completely absent, the entrepreneurial (market) process cannot operate.[34]

A well-known case where the market process is impaired is when entry in a market is restricted by legislation.[35] This is the case when a government grants a privilege in the production of a good to a producer or a group of producers. In doing so, the government enables the privileged producer to charge a higher price (i.e., a monopoly price, which results from restricted output) than it would if it were competing directly with others in the market. As long as freedom of entry exists, the market is always competitive. In so far as entry is restricted (by government), monopoly pricing becomes possible. In this sense, the government is always the source of monopoly pricing.[36] However, the producer may or may not derive monopoly rents from the situation; this will depend on the demand for its product. Over time, it is difficult to be shielded against the effect of the entrepreneurial process, as substitutes are developed and the value of the privilege to the producer diminishes.[37]

Ultimately what will determine the existence and the type of entrepreneurship is the quality of the institutional framework (i.e., the rules that govern human interactions and their enforcement), which determines whether (and to what extent) the three conditions above are present. Depending on their quality, institutions will direct the entrepreneurial process in different ways. As a result, some entrepreneurial discoveries may be socially beneficial while others may be socially unproductive (such as rent-seeking).[38]

7.6 Conclusion

Without the entrepreneurial process of discovery, our understanding of the market and competition is severely limited. It is because of the relentless actions of entrepreneurs that the market is seen as an ongoing process of simultaneous corrective activities. The development of this idea goes back, at least, to the work of Carl Menger. But it was really with Mises (and with Schumpeter) that the role of the entrepreneur in the market became more fully known. The genius of Mises was to explain the dynamic nature of markets by pointing out how individuals are capable of recognizing what had never been realized before and by showing how this activity explains the systematic, self-adjusting properties of the market system. It was left to Kirzner to explain the detail of that mechanism by putting together the work of Hayek on knowledge and that of Mises on the role of the entrepreneur. Kirzner developed a theory of entrepreneurial discovery that accounts for the emergence of novelty through the concept of alertness. He embedded entrepreneurship within the reality of economic calculation while integrating his approach with an emphasis upon knowledge, ignorance, creativity, and uncertainty. Kirzner made explicit the idea that the entrepreneurial market process goes beyond sheer entrepreneurial discovery (which is present in all sorts of non-market situations): it is the relentless process of error correction through which the introduction of new information in the market is effected.

Despite contemporary (marginal) disagreements concerning the nature of entrepreneurship among Austrian economists, it is the appreciation for the entrepreneurial character of the market process that has given those economists the ammunition to resist the temptations of the mechanistic understanding of social phenomena as seen in most twentieth-century economic theory. As Lavoie emphasized, it was the uniqueness of the Austrian position on the nature of the market system that enabled economists in this tradition to avoid, for instance, the fallacy of quasi-market solutions to socialism and to understand early on the negative effects of anti-trust policies. While on other aspects (e.g., the minimum wage), the conclusions of neoclassical economists are similar to that of the Austrian position, it is only through the entrepreneurial understanding of the market process that one can grasp the full nature of the market system and the order it creates. As one reflects over the nature of entrepreneurial competition and the market process, one can only be in awe contemplating a social phenomenon of an amazing complexity that Mises, Hayek, and Kirzner have helped us understand better.

Notes

*   I would like to thank Kyle McKenzie, Israel Kirzner, Virgil Storr, and Bryce Wilkinson for their comments on previous versions of this paper. The usual caveats apply.
1.   For more on the evolution of the use of equilibrium and the notion of markets, see Boettke (1997). See also Machovec (1995).
2.   See Kirzner (1996, 2000a and 2000b). See also Mises (1966, p. 257 and following) and Boettke and Sautet (2009).
3.   See Hayek (1946, 1978), Kirzner (1973), and Mises (1966).
4.   Knight held the view that no scientific study of the market in which radical uncertainty is present is possible. The second part of *Risk, Uncertainty, and Profit* (1921) presents the model of perfect competition, which was eventually adopted by the economics profession as it lent itself well to the use of mathematics.
5.   This is reflected in the following passage where Kenneth Arrow explains that price theory still cannot explain what it is meant to explain: "Even if we accept this entire story [of general competitive equilibrium], there is still one element not individual [i.e., that is not related to individual actions]: namely, the prices faced by firms and individuals. What individual has chosen prices? In the formal theory at least, no-one. They are determined on (not by) social institutions known as markets, which equate supply and demand" (1994, p. 4).
6.   See the section below for a presentation of competition as entrepreneurial discovery.
7.   Other economists have also made that claim. For instance, George B. Richardson explained that in the absence of the process generating the information (i.e., the entrepreneurial process), there cannot be any order emerging. As he put it: "It is most important to remember that the conditions of the real world are not those of perfect competition and that, if they were, it might no longer be possible for this order to be produced" (1960, p. 12).
8.   See, for instance, Baumol (2002).
9.   This is also true for neo-Schumpeterian theories, which attempt to integrate insights from Schumpeter's work on entrepreneurship into closed models of technological change. See, for instance, the work of Lipsey and Carlaw (2004) and Carlaw et al. (2006). See also the work on the disequilibrium foundations of equilibrium by Franklin Fisher (1989).
10.   See Kirzner (2000b, p. xiii).
11.   Ibid.
12.   See Kirzner (1973) for an elaborate critique of that point. Kirzner uses the term "Robbinsian maximizing" to describe optimizing behavior.
13.   See also Kirzner and Sautet (2006).
14.   In the words of Kirzner (1979, p. 181), "the essence of individual entrepreneurship is that it consists of an alertness in which the decision is *embedded* rather than being one of the ingredients *deployed* in the course of decision making." Italics are in the original.
15.   As Kirzner (1994, p. 109) puts it: "For any entrepreneurial discovery creativity is never enough: it is necessary *to recognize* one's own creativity. In other words, an essential ingredient in each successful creative innovation is its innovator's vision of what he can creatively accomplish." This also relates to the idea of "pre-scientific hunch" in scientific research. Researchers need to have an idea as to where to look when they want to engage in research, even before having devised any theory and done any experiment.
16.   The idea that alertness is the essence of entrepreneurship has divided the community of Austrian economists for some time. Rothbard (1985), for instance, has argued that this

is incompatible with the Misesian understanding of entrepreneurship. See also Klein (2007) for a defense of "judgment" as the core entrepreneurial function. See below for a brief discussion of Salerno's and Rothbard's position.

17. See Klein (2007), for instance, on this point.
18. This relates to the Schumpeterian (1947) distinction between invention and innovation. Innovation can be defined as socially beneficial invention. While an inventor is bound by the state of current reality, he is free to invent objects that are not socially desired. An innovator on the other hand brings his invention to market and aims to serve customers.
19. Crusoe could very well imagine using satellite-guided lasers to go fishing. However, this would not be entrepreneurial in the sense that Kirzner (and Mises and Schumpeter for that matter) is concerned with. Kirznerian entrepreneurship is not about creativity unrelated to reality. This crucial point has been completely overlooked by Kirzner's critics.
20. See Harper (2003) and Lavoie (1991).
21. The role of monetary profit in connection to knowledge and entrepreneurial discovery can be found in Mises as well. As Mises explains in *Profit and Loss* (1962, p. 109): "What makes profit emerge is the fact that the entrepreneur who judges the future prices of the products more correctly than other people do buys some or all of the factors of production at prices which, seen from the point of view of the future state of the market, are too low. Thus the total costs of production – including the interest on the capital invested – lag behind the prices which the entrepreneur receives for the product. This difference is entrepreneurial profit."
22. As Kirzner and Sautet (2006) explain: "Land, lumber, steel and the rest, are resources in the sense that they are deliberately deployed in the course of processes of production. Someone wishing to build a house must assemble land, labor, steel, lumber, and so on, in order to build the house. He must acquire land and use these resources. However, the idea that building the house would be a profitable venture is not deployed. One does not initiate a productive venture by first going into the market to acquire a good idea. One has the good idea that it would be profitable to acquire resources in the market for specific production processes. One does not deliberately produce entrepreneurial ideas; one serendipitously discovers them."
23. See Kirzner (1973). Mises did not refer to Robbinsian maximizing in his own work when he discussed the issue of monetary calculation in the context of the entrepreneur. I would argue that this is because the issue of discovery was implicit in his work.
24. See Salerno (2008) for a recent discussion of the issue.
25. For instance, see Jack High (1982, p. 166) who noted: "If entrepreneurship is completely separate from ownership, is it meaningful to speak of entrepreneurial loss? Can losses fall on the entrepreneur or must they fall on the resource owner?"
26. See Rothbard (1987) for an interesting critique of Schumpeter's approach.
27. Compared with his position in 1973, Kirzner (1999) now sees a smaller gap between his understanding of the entrepreneur and that of Schumpeter.
28. See also Rizzo (1990) for a discussion of equilibrium tendencies in the work of Hayek.
29. Market prices are "false" prices because they only reflect the revealed part of the underlying variables of the market (i.e., the current knowledge of market participants). Entrepreneurial discovery is fundamentally about unearthing the hitherto unrevealed parts of the underlying variables such that market prices more closely and truthfully reflect the underlying preferences of consumers. This is a gradual process. It is important to note that while market prices are false, they also are market-clearing, as they do reflect the revealed current knowledge available to market participants. However, they are not equilibrium prices in the neoclassical sense, as there remains information that is not reflected in market prices and that could be discovered.
30. Rothbard (1985, p. 284) also saw a role for equilibration tendencies in the market. As he put it: "It is one thing to say, with Mises and his followers, and in contrast to the neoclassical economists, that equilibrium does not and can never exist on the market.

It is quite another thing to say that the market does not even harbor equilibrating tendencies."
31. As Mises (1966, p. 392) put it: "What is called a price is always a relationship within an integrated system which is the composite effect of human relations."
32. For a development of this idea, see Kirzner (2000a) and Sautet (2007).
33. In addition to alienability, an important aspect of property rights for entrepreneurial discovery is divisibility. Entrepreneurs may find new ways to allocate resources by dividing existing property rights in new ways.
34. For a discussion of entrepreneurship and institutions, see Harper (2003), Chapters 4 and 5.
35. See also Ikeda (1996) and Kirzner ([1978] 1985) for detailed analysis of interventionism and the market process.
36. Mises held the view that monopoly pricing could, in some very rare cases, emerge in the unhampered market. For a detailed presentation of his view, see Kirzner (2001). See Rothbard (1993) for a critique of Mises' view. See also Sautet (2002).
37. For more on the issue, for instance, see Sautet (2007).
38. See Baumol (1990) for a discussion of the impact of institutions on entrepreneurship.

References

Arrow, Kenneth (1994) "Methodological Individualism and Social Knowledge," *The American Economic Review*, **84**(2), 1–9.
Baumol, William (1990) "Entrepreneurship: Productive, Unproductive, and Destructive," *The Journal of Political Economy*, **98**(5), 893–921.
Baumol, William (2002) *The Free-market Innovation Machine: Analyzing the Growth Miracle of Capitalism*, Princeton: Princeton University Press.
Boettke, Peter (1997) "Where Did Economics Go Wrong? Modern Economics as a Flight from Reality," *Critical Review*, **11**(1), 11–64.
Boettke, Peter and Frederic Sautet (2009) "Introduction to the Liberty Fund Edition," in Israel M. Kirzner *The Economic Point of View: An Essay in the History of Economic Thought*, Indianapolis: Liberty Fund.
Carlaw, Kenneth I., Leslie T. Oxley, Paul Walker, David Thorns and Michael Nuth (2006) "Beyond the Hype: Intellectual Property and the Knowledge Society/Knowledge Economy," *Journal of Economic Surveys*, **20**(4), 643–90.
Fisher, Franklin (1989) *Disequilibrium Foundations of Equilibrium Economics*, Cambridge: Cambridge University Press.
Harper, David (2003) *Foundations of Entrepreneurship and Economic Development*, London: Routledge.
Hayek, Friedrich A. (1945) "The Use of Knowledge in Society," reprinted in Friedrich A. Hayek (1948) *Individualism and Economic Order*, Chicago: University of Chicago Press.
Hayek, Friedrich A. (1946) "The Meaning of Competition," reprinted in Friedrich A. Hayek (1948) *Individualism and Economic Order*, Chicago: University of Chicago Press.
Hayek, Friedrich A. (1978) "Competition as a Discovery Procedure," in *New Studies in Philosophy, Politics, Economics, and the History of Ideas*, London: Routledge.
High, Jack (1982) "Alertness and Judgment: Comment on Kirzner," in Israel M. Kirzner (ed.) *Method, Process, and Austrian Economics: Essays in Honor of Ludwig von Mises*, Lexington, MA: D.C. Heath and Company, pp. 161–8.
Ikeda, Sanford (1996) *Dynamics of the Mixed Economy: Towards a Theory of Interventionism*, London: Routledge.
Kirzner, Israel M. (1973) *Competition and Entrepreneurship*, Chicago: University of Chicago Press.
Kirzner, Israel M. [1978] (1985) "The Perils of Regulation," reprinted in Israel Kirzner *Discovery and the Capitalist Process*, Chicago: University of Chicago Press.
Kirzner, Israel M. (1979) *Perception, Opportunity, and Profit: Studies in the Theory of Entrepreneurship*, Chicago: University of Chicago Press.

Kirzner, Israel M. (1984) "Economic Planning and the Knowledge Problem," *CATO Journal*, **4**(2), 407–18.
Kirzner, Israel M. (1994) "Entrepreneurship," in Peter Boettke (ed.) *The Elgar Companion to Austrian Economics*, Aldershot, UK and Brookfield, VT, USA: Edward Elgar.
Kirzner, Israel M. (1996) "Reflections on the Misesian Legacy in Economics," *Review of Austrian Economics*, **9**(2), 143–54.
Kirzner, Israel M. (1999) "Creativity and/or Alertness: A Reconsideration of the Schumpeterian Entrepreneur," *Review of Austrian Economics*, **11**(1–2), 5–17.
Kirzner, Israel M. (2000a) "The Limits of the Market: the Real and the Imagined," reprinted in Israel M. Kirzner *The Driving Force of the Market: Essays in Austrian Economics*, London: Routledge.
Kirzner, Israel M. (2000b) "Foreword," in Frederic Sautet (2000) *An Entrepreneurial Theory of the Firm*, London: Routledge.
Kirzner, Israel M. (2001) *Ludwig von Mises*, Wilmington: ISI Books.
Kirzner, Israel M. and Frederic Sautet (2006) "The Nature and Role of Entrepreneurship in Markets: Implications for Policy," *Mercatus Policy Series*, Policy Primer No. 4, Arlington: Mercatus Center.
Klein, Peter (2007) "The Place of Austrian Economics in Entrepreneurship Research," unpublished manuscript.
Knight, Frank (1921) *Risk, Uncertainty, and Profit*, Boston: Houghton Mifflin Company.
Lavoie, Don (1991) "The Discovery and Interpretation of Profit Opportunities: Culture and the Kirznerian Entrepreneur," in B. Berger (ed.) *The Culture of Entrepreneurship*, San Francisco: Institute for Contemporary Studies, pp. 33–51.
Lie, John (1997) "Sociology of Markets," *Annual Review of Sociology*, **23**(1), 341–60.
Lipsey, Richard and Kenneth Carlaw (2004) "Total Factor Productivity and the Measurement of Technological Change," *The Canadian Journal of Economics/Revue canadienne d'Economique*, **37**(4), 1118–50.
Lipsey, Richard, Kenneth I. Carlaw and Clifford Bekar (2006) *Economic Transformations: General Purpose Technologies and Long Term Growth*, Oxford: Oxford University Press.
Machovec, Frank. M. (1995) *Perfect Competition and the Transformation of Economics*, London: Routledge.
Marshall, Alfred [1890] (1936) *Principles of Economics*, 8th edition, London: Macmillan and Co.
Mises, Ludwig von (1962) "Profit and Loss," reprinted in *Planning for Freedom*, 2nd edition, South Holland, IL: Libertarian Press.
Mises, Ludwig von (1966) *Human Action: A Treatise on Economics*, 3rd edition, Chicago: Contemporary Books.
Mises, Ludwig von (1978) *Notes and Recollections*, South Holland, IL: Libertarian Press.
O'Driscoll, Gerald P. Jr. (1977) *Economics as a Coordination Problem: The Contributions of Friedrich A. Hayek*, Kansas City: Sheed Andrews and McMeel, Inc.
Richardson, George B. (1960) *Information and Investment*, 2nd edition, Oxford: Oxford University Press.
Rizzo, Mario J. (1990) "Hayek's Four Tendencies toward Equilibrium," *Cultural Dynamics*, **3**(1), 12–31.
Rothbard, Murray N. (1985) "Professor Kirzner on Entrepreneurship," *Journal of Libertarian Studies*, 7(2), 281–6.
Rothbard, Murray N. (1987) "Breaking Out of the Walrasian Box: Schumpeter and Hansen," *Review of Austrian Economics*, **1**(1987), 97–108.
Rothbard, Murray N. (1993) *Man, Economy, and State: A Treatise on Economic Principles*, Auburn: Ludwig von Mises Institute.
Salerno, Joseph (1990) "Ludwig von Mises as a Social Rationalist," *The Review of Austrian Economics*, **4**(1), 26–54.
Salerno, Joseph (1993) "Mises and Hayek Dehomogenized," *The Review of Austrian Economics*, **6**(2), 113–46.

Salerno, Joseph (2008) "The Entrepreneur: Real and Imagined," *Quarterly Journal of Austrian Economics*, **11**(3), 188–207.

Sautet, Frederic (2002) "Kirznerian Economics: Some Policy Implications and Issues," *Journal des Economistes et des Etudes Humaines*, **12**(1), 131–51.

Sautet, Frederic (2007) "The Shaky Foundations of Competition Law," *New Zealand Law Journal*, June, 186–90.

Schumpeter, Joseph (1942) *Capitalism, Socialism, and Democracy*, New York: Harper & Brothers.

Schumpeter, Joseph (1947) "The Creative Response in Economic History," *Journal of Economic History*, 7(Nov), 149–59.

Schumpeter, Joseph (1982) *The Theory of Economic Development: An Inquiry into Profits, Capital, Credit, Interest, and the Business Cycle*, Piscataway, NJ: Transaction Publishers.

Smith, Adam [1776] (1981) *An Inquiry Into the Nature and Causes of the Wealth of Nations*, Indianapolis: Liberty Fund.

PART III

MACROECONOMICS

8 Money is non-neutral

J. Robert Subrick

8.1 Introduction

The neutrality of money holds a central place in modern macroeconomics and monetary economics. In the long run, changes in the supply of money do not affect real variables such as the level of gross domestic product (GDP), the growth rate of GDP, or the rate of unemployment. Changes in the money supply do not alter relative prices; that is, the ratio of prices between goods and services remains the same after a monetary contraction or expansion takes place. Variations in the money supply only influence the aggregate price level. All prices change equally when the money supply changes. Increases or decreases in the money supply alter only the level of nominal variables. Most macroeconomic models accept this proposition, at least for the long run. For example, both Monetarism and New Keynesianism accept the long-run neutrality of money. Models of real business cycles begin with the assumption that money is neutral in both the long and short run.

In sharp contrast, the *non-neutrality* of money has a central role within the Austrian approach to monetary economics. Increases in the money supply do affect relative prices and real variables in the short run. Changes in the supply of money alter relative prices, which influence individual decision-making regarding the types of goods and services to consume. Either increases or decreases in the money supply affect the market rate of interest. As a result, savings and investment patterns change. Money has a non-neutral impact on the economy.

The non-neutrality of money forms one of the central pillars for explaining the business cycle according to Ludwig von Mises, F.A. Hayek, and their followers. When the monetary authority increases the supply of money, the rate of interest falls and relative prices between consumption and investment goods change accordingly. Investment increases. As people make more investments and consume less, differences emerge between the amount and types of goods produced and types of goods demanded. Over time, malinvestment takes place as certain markets have an excess supply of goods and other markets have excess demand. The downturn occurs once the divergence between them becomes too great.

F.A. Hayek introduced the term neutral money into English-speaking economics in the 1930s. He credited the term to Knut Wicksell, although

Wicksell does not use the term but other writers cited by Hayek do (Patinkin and Steiger, 1989). Hayek criticized Wicksell's usage and used the term neutral to explain how a change in the interest rate induced by monetary policy affects relative prices between consumption and investment goods. Money had a neutral impact when it did not change relative prices. It served as a goal of monetary policy.

The concept of neutral money predates Hayek's discussion by many decades. David Hume ([1742]1987), in his essays 'Of Money' and 'Of Interest' contain early statements of the non-neutral aspects of money as does Richard Cantillon's ([1755] 1931) *Essay on the Nature of Commerce*.[1] They discussed both the short-run and long-run effects of changes. Monetarists and New Classicists have claimed Hume as a predecessor but they have ignored the relative price changes that arise from changes in the money supply that drive parts of his analysis (Mayer, 1980; Lucas, 1996). Keynes emphasized the non-neutrality of money in his *Tract on Monetary Reform* (1923). His famous remark that "In the long run we are all dead"[2] referred to irrelevance of the long-run monetary neutrality proposition discussed by proponents of the quantity theory of money. Like the Austrians, Keynes stressed the non-neutrality of money.

This chapter briefly restates the logic of claims of monetary neutrality. It then examines the sources on non-neutrality both mentioned by Hayek and later writers both within and outside of the Austrian tradition. Then it turns to the question of why non-neutral money matters for Austrian economics. In particular, it places non-neutral money within the Austrian theory of the business cycle. Finally, it considers the New Classical challenge; in particular, the claims made by rational expectations-based macroeconomics and offers reasons to expect further development of its implications for understanding fluctuations in GDP that take place.

8.2   What is neutral money?

The neoclassical definition of neutral money emphasizes the long-run relationship between changes in the money supply and the aggregate price level. Money has neutral properties when an increase or decrease in its supply only affects the price level and does not affect real variables. Formally, neutral money refers to a demand function that is homogeneous of degree zero in money prices and in the initial quantity of financial assets. But the neoclassical definition is only one of several possible definitions of neutral money. There are at least four different propositions that describe neutral money (Visser, 2002, p. 527). All the propositions have one thing in common: changes in the money supply do not affect real variables. The four propositions are:

1. Money acts only as a veil. The introduction of money does not affect resource allocation and the economy acts as if it were a barter economy.
2. Monetary equilibrium holds at all times; that is, no excess demand for or supply of money exists.
3. Changes in the money supply only affect the aggregate price level as described in the quantity theory of money.
4. Changes in the rate of inflation do not affect real variables. This is the super-neutrality proposition.

Hayek (1935, p. 130) discussed the proposition that money serves only as a veil and does not affect real variables. He wrote that the concept of neutral money "refers to the set of conditions under which it be *conceivable* that the events of a monetary economy would take place, and particularly under which, in such an economy, relative prices would be formed, as if they were influenced only by 'real' factors" (italics original). Money only serves as a veil. The introduction of money into the economic system does not change relative prices. Real factors solely determine prices. Money only provides a scalar to facilitate exchange by reducing transaction costs but does not influence production or consumption decisions. This definition of neutral money was a policy ideal unlikely to be attained in the modern world.

The Austrian tradition has addressed the impact of monetary disequilibrium much more thoroughly. Hayek's writings emphasize the effects of changes in the money market on aggregate outcomes. Monetary equilibrium occurs when there is no excess supply of or demand for money. Individuals hold their optimum quantity of money based on their subjective expectations and information they have. When the monetary authority introduces new money into the economic system, individuals alter their demand for money. Prices change as the new recipients use their money to purchase goods and services. The rise in prices that results from the new money forces others to change the amount of money they hold for consumption. Individuals alter their behavior to adjust to the new monetary situation. Similarly, when changes in productivity take place, the demand for money changes and monetary disequilibrium occurs. For example, an increase in productivity reduces prices and individuals demand less money. As they adjust the quantity of money they hold, prices change and resources are reallocated.

The third definition of neutral money follows from the quantity theory of money. In the equation of exchange ($MV = PQ$ where M is the money supply, V is the velocity of money, P is the general price level, and Q is the quantity of output), money has a neutral affect when V and Q are held constant. Under these assumptions, changes in M only affect P. This is the fundamental truth of the quantity theory. As Milton Friedman stated: "inflation is always and everywhere and a monetary phenomenon" (1963). Hayek (1935, p. 4) dismissed the quantity theory as relatively useless because: "For none of these magnitudes as such ever exerts an influence on the decisions of individuals; yet it is on the assumption of a knowledge of the decisions of individuals that the main propositions of non-monetary economics theory are based." In other words, the neutrality of money in the quantity theory refers to long-run properties of a monetary economy. But, again, as Keynes so memorably wrote, "In the long run we are all dead." In the real world, the neutrality proposition holds only after decades have passed and the ups and downs of the business cycle have occurred. It does not address the issues that arise as the economy shifts from one equilibrium to another. The process of how prices change remains unexplained or is assumed away. Milton Friedman (1969), in a well-known analogy, depicted the money supply process as the monetary authority dumping money from a helicopter to all the citizenry equally. In the modern economy, helicopters do not have a role in money supply process. The new money is not distributed equally. As a result, money has non-neutral effects.

The fourth neutrality proposition addresses the super-neutrality of money. An increase in the money supply may not affect real variables and leave relative prices the same, but changes in the growth rate of money supply may affect the real economy. In other words, changes in rate of inflation can have effects on the real economy, especially the rate of economic growth and the distribution of income. Inflation has distributional effects. For example, the wealthy often have the means to adjust their portfolio to assets less affected by inflation than the poor. As a result, the harmful effects of inflation are disproportionally borne by the poor. Similarly, changes in the variance in inflation can affect economic growth by increasing uncertainty in an economy. As investors become less able to predict future inflation rates because it lacks stability, they choose to invest their resources elsewhere. As investment falls, so does the rate of economic growth. Traditional Austrian approaches have said little about the likelihood of super-neutral money although it does not present an analytical problem.

To sum up, neutral money has several definitions. Conventional macroeconomic wisdom contends that the effect of money in the long run is neutral. Changes in the quantity of money do not affect real economic variables. Nearly all empirical evidence has supported the claims that money has neutral effects in the long run. It would seem that the Austrian approach to monetary economics has little, if any, empirical support.

However, studies of the short run effect of changes in the money supply do find non-neutral effects. Changes in the money supply affect the real economy.

8.3 Sources of non-neutrality

A number of reasons exist to explain the non-neutrality of money. Hayek offered several reasons in his writings in the 1930s. They include forced savings, sticky prices, Cantillon or distribution effects, and the effects of long-term contracts on the flexibility of prices. The classical economists included additional reasons as have recent contributors to macroeconomics. The recent models stress traditional Austrian themes – the importance of imperfect information and subjective expectation formation.

Humphrey (1984) and Visser (2002, p. 530) summarized the reasons for non-neutral money. Their combined lists include the following:

- Cantillon effects;
- forced savings;
- money illusion;
- sticky prices and long-term contracts;
- Mundell-Tobin effect;
- commodity money.

8.3.1 Cantillon effects

The most well-known source of the non-neutral effects of money within the Austrian tradition stems from ideas contained in Cantillon's ([1755] 1931) *Essai* (and Hume's [1742] 1987 economic writings) and extended by Hayek in his LSE lectures. Cantillon emphasized the path by which money entered an economy. When the monetary authority increases the money supply, all consumers do not receive the amount necessary to prevent relative prices from changing. The money ends up in the hands of some and not others. Monetary contractions or expansions do not affect everyone equally. The people who first receive the money spend it on goods and services that they prefer. They have increased purchasing power relative to the rest of the citizenry. As a result, the prices for these goods and services increase. Investors and firms respond by allocating more resources to the production of these goods and services because of the higher prices. Resource reallocation takes place.

The Cantillon process continues as the money passes through the hands of various members of society. Those people who receive the money early have greater purchasing power than those who receive it later. They alter the structure of relative prices. By the time the money becomes neutral in the long run, a new distribution of prices has emerged. The Cantillon effect arises, in part, because citizens lack the relevant information about the source of the change in prices. They confuse real and nominal changes and money has a non-neutral effect. They have interpreted changes in the money supply with a change in either supply or demand conditions. As a result, money has a non-neutral effect.

8.3.2 *Forced savings*
Although the doctrine of forced savings originated with Jeremy Bentham, Hayek developed the idea to explain how changes in the supply of money affected relative prices between consumption and capital investment. When the money supply increases, capital formation increases because of a reduction in the interest rate. Inflation follows the increase in the money supply and those people with fixed incomes are forced to use their savings in order to purchase goods. Their existing savings have lost some purchasing power. Horwitz (2000, p. 115) summarized the forced savings as "the forced reduction in the purchasing power of non-recipients of excess supplies of money."

8.3.3 *Money illusion*
The critical assumption behind the neutrality of money is that individuals do not suffer from money illusion (Patinkin, 1987). People understand the difference between a change in real variables and nominal variables. Only changes in real variables affect behavior; changes in nominal variables do not. For example, a change in economic growth rates (a real variable) lead consumers to alter their behavior whereas a change in inflation (a nominal variable) does not change anyone's behavior. Much of modern monetary theory assumes that money illusion does not exist.

Nominal values do not affect real variables. More formally, Patinkin (1965, p. 22) wrote that "an individual will be said to be suffering from such an illusion if his excess demand functions for commodities do not depend solely on relative prices and real wealth." Standard microeconomic theory supports the absence of money illusion as only relative prices affect behavior. James Tobin (1972, p. 3) wrote "an economic theorist can, of course, commit no greater crime than to assume money illusion." Yet the Austrian approach does allow for money illusion and has committed no crime. Confusion between nominal and real changes plagues people. Anyone who has taught principles of economics courses knows that many students confuse the difference between real and nominal variables.

Money illusion complements other sources of monetary non-neutrality. Horwitz (2000, p. 163) discusses money illusion as a source of price stickiness. He wrote that "it is possible that people do not understand that nominal wage cuts when output prices are falling will leave them more or less the same as they were before." A common explanation for money illusion stems from the costs of obtaining information. If nominal prices change slowly and by relatively small amounts, what incentives exist for people to collect information about the inflation adjusted prices? Similarly, people often fail to collect information about the source of price changes. Whether supply or demand changed because of a real or nominal change involves costs that people often view as relatively high. In most costs, not knowing the real price of a good has very little impact on behavior.

An alternative Austrian explanation exists but has been little explored. Hayek's *The Sensory Order* (1952) argues that people's perceptions evolve in response to repeated interaction with the external environment. If people operate within an environment of nominal prices (as they do), they will think in nominal terms. It should not be surprising that they confuse real and nominal variables as their minds have evolved to operate within the nominal world. Future research may examine the relationship between Hayek's psychological writings and their relationship to the monetary economy.

8.3.4 Sticky prices and long-term contracts

For money to have neutral effects, wages and prices must adjust to changing demand and supply conditions. If prices respond to changes in the monetary contraction or expansion, money is neutral. Yet, in many markets, prices do not adjust immediately to new conditions. They remain the same after the monetary authority has adopted a course of action that either reduces or increases the money supply. A number of reasons have been posited to explain the lag in changing prices after a change in the money supply.

Long-term contracting limits the neutrality of money in the short run. Hayek (1935, p. 131) wrote that "the existence of a generally used medium of exchange will always lead to the existence of long-term contracts in terms of this medium of exchange, which will have been concluded in the expectation of a certain future price level." Individuals guess as to what future prices will be. Sometimes they correctly guess future prices and sometimes they do not. They negotiate contracts in order to minimize uncertainty about the future. When they guess wrong about the future, money has a non-neutral effect. For example, wage contracts are denominated in nominal terms. If actual inflation exceeds expected inflation, then the real wage falls. If the workers realized their real wages have fallen, they may respond by reducing productivity.

New Keynesian models formalized and extended the sources of price stickiness. Menu costs offered a simple example. When price changes are small, it may be too costly to print up new menus. The benefits from posting new prices are less than the cost. Although the empirical literature has not found much support for menu cost models, more recent studies that include the costs associated with deciding whether or not to change prices indicate that menu costs can explain how money has a non-neutral effect.

8.3.5   *Mundell-Tobin effect*

The Mundell-Tobin effect occurs when nominal interest rates increase less than one-for-one with inflation due to the impact of changes in individual behavior that arise from increased inflation. Increases in the money supply cause the nominal interest rate to differ from the real interest rate. The increase in inflation reduces the value of money. Consumers respond by holding less money. They hold other assets instead and, as a result, demand less money. Real interest rates fall in response. The change in the rate of inflation has caused real changes in the economy.

8.3.6   *Commodity money*

When money has a commodity basis, it has non-neutral effects. When Hayek first wrote, the remnants of the gold standard remained in use. Implicitly, he accepted that some real resource would provide the value of money. But since the breakdown of the Bretton Woods system under the Nixon administration, fiat money has become the norm (for developed nations at least). Under commodity money, an increase in the supply of gold or silver would increase the price level and change the relative prices between gold and silver and other goods and services would take place. Real changes would take place in the economy. The introduction of fiat money does not affect relative prices between the commodity basis of money and other goods and services. The change from commodity money to fiat money removed this as a source of non-neutral money.

8.4   Non-neutral money and economic fluctuations

The Austrian explanation for economic fluctuations stresses how monetary factors cause real changes that increase and decrease GDP in the short run. Money exerts a large effect on the aggregate economy and becomes a source of the business cycle. The Austrian explanation for economic fluctuations begins with understanding the role of interest in a monetary economy. Interest rates reflect the subjective preferences of those who save and those who want to borrow. Interest emerges from their interactions. Assume that intertemporal preferences do not change. That is, the interest rate does not change because people have altered their preferred trade-off between present and future consumption. This is the natural rate of interest. It is natural in the sense that it reflects the preferences and constraints of borrowers and lenders. Now suppose that the central bank expands the money supply, thereby increasing the supply of credit available. This is the market rate of interest. The market interest rate declines as a result as more credit is available. It is below the natural rate of interest. Saving falls and investment increases at the lower interest rate. Consumption declines and investment rises.

The Austrian approach differs from more conventional approaches, in that it stresses the effects of the injection of credit on the capital structure. The central bank provides the money to banks and the central government through the purchase of bonds. If they use the new credit to make investments in capital, prices for those goods rise. The initial recipients of the new money have increased their purchasing power relative to those who have not received the money. The non-neutral effects of money occur because of the "loose joint" aspects of money. Money permeates all markets. When new money enters an economy, people have to adjust their money holdings.

Horwitz (2000, pp. 96–103) emphasized the monetary disequilibrium understanding of neutral money and its relation to the capital structure. Capital is a heterogeneous good that is characterized by complementarity and substitutability, the path by which money enters the economy matters (see Chapter 9). He wrote that:

> If the capital structure is understood as being comprised of the various inter-temporal prices existing in the market, then money is neutral if the current monetary policy or regime is not a cause of any systematic distortion in those prices, leading to the potential unsustainability of that structure. Changes deriving from the money supply process are not providing too much or too little investment in comparison to voluntary savings, creating the possibility of a sustainable capital structure. In monetary disequilibrium, the mismatch of savings and investment implies a lack of synchrony between the signals facing entrepreneurs and the preferences of consumers, leading to the creation of a capital structure that is unsustainable and must eventually be reversed. It is in this sense that money is neutral in monetary equilibrium.

Money is non-neutral when expected relative price changes and resources are reallocated to activities they would not be allocated to if new money was not introduced.

8.5 The New Classical challenge

The emergence of the New Classical approach to monetary economics and macroeconomics more generally has greatly reduced the importance of money in explaining the effects of changes in its supply. Their rise to dominance virtually eliminated any discussion of Austrian approaches to non-neutral money. Early New Classical models assumed away the sources of non-neutral money. Changes in the money supply lead to nearly simultaneous changes in prices. Many real business cycle models posit instantaneous price adjustment. If prices adjust quickly to changes in the money supply, then monetary neutrality becomes the norm. Furthermore, distributional concerns, money illusion, and systematically incorrect expectations have been assumed away. Given these assumptions, there is no need to include Austrian macroeconomics in the discussion of short-run macroeconomic problems since it begins with a fundamentally incorrect starting point of analysis. As a result, Austrian macroeconomics has virtually disappeared from academic and public policy discussion.

The New Classical challenge extends beyond simply denying the non-neutrality of money. Real business cycle theorists have challenged the causal impact of money on output. They do not interpret the evidence as supporting claims that monetary contractions lead to reductions in output. Instead, they argue that the causation runs the other way; changes in output cause changes in the money supply. For example, increases in output cause individuals to increase their demand for money. As money demand rises, the monetary authority increases the money supply. Economic expansion causes monetary expansion. If output falls, then the demand for money declines and the monetary authority decreases the money supply. They argue that Austrian macroeconomics (and Monetarism) has it exactly backwards. Changes in the money supply do not lead to changes in output. Rather changes in output cause the money supply to change.[3]

Finally, the New Classical approach assumed that people have rational expectations. In its most simple form, the rational expectations hypothesis states that individuals form the expectations rationally. They consider the costs and benefits of collecting additional information and optimize accordingly. The rational expectations hypothesis implies that people do not make systematic mistakes because they are costly. If they make a mistake, then they update their expectations. Systematic errors do not persist. Individuals with rational expectations also have a correct theory of how the economy operates. They understand how changes in the money supply only affect nominal variables. They do not suffer from money illusion and only include real variables in the decision-making function.

Austrian models have responded to the first claim about the amount of time between changes in prices. They have offered plausible explanations for sticky prices that have empirical support. On the second point (changes in output lead to changes in the money supply) little Austrian research has addressed the literature directly. For example, Horwitz (2000) and Garrison (2000) do not address the question of the causal direction of money and output. Little empirical evidence has been provided to support the causal claims of the Austrian theory from an Austrian perspective. Friedman and Schwartz (1963) and Romer and Romer (2004) have documented the causal impact of the money supply on output by examining the historical record. Finally, on the third point, Austrians have responded to the rational expectations hypothesis. In an early contribution, Haberler (1980, p. 836) argued that rational expectations contained a basic truth that "agents in the market must not be assumed simply to extrapolate mechanically the current rate of inflation. . .but to make use of all the information available, including the probable consequences of government policies." He continued by noting that "but to say that systematic policies are ineffective even in the short-run seems to me unacceptable." Ironically, the New Classical approach began from Austrian foundations. The early New Classical models, such as the Lucas island model, built explicitly on Hayek's ideas in the 1930s. They accepted the non-neutrality of money. Later, they rejected the non-neutrality of money and offered other explanations for the role of changes in the money supply on output. Information regarding the behavior of the monetary authority can be collected relatively cheaply. Similarly, real business cycle models began with Eugen von Böhm-Bawerk's notion of capital as a time-consuming process. Real business cycles initially emphasized the time to build aspects of the capital structure to produce new goods and the amount of time needed to reallocate capital to random shocks. They later moved away from the Austrian notion of the time structure of capital. The Austrian response to these developments has been largely focused on the early models and relatively little has focused on the real business cycle models.[4]

8.6 Conclusions

The non-neutrality of money forms the basis of Austrian claims regarding the role of money in a dynamic economy. As Hayek noted, money serves as a loose joint in the economic system. Money permeates all formal markets, and some informal markets as well. When the money market is out of equilibrium, it affects all markets as people adjust their cash balances to the changing structure of prices. The adjustment process reflects the non-neutral effects of money. Whether for traditional reasons related to sticky prices or non-indexed long-term contracts or less conventional reasons based on money illusion, increases in the money supply affect real behavior and variables. It is not simply a veil that exerts an impact on the real economy in the short run.

Although Austrian macroeconomics began in the 1930s with monetary non-neutrality as a cornerstone of its approach, subsequent decades have yielded relatively little research into the sources of non-neutrality (the New Keynesians did much of the legwork). Furthermore, incorporating the effects of non-super-neutral money has yet to occur. Given that money is non-neutral in Austrian explanations of the business cycle, it seems likely that integrating the effect of non-super-neutral money will not be difficult. It may offer new insights into how changes in the growth rate of the money supply affect the evolution of economies over decades.

The improved psychological foundations of economic theory offer an opportunity to reassess Austrian monetary theory. Given the limited capabilities of economic agents to understand all the interdependencies of a modern economy and the emergence of interest in Hayek's writings on psychology, a new look at the Austrian macroeconomics may be in order.

Hayek's introduction of neutral money into macroeconomic analysis greatly improved understanding of business cycles. The larger project of developing the implications of non-neutral money in the short and long run offers many avenues for further inquiry. Various schools of thought have offered explanations for the non-neutrality of money. The Austrian school will, in all likelihood, continue to make contributions to the development of empirically supported macroeconomic theory and insights into the evolution of the macroeconomy.

Notes

1. Thornton (2007) offers compelling evidence that Cantillon's significant essay influenced Hume. Hayek suspected this to be true. Humphrey (1984) documents a number of reasons offered by the Classical economists why money had non-neutral effects.
2. *Tract on Monetary Reform* (1923), Chapter 3.
3. Freeman and Kydland (2000) offer empirical support for the claims that changes in output lead to changes in the money supply.
4. Of course, there are exceptions. See Cochran (2001).

References

Cantillon, Richard. [1755] 1931. *Essai sur la Nature du Commerce en General.* New York: August M. Kelley.
Cochran, John. 2001. "Capital-based Macroeconomics: Recent Developments and Extensions of Austrian Business Cycle Theory," *Quarterly Journal of Austrian Economics* **4**(3): 17–25.
Freeman, Scott and Finn Kydland. 2000. "Monetary Aggregates and Output," *American Economic Review* **90**(5): 1125–35.
Friedman, Milton. 1963. *Inflation: Causes and Consequences.* New York: Asia Publishing House.
Friedman, Milton and Anna Schwartz. 1963. *A Monetary History of the United States, 1967–1960.* Princeton: Princeton University Press.
Garrison, Roger. 2000. *Time and Money: The Macroeconomics of Capital Structure.* New York: Routledge.
Haberler, Gottfried. 1980. "Critical Notes on Rational Expectations," *Journal of Money, Credit and Banking* **12**(Nov.): 833–6.
Hayek, F.A. 1935. *Prices and Production.* New York: August M. Kelley.
Hayek, F.A. 1952. *The Sensory Order.* Chicago: University of Chicago Press.
Horwitz, Steven. 2000. *Microfoundations and Macroeconomics: An Austrian Perspective.* New York: Routledge.

Hume, David. [1942] 1987. *Essay: Moral, Political, and Literary*. Indianapolis: Liberty Press

Humphrey, Thomas. 1984. "Non-neutrality of Money in Classical Monetary Thought," Federal Reserve Bank of Richmond.

Lucas, Robert E. 1996. "Nobel Lecture: Monetary Neutrality," *Journal of Political Economy* **104**(4): 661–82.

Mayer, Thomas. 1980. "David Hume and Monetarism," *Quarterly Journal of Economics* **95**(1): 89–101.

Patinkin, Don. 1965. *Money, Interest, and Prices*. New York: Harper & Row.

Patinkin, Don. 1987. "Monetary Neutrality," in John Eatwell, Murray Milgate, Peter Newman (eds), *The New Palgrave*, London: Macmillan Press Ltd.

Patinkin, Don and Otto Steiger. 1989. "In Search of the 'Veil of Money' and the 'Neutrality of Money': A Note on the Origin of Terms," *The Scandinavian Journal of Economics* **91**(1): 131–46.

Romer, Christina and David Romer. 2004. "A New Measure of Monetary Shocks: Derivation and Implications," *The American Economic Review* **94**(4): 1055–84.

Thornton, Mark. 2007. "Cantillon, Hume, and the Rise of Anti-Mercantilism," *History of Political Economy* **39**(3): 453–80.

Tobin, James. 1972. "Inflation and Unemployment," *American Economic Review* **62**: 1–18.

Visser, Hans. 2002. "The Neutrality of Money," in Brian Snowdon and H.R. Vane (eds), *An Encyclopedia of Macroeconomics*, Cheltenham, UK and Northampton, MA, USA: Edward Elgar.

9 Some implications of capital heterogeneity
Benjamin Powell*

9.1 Introduction

A tractor is not a hammer. Both are capital goods but they usually serve different purposes. Yet both can be used to accomplish more than one goal. A tractor can be used to plow a field, pull a trailer, or any number of other tasks. A hammer could be used by a carpenter to build a house or by an automobile mechanic to fix a car. The fact that a tractor and hammer serve different purposes but yet each is capable of serving more than one single purpose should seem obvious. Yet the consistent application of this observation to economic theory is one of the unique aspects of the Austrian school and it has led the Austrian school to come to unique conclusions in areas ranging from socialist calculation, to business cycles and to economic development among others.

Capital goods are those goods that are valued because of their ability to produce other goods that are the ultimate object for consumption. Because these capital goods are heterogeneous and yet have multi-specific uses we must coordinate economic activity to best align the structure of capital goods to most efficiently produce consumer goods without leaving any higher valued consumption wants unsatisfied. The coordination of consumption plans with the billions of ways the capital structure could be combined to satisfy those consumption plans is one of the major tasks any economy must accomplish. Yet, often formal economic models reduce capital to a single homogeneous stock "K" and by doing so they assume away one of the greatest coordination tasks an economy has to solve.

The following section briefly outlines Austrian capital theory. Sections that follow trace out the implications of capital heterogeneity in a variety of applied research areas. Socialist calculation, business cycles, economic development through the Solow model, World Bank aid for investment schemes, and industrial planning are all studied and the conclusions of the Austrian school are contrasted to those that are reached by theorists who fail to appreciate the importance of capital heterogeneity.

9.2 Austrian capital theory

Capital theory is an important area that makes Austrian economics unique. In fact, Horwitz (2000, p. 41) has argued that, "Although its capital theory does not define Austrian economics, understanding that theory and its implications will give one a good grasp on precisely what is distinct about the Austrian approach." Austrian capital theory draws on other key aspects of Austrian economics such as subjectivism, expectations, the role of time, and markets as a process of adjustment to illustrate the importance of capital heterogeneity. When these insights are applied to areas of inquiry, its capital theory is often what differentiates Austrian explanations of phenomena from other schools' conclusions.

The first task of Austrian capital theory is to explain why capital heterogeneity is important. It is obvious that a hammer is not a tractor but why is that fact going to be important for economic theory? Why isn't the simplifying assumption of capital homogeneity justified? First we must define in what ways capital is heterogeneous.

Of course a hammer and a tractor have different physical properties. However, that is not the only feature that makes them heterogeneous. They are also heterogeneous because of the different plans they will satisfy for a particular human actor. In fact, whether a good is capital or not depends crucially on the plans of its owner. A computer placed in a home to play video games is a consumption good, not a capital good. But if that same computer were placed in an office where a person planned to type economics articles on it then it would be a capital good. Goods are heterogeneous both because of their physical dimensions and also because of the different plans that they can satisfy.

This leads us to the problem of aggregating the capital stock. How can it be summed together? Lachmann famously wrote, "[W]e cannot add beer barrels to blast furnaces nor trucks to yards of telephone wire" (1978, p. 2). Since these are all different goods they obviously cannot be directly added together. A common denominator is required. Neoclassical economics typically sums the monetary value of these heterogeneous capital goods to arrive at a value of the capital stock.[1] However, this is justified only if all of the heterogeneous plans of all of the people using all of the capital goods are perfectly coordinated.

To see why, consider how capital goods get their value. Consumer goods are valued because they satisfy subjective desires of the individuals consuming them. Capital goods are valued because of their ability to produce the consumer goods that are the ultimate aim of production. However, because capital goods are heterogeneous they cannot be perfectly substituted for one another to produce the consumer goods. Yet capital goods are also multi-specific; each is capable of fitting into more than one single production plan for one consumer good. So capital goods derive their value from the entrepreneurs who bid on them with the aim of incorporating those capital goods into a specific plan to produce the final consumer goods of ultimate valuation. The monetary value of capital goods will be the outcome of the bidding process of entrepreneurs that was based on their expectations of fulfilling particular plans to profitably produce particular final consumer goods.

Because the monetary value of capital goods was derived from the values placed on them based on expectations of incorporating them into individual production plans, the values for the various capital goods can only be summed together if all of the various individual plans are mutually compatible. If all of the individual production plans are not mutually compatible some of the capital used will not result in producing the final consumption goods it was intended to produce. Thus, it will not create the final value that its ex ante monetary price reflected. It is meaningless to add the monetary value of capital good A to the monetary value of capital good B if the only way the production plan for capital good A could be fulfilled is if it used other resources that precluded the possibility of the production plan for capital good B coming to fruition. The end result of these two plans would not create the intended consumer goods the plans called for. Hence adding their ex ante monetary values is still like adding blast furnaces to beer barrels.

The only time that capital can be summed up using monetary values is if all plans are perfectly coordinated so that all come to final fruition and produce the intended goods for final consumption. This only happens in equilibrium. But as Austrians have long recognized, the actual economy is never in equilibrium. An actual economy is always in a process of adjustment where we learn and discover new information and continually adjust our plans. We are always moving towards an equilibrium that itself is ever changing. Since we are never in general equilibrium, plans are never perfectly coordinated and prices of capital goods are not equilibrium prices that can be meaningfully summed.[2] Thus, Austrian capital theory does not focus on or measure "the" capital stock. Instead, Austrian capital theory focuses on the structure of the capital stock.

Because capital is both heterogeneous and multi-specific, Austrian capital theory focuses on how these individual units of capital fit together, or in other words, they study the capital structure. This is precisely where Austrian capital theory differs from the neoclassical mainstream. Austrians have to grapple with issues of capital complementarity and capital substitutability while these issues never arise if capital is modeled as homogeneous.[3]

Capital complementarity stems from the fact that it most often requires more than a single capital good to produce the final consumption good. Few cars will be produced if only the physical building for the assembly line is constructed but the individual assembly machines are not included in the structure. The assembly machines and physical building complement each other and make greater production of cars possible. One of the tasks of entrepreneurs in the market economy is not just to invest and create new capital but to invest in creating the *right* capital that will best complement the existing capital. That means creating capital that fits into and complements other production plans.

All investment takes place in time. From the time the decision is made to invest, to when the actual capital good is created, time has elapsed and often revealed that original plans will need to be altered. Also, because capital is often durable, even if it at first serves its original purpose, later developments may indicate that the plan should be changed. Because investment decisions are made ex ante and the world is uncertain some plans will have to be altered as market conditions evolve. This raises the issue of capital substitutability. If all capital were perfectly homogeneous, substitutability would not raise any problems. Each capital good would be a perfect substitute for every capital good and changing plans would not involve any losses. If each capital good were perfectly specific (capable of fulfilling only a single function in a single plan) then substitutability would be impossible and when plans needed to change, existing capital would be useless. Because capital is both heterogeneous and multi-specific capital substitutability becomes an issue.

When an existing production plan changes to no longer require a capital good that was created to serve that plan the capital good must be integrated into another plan or else it will no longer be maintained. Substitutability is usually a matter of degree. It is a matter of how well an existing capital good serves a new purpose for which it was not intended and how large the adjustment costs are to putting the capital good into the new use.

Whether a society is prospering or stagnating does not just depend on how much capital it has or is in the process of creating because of capital complementarity and substitutability. Prosperity depends on both how much capital there is and how well fit together the existing capital structure is.

Horwitz (2000, p. 40) has labeled Austrian capital theory the "missing link" that bridges microeconomic foundations to macroeconomic analysis. Because of their different capital theory, Austrians ask different macroeconomic questions than other schools of thought. When capital is heterogeneous and multi-specific, economic growth theory doesn't simply ask how to create more investment. It asks how to get the type of investment that best complements the existing capital stock. Policy-makers no longer have to stimulate aggregate demand to get out of a depression but instead have to deal with a situation where there were a cluster of errors in planning that created heterogeneous capital that now will have to serve purposes other than what it was created for. Austrian business cycle theory asks how capital should be reallocated.

Before we turn to the role of capital heterogeneity and multi-specificity in long-run growth and in business cycles it is first worth examining the role it plays in one of the most important debates in the twentieth century – the socialist calculation debate.

9.3   Socialist calculation

The debate sparked by Mises' 1920 article, "Economic Calculation in the Socialist Commonwealth" is probably one of the most important debates that occurred in the economics profession in the twentieth century. In many ways the debate illustrated how the evolving neoclassical paradigm differed from the Austrian school. In fact, Boettke (2001) argues that economic calculation is *the* contribution of Austrian economics to political economy in the twentieth century: "[*A*]*ll* the unique contributions of the Austrian school of economics to substantive economics can be traced back to the central importance of economic calculation for human cooperation" (p. 30; emphasis original). Yet for much of the twentieth century most economists believed the Austrians lost the economic calculation debate.

The mainstream of the economics profession failed to appreciate the Austrians' contribution to the socialist calculation debate both because of their preoccupation with equilibrium analysis and because of their tendency to model capital as homogeneous. The mainstream's preoccupation with equilibrium analysis led them to assume much of the information that it is the market processes' job to discover. This problem has been dealt with extensively in the Austrian literature and elsewhere in this volume (see Chapters 5 and 7) so it will not be further discussed here. However, the assumption of capital homogeneity is directly relevant for our purposes.

Mises ([1920] 1990) adopts the definition of socialism as collective ownership of the means of production. A postcard version of his argument reads:

- Socialism is the collective ownership of the means of production (MOP).
- Without private property in the MOP there is no market for the MOP.
- Without a market for the MOP there are no prices for the MOP.
- Without prices for the MOP there are no relative scarcity indicators for the MOP.
- Without relative scarcity indicators economic calculation is impossible:

    – that is, you have no way of knowing which capital goods to combine in which proportions to produce the final consumer goods most economically.

Because socialism is defined as the collective ownership of the means of production, whether capital goods are homogeneous or heterogeneous is crucial because the economic calculation problem stems from the fact that we have no relative scarcity indicators for these capital goods.

If capital goods are all perfectly specific then no problem arises when you have no relative scarcity indicator for them. Each is only suitable to one task. An economy need only know the final consumer goods it wants and then the planner can choose to accumulate the capital necessary to make those goods. Similarly if all capital goods are perfectly homogeneous their relative scarcities do not matter. Each can be perfectly substituted for every other. A planner again only needs to know the desired type and quantity of consumer goods. Any structure of capital goods used to produce those consumer goods is equally efficient.

With perfect capital specificity or perfect homogeneity the economic calculation problem collapses into a technical production problem. Schumpeter (1942, p. 175) argued that an economy could have economic calculation for factors of production without private property for the MOP because "[C]onsumers in evaluating ('demanding') consumers' goods *ipso facto* also evaluate the means of production which enter into the production of these goods." However, the "ipso facto" does not hold precisely because capital is heterogeneous. If each capital good could only produce one consumption good then the valuation of consumer goods would suffice to value the capital good. But because capital goods are multi-specific we need to know the relative scarcity of the capital good in its alternative uses in order to have economic efficiency. Hayek (1945) pointed out that Schumpeter's ipso facto only holds if all the facts are given to one mind. Alternatively it is also accurate to say that with dispersed knowledge the ipso facto would hold only if all capital was perfectly specific or all capital was homogeneous.

The economic calculation problem only exists because capital is heterogeneous and multi-specific. These same factors also drive the Austrian business cycle theory, much of which was developed contemporaneously with the socialist calculation debate.

9.4 Business cycles
Its capital theory is a distinguishing characteristic of Austrian business cycle theory (ABCT). Most macroeconomic schools of thought model capital (or investment) as homogeneous. Thus, when examining business

cycle fluctuations they can only talk about increases or decreases in the quantity of investment. ABCT integrates its capital theory to model the heterogeneous and multi-specific nature of capital. Therefore ABCT examines how misalignments in the structure of production occur. ABCT is sometimes characterized as a theory of over-investment but in fact it is better described as a theory of mal-investment because it addresses the dis-coordinated nature of the capital structure.

Austrian capital theory is both the microfoundation for macroeconomics (Horwitz, 2000) and the link between the short run and the long run (Garrison, 2001). Entrepreneurs make decisions based on the price signals from consumer goods, capital goods, and the interest rate to make investment decisions. The first of these signals what consumption goods are desired, the second signals the most economical way to produce them, and the third provides intertemporal coordination. Entrepreneurs' investments take the form of heterogeneous multi-specific capital goods. Because these goods are durable and have multiple uses they provide a bridge between the short and long run.

Not all ex ante entrepreneurial forecasts are correct. So capital goods will need to be reallocated ex post to alternative production processes. A business cycle occurs when there are a cluster of systematic entrepreneurial errors. Consistent with real business cycle theory (RBC) the cluster of errors could be created by a technological shock or an unexpected government regulation. However, unlike RBC theory, because Austrians believe money is non-neutral (see Chapter 8) the cluster of errors could also be created by monetary manipulations that distort inter-temporal coordination.

When the cluster of errors stems from artificially depressing the interest rate it will encourage a "lengthening" of the structure of production where more "round-about," or longer-term, production processes will be employed than is optimal. It is beyond the scope of this chapter to examine and evaluate all of the possible sources of the cluster of errors or go into depth on the nature of credit-induced boom (see Garrison, 2001). For our purposes we are interested in what the implications of capital heterogeneity and multi-specificity are once a cluster of errors has occurred.

Where Keynesians and Monetarists see a lack of aggregate demand, and RBC theorists see an optimal equilibrium given the shock, Austrian theorists see a mismatch between the heterogeneous capital goods structure and the structure of those capital goods necessary for satisfying consumer desires. There is no lack of aggregate demand; there is a lack of enough particular demand for the consumer goods produced by the existing combinations of capital goods. To recover from a depression Austrian theory shows bad investments must be liquidated and capital reallocated.

Depressions can persist as long as the structure of production is not in line with consumer preferences for consumption goods.

The policy implications of ABCT stem directly from the fact that capital is heterogeneous and multi-specific. Bad investments were made. The existing capital goods are imperfect substitutes for what capital should have been created but the capital goods, if transformed into another production plan, can still be useful. How best to do this? First, stop distorting the price system in a way that led to the cluster of errors in the first place. This means if it was an inflation-induced boom-bust, stop inflating the currency. Second, do not bail out bad investments in a way that would preserve the current structure of production. Business failure will not destroy the heterogeneous capital goods; it will free them up to be reallocated according to consumer preferences.

These recommendations stand in stark contrast to Keynesian and Monetarist prescriptions that call for attempts to stimulate aggregate demand through either monetary or fiscal policy. In fact, as a historic matter, government attempts at fiscal stimulus often serve to artificially create demand for goods produced by the existing structure of production and thus slow economic recovery. Rothbard's ([1963] 2000) *America's Great Depression* forcefully argues that interventions starting with the Hoover administration maintained an existing structure of production and delayed economic recovery. Powell (2002) makes a similar argument about Japan's depression in the 1990s.

Because ABCT allows monetary distortions to change the capital structure away from consumer preferences it is also capable of explaining stagflation. During stagflation prior inflation distorted the capital structure away from that required for full employment and then continual inflation prevented the realignment of the capital stock and economic recovery.

Most macroeconomic schools of thought focus on aggregate levels of economic activity. In doing so they miss describing the ways capital combines and recombines to produce final consumer goods. Because of the Austrian school's unique capital theory they are able to focus on discoordination within an aggregate category such as investment. Austrian capital theory better enables Austrians to explain depressions, recovery, and stagflation.

9.5 Economic development

Capital goods have played a prominent role in Austrian explanations of the wealth of nations. Mises writes, "The heritage of the past embodied in our supply of capital goods is our wealth and the foremost means of further advancement in well-being" ([1949] 1998, p. 510). Perhaps even more forcefully, Rothbard refers to the "relative unimportance of technology in production as compared to the supply of saved capital" ([1962] 1993, p. 490). Yet ironically the textbook neoclassical growth model demonstrated that capital was not the cause of long-run growth. It is capital heterogeneity again that explains the differing conclusions.

In the Solow growth model, output is a function of capital and labor. Savings is a fraction of total output but there are assumed to be diminishing returns to capital. So as the capital stock grows, the marginal increases in output become increasingly smaller eventually leading to a steady state with no more growth due to capital accumulation. Once this point is reached only technological change can cause long-run growth.

Homogeneous capital is one reason for the diminishing returns. When capital is heterogeneous there could be constant or increasing returns because of complementarity rather than the Solow model's decreasing returns. Hayek (1937, p. 174), when writing on business cycles well before Solow's model was created anticipates this:

> The effect which the current production of capital goods will have on the future demand for investable funds will depend not so much on the quantity of capital goods produced, as on the kind of capital goods which are produced. . .an increase in the current output of capital goods will frequently have the effect not of lowering but of raising the future demand for investable funds, and thereby the rate of interest [marginal productivity].

Capital heterogeneity does not make the Solow model wrong in theory but it can make it irrelevant in practice. The model measures what happens to output when capital per worker is increased. Since the model is measuring income per capita, whatever the rate of population growth, the rate of capital accumulation must exceed it for there to be growth, so eventually diminishing returns must set in as more and more capital *per worker* is accumulated. The unit "worker" is essentially fixed so diminishing returns must eventually occur. However, the tacit assumption when the Solow growth model is invoked is that wealthy countries are now somewhere approximately near the steady state. Because capital is heterogeneous we could have capital complementarity and the growth that comes from accumulating more capital up to much higher income levels. If income levels in the steady state are $1 billion per capita because of capital heterogeneity it does not mean the Solow model is theoretically wrong but it does mean that the model is not an accurate description of growth in the current state of the world. Capital heterogeneity allows Austrians to coherently claim that for the foreseeable future long-term growth can result from capital accumulation.

The Solow model was the leading theoretic growth model of the twentieth century but the World Bank's financing gap model may be the most implemented growth model during the last 60 years. The idea behind the financing gap model is that poor countries are in a low-growth equilibrium where they do not have enough savings to finance capital accumulation so aid for investment should be used to create capital accumulation.

The financing gap model fails to fully appreciate the importance of capital heterogeneity and economic calculation. In fact, it was even inspired by a former socialist central planning model! Poor countries do not simply need "investment." They need investment in capital that complements the existing structure of production. Investments need to be made on the basis of expected profit and loss. Private investment accomplishes this. Aid for investment often takes the form of infrastructure investment or other projects that are not bought and sold on the market. Therefore, much of the investment financed by the financing gap model has been outside of the sphere of economic calculation. The impact of poor incentives created by aid for investment programs has been well documented. The epistemic problems associated with using aid to finance the right heterogeneous capital have been less emphasized but are no less real.

National economic development planning is another area where an appreciation of capital heterogeneity has led Austrians to conclusions different from the mainstream. Advocates of state development planning do not assume that capital is homogeneous. In fact, their rationale for planning is that capital is heterogeneous but that they can select the capital better than the market. But by selectively promoting some industries they enable those industries to bid capital away from other industries and by doing so they interfere with the very process that reveals the relative scarcity of the heterogeneous capital goods. Lavoie (1985, p. 95) summarizes the problem:

> The same lack of knowledge on the part of any single person or organization which makes it impossible for comprehensive planning to replace the market also makes it irrational for a noncomprehensive planning agency to try merely to "guide" the market. If the guiding agency is less knowledgeable than the system it is trying to guide – and even worse, if its actions necessarily result in further undesired consequences in the working of that system – then what is going on is not planning at all but, rather, blind interference by some agents with the plans of others.

When the state actively plans development, it forces heterogeneous capital goods to particular industries. The decision-makers in the government planning bureau have no method to evaluate the opportunity cost of another industry's potential use of those capital goods. The opportunity cost is the subjective loss suffered by the person who would have received resources if the government had not interfered with the market process.

Since the planning bureau has no way of evaluating this loss, it cannot determine if the loss in output from other industries caused by promoting one industry is greater or less than the benefit produced. The planning agency has no way to know if it is promoting development or retarding it. Because capital is heterogeneous and multi-specific whenever competitive market forces are not allowed to dictate the capital structure an economy will not generate the level of prosperity that it is capable of.

9.6   Conclusion

The fact that capital is both heterogeneous and multi-specific should be obvious. But economic models that have failed to incorporate this fact have done a poor job at explaining real world phenomena. Some of the biggest economic events of the twentieth century; the failure of socialist planning, the length and severity of the Great Depression, stagflation, and the failure of official development assistance, have been explained coherently by Austrian economists. In each case, the unique Austrian conclusions stemmed, in part, from the fact that Austrians were relying on realistic models of heterogeneous and multi-specific capital while competing theories modeled capital as homogeneous. Boettke claimed that all of the unique contributions to substantive economics made by Austrian economists stem from the importance of economic calculation. He may be right, but it is because Austrian capital theory seriously grapples with the fact that capital is both heterogeneous and multi-specific, that allows Austrians to reach unique conclusions about economic calculation and thereby reach similarly unique conclusions in other applied research areas.

Notes

*   I thank Jeffery Hummel and Andrew Young for helpful suggestions on an earlier draft. The usual caveat applies.
1. Austrians are certainly not alone in critiquing neoclassical capital theory. For an alternative critique see the Cambridge Controversies. A short retrospective summary of the debate appears in the *Journal of Economic Perspectives* **17**(1): 199–214, "Whatever Happened to the Cambridge Capital Theory Controversies?" by Avi Cohen and G.C. Harcourt (2003).
2. Measurement inaccuracy can be a matter of degree. With a strong tendency toward equilibrium and a huge proportion of plans that do turn out to be ex post compatible then summing the monetary value of capital would yield an approximation of the capital stock. These arguments should also not be taken as a complete condemnation of equilibrium theorizing in Austrian economics. Hayek's classics, *Prices and Production* ([1931] 2008) and *Pure Theory of Capital* ([1941] 1975) and more recently Garrison's *Time and Money* (2001) all fruitfully begin with a macroeconomic equilibrium analysis of the capital structure and study deviations from that equilibrium.
3. This is not to claim that the issue of capital heterogeneity has not been raised in the mainstream. Certainly Solow and others involved in the Cambridge controversies did debate it and there are still attempts by some mainstream economists to incorporate

heterogeneity into their models. The point is that the main thrust of neoclassical growth theory, whether the Solow model, or later endogenous growth theory, has failed to adequately incorporate capital heterogeneity and usually chooses to assume it away.

References

Boettke, Peter. 2001. *Calculation and Coordination*. New Brunswick: Routledge.

Garrison, Roger. 2001. *Time and Money*. New Brunswick: Routledge.

Hayek, Frederic von. [1931] 2008. *Prices and Production*. Auburn: Ludwig von Mises Institute.

Hayek, Frederic von. 1937. "Investment that Raises the Demand for Capital," *Review of Economic Statistics* **19**(4): 174–7.

Hayek, Frederic von. [1941] 1975. *Pure Theory of Capital*. Chicago: University of Chicago Press.

Hayek, Frederic von. 1945. "The Use of Knowledge in Society," *American Economic Review* **35**(4): 519–30.

Horwitz, Steven. 2000. *Microfoundations and Macroeconomics*. New Brunswick: Routledge.

Lachmann, Ludwig. 1978. *Capital and its Structure*. Kansas City: Sheed, Andrews and McMeel.

Lavoie, Don. 1985. *National Economic Planning: What is Left?* Cambridge: Ballainger Publishing Company.

Mises, Ludwig von. [1920] 1990. *Economic Calculation in the Socialist Commonwealth*. Auburn: Ludwig Von Mises Institute.

Mises, Ludwig von. [1949] 1998. *Human Action*. Auburn: Ludwig Von Mises Institute.

Powell, Benjamin. 2002. "Explaining Japan's Recession," *Quarterly Journal of Austrian Economics* **5**(2): 35–50.

Rothbard, Murray. [1962] 1993. *Man, Economy, and State*. Auburn: Ludwig Von Mises Institute.

Rothbard, Murray. [1963] 2000. *America's Great Depression*. Auburn: Ludwig Von Mises Institute.

Schumpeter, Joseph. 1942. *Capitalism, Socialism, and Democracy*. New York: Harper & Row.

10 Anarchy unbound: how much order can spontaneous order create?
Peter T. Leeson

10.1 Introduction

Narrowly speaking, spontaneous order is "the result of human action, but not the execution of any human design" (Ferguson [1767] 1966: Part III, Section 2, p. 122). More broadly speaking, spontaneous order is any order that private actors generate. In both the narrower and broader conception, spontaneous order is "decentralized," as opposed to the centrally created order of the state. Similarly, in both conceptions the resulting order emerges endogenously from private individuals acting "within the system" rather than being created and imposed by political agents acting "outside the system."[1]

This chapter considers spontaneous order in the broader sense of the term, which includes, but is not limited to, invisible hand-type processes. It also considers spontaneous order resulting from private but visible hands. Spontaneous order has long been central to Austrian economics. Austrian school founder Carl Menger ([1871] 1950) famously argued that money has a spontaneous origin. Following Menger, F.A. Hayek emphasized that language, law, and even the price system that coordinates markets have spontaneous origins (see, for example, Hayek 1948; 1973–79). Long before either of these men discussed spontaneous order, however, there was Adam Smith ([1776] 1976) whose "invisible hand" described the marketplace itself as a spontaneous order.

Whether they refer to these institutions as "spontaneous orders" or not, today, most economists recognize that many important institutions that facilitate social cooperation have their origin in the self-interested activities of private individuals, not in the intentional designs of government. But recognition that spontaneous order exists does not tell us anything about the extent of the order it creates. According to conventional wisdom, spontaneous order may be able to create some limited order in the "shadow of the state." But it cannot create enough order to make the state unnecessary. Spontaneous order may flourish within the government-created meta-rules of social order. But it cannot create such meta-rules itself. Even if spontaneously ordered "meta-rules" were possible, most economists doubt their ability to facilitate the same level of cooperation that government-designed institutions facilitate. For instance, we have no examples of spontaneously ordered societies that generated volumes of cooperation sufficient to create the levels of wealth we observe in places where political authorities centrally designed meta-rules.

This chapter investigates these issues and seeks to shed light on the question of how much order spontaneous order can create. To do this, I consider three separate "classes" of spontaneous order emergence and operation. First, I consider the "easy case," spontaneous order in the "shadow of the state." Next, I consider the "harder case," spontaneous order over meta-rules themselves where government is absent. Finally, I consider the "hardest case," the possibility of a spontaneous order capable of generating cooperation that equals or surpasses the levels we observe in societies that rely on government for this purpose.

I find that spontaneous order is possible in the "easy" and "hard" cases. The verdict is still out on the "hardest" case. But there is reason to be optimistic about spontaneous order even here. Further, as I discuss below, while it is important for analyses of spontaneous order to go beyond mere "existence proofs" – evidence that some spontaneous institutional arrangements will emerge without government – it is equally important to get the benchmark right for assessing spontaneous order's ability to produce cooperation relative to government. Correct benchmarking makes the possibility of the "spontaneous order unicorn" – the privately-ordered society that is as, or more, productive than state-governed society – not so unimaginable after all.

10.2 The easy case: spontaneous order in the shadow of government

Even where government exists and functions well, the cost and imperfection of state enforcement creates ample space for spontaneous order. One of the most prevalent examples of this is extra-legal institutions of contract enforcement, such as reputation. Suing Jimmy B.'s Burger Shack because it gave you a small drink instead of the large drink you ordered and paid for, for example, is prohibitively costly. Even if you win your lawsuit against Jimmy B. for perpetrating this fraud, you will likely be worse off than if you had not bothered suing him in the first place. The simple time-cost of the procedure outweighs what you can hope to recover for the average meal. Situations like this create latitude for post-contractual opportunism on the part of exchange partners despite state enforcement's existence. If individuals cannot prevent such opportunism, they won't enter exchange agreements with others and the market shrinks along with individuals' ability to capture the gains from cooperating. Contracts with a credit component to them create another kind of post-contractual opportunism. Here, since payment is separated from provision, the debtor has an incentive to default on repayment with the same baneful effect on cooperation and exchange as cases of fraud, per the example above. Many other varieties of potential post-contractual opportunism pose essentially the same problem.

Reputation – a spontaneously ordered mechanism of contractual enforcement – often solves this problem where state enforcement is a costly or otherwise impractical means of securing contractual compliance. Instead of suing Jimmy B., for example, you boycott his establishment and encourage others to do so as well, warning them of his penchant for fraud. By boycotting Jimmy B. and damaging his reputation, you reduce his future income stream. Provided he does not discount the future too heavily, in the face of this possibility, he finds that he makes more money by satisfying his customers than by cheating them. Because of reputation, Jimmy B.'s contracts with his customers are self-enforcing.

The basic idea here can be extended to much more valuable exchanges and many more kinds of contracts. For instance, as I discuss below, international traders rely on a similar spontaneously ordered mechanism to secure their exchange partners' compliance with contracts worth many millions of dollars involving the transnational movement of goods. Also, on the Internet, reputation supports exchange agreements through seller rating and feedback systems, such as eBay's. These systems appear to work quite well. According to eBay, less than one-hundredth of 1 percent of its online exchanges involve fraud or other kinds of post-contractual opportunism. I discuss the equally impressive evidence of contractual compliance in the international arena below.

Reputation is not the only privately created institution of contract enforcement. There are others that work in conjunction with reputation to improve its effectiveness. Costly specific investments are one example of this (see, for instance, Williamson, 2005). Producers credibly commit themselves to cooperate with potential customers by making costly, upfront, firm-specific investments that they lose if they go out of business. Investments in firm-specific physical capital, logos, and even signage are examples of such investments. Since these investments only have value to the producer if his firm stays open, and his firm can stay open only if his customers are satisfied, these investments enhance the producer's incentive to comply with his contracts, reducing his temptation to behave opportunistically. They act as a sort of hostage or bond the producer loses if he fails to comply with his customer agreements, imposing a large cost on the producer that he wants to avoid.

The frequent use and success of these particular spontaneous orders in preventing opportunism has led some to suggest that social interactions in general could be based in these arrangements (see, for instance,

Stringham, 2006). A common objection to this suggestion is that spontaneous orders, such as reputation and bonding, emerge and work precisely because the specter of the state lurks in the background ready to enforce contractual agreements if for some reason private arrangements break down. If, for instance, Jimmy B. is very impatient and so doesn't care if he loses some future customers if he defrauds you or, say, the value of a producer's firm-specific investments for some reason plunge below what he can earn by defaulting on his contracts, the threat of state enforcement can facilitate contractual compliance nonetheless.[2] According to this reasoning, ultimately, it is government-created order that makes spontaneous order work.

Those who hold this popular position point out that the state supports spontaneous orders in another important way as well: it provides the physical security that individuals need to feel confident interacting. If, for instance, government didn't ensure that you wouldn't be stabbed or mugged when you left your home in the morning, you wouldn't be able to realize the benefits of cooperation whether spontaneously ordered contract enforcement prevented post-contractual opportunism or not. This criticism of the magnitude of the order that spontaneous order can create is closely related to another, which argues that spontaneous orders only work under certain, rather limited conditions, such as in small populations (although eBay seems to belie this) and where individuals are socially close (although international trade, discussed below, belies this).

None of this means what those who most frequently make these criticisms think it means, which is that spontaneous order can therefore create very little order. Rather, what it means is that spontaneous order must move beyond simple reputation mechanisms to secure more widespread social order. And this is precisely what we observe.

10.3 The harder case: spontaneous order without government

The "shadow of the state" limitation on spontaneous order is not a limitation if in fact individuals' private actions are capable of generating spontaneously ordered "meta-rules" – that is, if they are capable of going beyond facilitating contractual enforcement where commercial law already exists and can produce such law itself, as well as produce and enforce laws regulating violence, theft, and other kinds of socially destructive behavior. For meta-rule-creating spontaneous order to emerge, there must be either "pockets of anarchy" or "utter anarchy," which create a need for private meta-rules in the first place. For both types of anarchy, spontaneous meta-rules emerge not because government institutions exist but are impractical or costly to use. They emerge because for some or all kinds of interaction, government institutions do not exist.

Pockets of anarchy involve the absence of government with the power to govern particular and limited social interactions. If, for instance, there were no formal law governing certain kinds of commercial agreements and state courts did not exist or have the authority to enforce related commercial contracts, or they did but were simply too weak or uninterested in doing so, we would have a pocket of anarchy for these contracts. Criminalized trades, such as prostitution and the sale of illegal drugs, for example, constitute pockets of anarchy. So do many other commercial interactions in parts of the developing world where in principle state legal systems exist but they are so dysfunctional that in practice they do not.

In addition to pockets of anarchy, there may also be "utter anarchy." Under utter anarchy, anarchy is pervasive; the pockets of anarchy discussed above cover all interactions such that there is no (effective) centralized monopoly on violence to create or enforce rules for any social interactions. Somalia, which I discuss in Section 10.4, is one example of this. Stateless tribal societies, some of which existed into the twentieth century, and in a few cases exist to this day, are another example. Further back in history, many other societies also existed in utter anarchy. I discuss several of these below.

On the surface, at least, it seems that spontaneously ordered meta-rules would be far less likely to emerge than spontaneous order in the shadow of the state. This intuition is unsupported, however. The potential losses – unrealized gains from cooperation – associated with the absence of functional meta-rules are considerably larger than those associated with absent or dysfunctional rules at lower levels. If individuals cannot leave their homes for fear of being shot, society will be significantly poorer than if individuals cannot enforce credit agreements. Thus, individuals' incentive to find private solutions in the absence of government-created meta-rules is correspondingly larger than their incentive to develop private institutions of order where government provides such rules.

10.3.1   Pockets of anarchy: international trade

One of the best examples of this is the medieval "law merchant," or *lex mercatoria*. Bruce Benson's (1989) excellent paper, "The Spontaneous Evolution of Commercial Law," discusses this spontaneous order. International trade in the late tenth and early eleventh century, like international trade today, was conducted in the absence of a formal, supranational agency of commercial contract enforcement – that is, in the absence of a world government or legal system. The long-standing persistence of "international anarchy" created a large, formally ungoverned interstice – a significant pocket of anarchy. Since no universal, formal commercial law existed to regulate international commerce, and no formal court system existed to adjudicate international commercial disputes even if such law had existed, international traders faced a significant obstacle to realizing the gains from exchange. Rather than throwing up their hands and forgoing these gains in the absence of government-created commercial law, however, international traders relied on customs to regulate their dealings and "merchant courts" – private adjudication venues specifically for international commercial disagreements, adjudicated by merchants themselves – to resolve disputes. Over time, this spontaneous order evolved into a full-blown body of private international commercial law called the *lex mercatoria*. This spontaneously ordered legal system governed the bulk of international commerce throughout Europe until the sixteenth century.

Since the sizeable pocket of anarchy that gave birth to the medieval *lex mercatoria* – international anarchy – remains to this day, modern international commerce is also governed by this spontaneously ordered system. The modern *lex mercatoria* is applied to international commercial contracts in private international arbitration associations instead of merchant courts. But the essence of the system is similar. Hundreds of such associations exist globally. The largest and most significant of these is the International Chamber of Commerce's (ICC) International Court of Arbitration. Ninety percent of parties to private international commercial contracts provide for private arbitration in their agreements in the event they have a dispute (Volckart and Mangels, 1999). Parties may select their arbitration venue; in some cases they may select who their specific arbitrators will be; they may also select the law they want to apply to their contract, including the *lex mercatoria* itself, and other aspects of the private adjudication process.

Because international arbitration associations are private, they cannot formally enforce their decisions. However, a reputation mechanism among international traders similar to the process described in Section 10.2 ensures compliance nonetheless. The ICC, for instance, estimates that 90 percent of all parties that seek its arbitration services voluntarily comply with arbitrators' decisions even though they have no formal force (Craig et al., 2000). Apparently the spontaneously ordered "meta-rules" of international commerce are working quite well. International commerce now constitutes between 20 and 25 percent of world GDP – a remarkable volume of commerce supported by a spontaneous order.

Those who believe that spontaneous order cannot function outside the "shadow of the state" insist that in international trade, too, the state's shadow is responsible for flourishing exchange under the *lex mercatoria*. International anarchy is very real, they acknowledge; but private international arbitration decisions are in fact enforceable in state courts. The reason there is 90 percent voluntary compliance with private arbitral decisions at the arbitration stage is only because traders know that if they do not comply, a state court can compel them to.

Although I have never found an adherent to this position who could actually identify what specifically enables national courts to enforce private international arbitral awards, there is partial truth behind part of their claim. In 1958 several of the world's governments signed a treaty called the United Nations New York Convention on the Recognition and Enforcement of Foreign Arbitral Awards. According to this treaty, signatories agree to enforce the private international arbitration decisions of traders who approach them in their state courts. In principle, then, the New York Convention (NYC) provides formal enforcement to private international commercial contracts.

Those who (unwittingly) point to the NYC as evidence that the spontaneous order of the *lex mercatoria* operates in the shadow of the state are mistaken, however. First, the NYC didn't exist until 1958. And yet, international trade was large and growing before then (though admittedly not as fast as it has since then). This international exchange did not have the ostensible benefit of ultimate backing by state enforcement and flourished nonetheless. Second, I have empirically investigated the effect of the NYC on modern international trade using a gravity model of bilateral exchange and find that its effect on trade has been positive but economically small (see Leeson, 2008).

Third, the NYC's terms permit signatories to sign subject to reservation conditions, such as the condition that arbitral awards seeking formal enforcement must have been rendered in an NYC-member country, or the condition that requires arbitral awards seeking enforcement to relate to strictly commercial matters, with their commerciality being decided by the state court where enforcement is sought. Since such reservation conditions put a potentially large number of private international arbitral awards outside the purview of state enforcement, they significantly reduce even the theoretical scope of state enforcement under the NYC. And they are used widely by NYC members. Of the 109 countries that had signed the NYC as of 1999, for example, 68 of them, or more than 62 percent, were only "qualified" signatories subject to the reservation condition regarding reciprocity. Further, not all countries are members of the NYC. More than 50 countries remain non-members to this day and several "big players," such as the United Kingdom, remained non-members until as late as 1975. Similarly, the United States did not join the NYC until 1970.

Finally, and most important, however, the NYC is a multinational treaty and, like all such treaties, is not itself formally enforceable owing to absence of a supranational sovereign. What gives the NYC its force, if it has any, is the mere promises of its signatories to abide by its terms.

Failing to make good on such a promise brings no formal sanctions. The other signatories do not roll tanks into the NYC-reneging nation. In many cases, signatories have no way of even knowing whether their fellow signatories are enforcing foreign arbitral awards, per their promises, or not. The NYC's reservation conditions, discussed above, which allow signatories to back out of NYC at their discretion, exacerbate this monitoring problem.

For these reasons, spontaneously ordered mechanisms of enforcement, such as reputation, must be the source of any effect the NYC has on trade. In this sense, rather than spontaneous order existing in the shadow of inter-state agreements, it is actually inter-state agreements that exist in the shadow of spontaneous order. The argument that that shadow of the state ultimately underlies the success of spontaneous order in the international arena, then, is not only wrong. It has things precisely backwards.

10.3.2   *Utter anarchy: early eighteenth-century pirate society*

The *lex mercatoria* is an example of spontaneously ordered, commercial meta-rules outside the state's shadow. It illustrates spontaneous order's emergence in a pocket of anarchy created by the absence of a supranational sovereign in the international arena. But spontaneous order has emerged in the face of utter anarchy as well, where individuals could not rely on government for any purpose at all and where they therefore required encompassing spontaneous order that could govern not only their commercial interactions but all manner of other potential interactions, including violence and theft.

One of the most striking examples of this comes from early eighteenth-century pirates. In many ways, pirate ships were like floating societies. And, like other societies, pirate ships confronted problems of theft and violence. Since they were outlaws, pirates did not enjoy state protection for any of their interactions. Government did not enforce employment agreements between pirates or other piratical "contracts," nor did it prevent or punish theft or violence between pirates, and so on. Pirates existed in a state of utter anarchy.

Notably, the utterly anarchic environment that maritime bandits operated in did not lead them to abandon the idea of their criminal enterprise. On the contrary, the prospect of mutual gains from organizing this enterprise provided pirates with the incentive to find private ways of securing cooperation and order. Even by modern standards the spontaneous order that supported pirate society was remarkably sophisticated.

Pirates created written constitutions they called their "articles," which codified many of the laws that governed their ships, as well as punishments for lawbreakers. These included laws specifying the division of booty, laws against theft and violence, and even social insurance to support crew members injured in battle. To apply punishments and resolve disputes between crew members, pirates created an office called the "quartermaster." Crew members controlled quartermasters both through their constitutions, which prescribed the laws quartermasters could enforce and how they could enforce them, and by democratically electing crew members to this office.

The office of the quartermaster allowed pirates to overcome another obstacle anarchy posed for their organization – restraining potentially abusive pirate captains. A captain endowed with unlimited authority would be able to prey on his crew, skimming booty, mistreating crew members, and so on. To prevent such abuse, pirates initiated a system of separated powers, which transferred authorities susceptible to captain abuse to the quartermaster instead. In conjunction with also democratically electing their captains, pirate checks and balances overcame the threat of captain predation.

Pirates' private system of governance appears to have very effective. Inter-pirate conflict was rare, order was well maintained, and pirates cooperated regularly, permitting them to take massive hauls. What is remarkable about the spontaneous order of pirate society is not only its success; it is this order's success in a society of violent, dishonest, and debauched rogues – a literal society of criminals.

Terry Anderson and P.J. Hill's (2004) excellent study of *The Not So Wild, Wild West* provides another example of spontaneously ordered meta-rules – this time in a society of mostly law-abiding citizens rather than criminals. Between 1830 and 1900, much of the American West was without effective government. Rather than this absence leading to society's collapse, society seems to have gotten along quite well relying on spontaneous order. In the early nineteenth century, Americans began migrating westward in search of gold, land, and whatever else the expansive, unsettled region might be able to offer a resourceful family. Without a formal government to promote cooperation in the American West, people who Anderson and Hill call "institutional entrepreneurs" privately developed associations and arrangements to provide law and order to westerners' interactions instead.

To create and enforce property claims to previously unowned land, for instance, frontiersmen established a variety of "claims clubs," each complete with its own set of bylaws that created procedures for registering and protecting property claims and private courts for resolving land-related disputes. To protect westerners' cattle and create cooperation for the purposes of grazing and recovering stray animals, westerners also created "cattlemen's associations." Like claims clubs, cattlemen's associations also privately provided rules for their members and hired cattle detectives/

protectors to prevent cattle rustling and recover stolen animals. Miners and the members of wagon trails devised their own, similar institutions of governance to facilitate cooperation in the American West.

These private institutions of governance seem to have worked quite well. Popular Wild West fiction has promoted the idea of widespread western chaos, complete with lawless cowboys, gun-slinging showdowns, and frequent shoot-outs like the one at the O.K. Corral. But the evidence of spontaneous order's effectiveness in the Wild West paints a rather different picture. Between 1870 and 1885, for instance, in five of the largest cattle towns in the American West, Abilene, Ellsworth, Wichita, Dodge City, and Caldwell, there were a total of only 45 homicides for the entire 15-year period in all five cattle towns combined. That's an average of about 1.5 homicides per cattle-trading season (Dykstra, 1996). Historian Robert Dykstra provides some additional data on the not so Wild West. In the infamous Deadwood mining camp's first year, when there was no government to protect persons or property, there was a total of four homicides. Or consider Jesse James' infamous gang of bandits, which averaged only about one murder per year over the course of its career (ibid., p. 512).

Despite claims to the contrary, spontaneously ordered meta-rules – encompassing, private institutions of social order – evidently can emerge and secure social cooperation. In the international realm, spontaneously ordered merchant law and an attendant dispute resolution system developed to facilitate international commerce despite the pocket of anarchy that multiple international sovereigns create. In pirate societies and the American West there was utter anarchy. Far from preventing social order from emerging, the complete absence of formal government in these cases created strong incentives for individuals to devise private governance solutions that would permit them to realize the gains from cooperation. In the case of pirates, the result was a private system of constitutional democracy and separated powers that predated its adoption by governments in the legitimate seventeenth- and eighteenth-century world. In the case of the American West, the result was private associations that defined and enforced property rights where they previously did not exist. Both systems of spontaneously ordered meta-rules succeeded in generating social order.

Despite this success, neither system generated wealth for their participants that approaches the level of wealth enjoyed by citizens under some governments today. Critics of the idea that spontaneous order can create significant order are fond of pointing this out. Perhaps spontaneous order can function without the shadow of the state; perhaps it can generate meta-rules of social order. But it cannot do so more effectively than government. Where, these critics ask, are the examples of rich, spontaneously ordered societies?

10.4   The hardest case: beyond "existence proofs"

To address the issue this question is concerned with and, more generally, to evaluate spontaneous order's effectiveness in facilitating social coopera- tion relative to government, it is important for analyses of spontaneous order to go beyond "existence proofs," which point out that spontaneous orders will or did emerge but not whether the order they generate is as effective as government-created order. This is not to say that identifying the emergence of spontaneous social order and analyzing its operation in particular cases is unimportant. Precisely because the critics of spontane- ous order's widespread applicability have traditionally set up their argu- ments in the form of: "problems x, y, and z mean that private institutions of governance cannot emerge/work in scenarios a, b, and c," showing that private individual action has in fact overcome problems x, y, and z in sce- narios a, b, and c is important and valuable in and of itself. But existence, of course, does not imply superiority.

There are several difficulties with evaluating the comparative effective- ness of government- vs. spontaneously-created social orders. In the first place, there simply is not that much contemporary evidence to work with on the spontaneous order side of things. Officially at least, most of the world today has government. Only one country in recent history – Somalia – has transitioned from government to sustained anarchy, allowing a rea- sonable comparison to be made (more on the results of this comparison below).

Critics of spontaneous order often invoke the near-universal prevalence of government as if it were somehow evidence that government is superior to private, spontaneous arrangements in producing social order. I cannot figure out why. There is an entire field of political economy called public choice, the overriding point of which is that inefficient political outcomes abound. Of course, this basic insight also applies to the very existence of government itself. No one would conclude from the fact that essentially every country in the world has tariffs that protectionism must be more economically efficient than free trade. It is strange, then, that anyone would conclude from the fact that nearly every country in the world has government that government must be more economically efficient than spontaneous order. The fallacy involved in both conclusions is the same. The difficulty of evaluating spontaneous order's comparative efficiency is not that we know it is always comparatively inefficient because nearly all the world has government. The difficulty is that because nearly all the world has government, we have few contemporary cases of spontane- ously ordered societies that could shed empirical light on the comparative efficiency question.

Since most of the world for most of its history had no effective government, there are plenty of *historical* examples of spontaneous order to consider. However, as noted above, over time, virtually all of these orders were supplanted by governments. We therefore don't know how they might have developed if this hadn't occurred and what level of progress they might have supported. But we do know this much: it is wrong to conclude from the poverty of, say, spontaneously ordered medieval Iceland, *relative to the wealth in any society with government in the world today*, that spontaneous order cannot support higher standards of living, comparable to, or even greater than, those that some modern governments support.[3] The relevant comparison is not medieval Iceland vs., say, modern-day USA. Modern-day USA's standards of living were not available to or enjoyed by anyone – whether their society was ordered spontaneously or through government – in the Middle Ages. The relevant comparison is how spontaneously ordered medieval Iceland fared relative to, say, centrally ordered medieval European countries. Medieval Iceland's poverty from today's perspective says exactly nothing about spontaneous order's ability to generate wealth if it had been allowed to flourish, or how this wealth compares with what government delivered.

This point is simple enough and has many counterparts that economists are familiar with and accept when it comes to making other comparisons. For example, economists often point out that the Industrial Revolution, which non-economists commonly view as a time of economic retrogression for the average nineteenth-century laborer, in fact generated remarkable progress for these laborers. The non-economist's error is in comparing wages and work standards during the nineteenth century with those we enjoy today. Modern wages and work conditions are, of course, irrelevant. They were not available – not affordable – to nineteenth-century society. The relevant benchmark of comparison for assessing the Industrial Revolution's impact on laborers' welfare, then, is not the contemporary United States or Western Europe. It is the wages and work conditions that *feasible*, alternative economic arrangements could have generated in the nineteenth century – namely, continued focus on agricultural production. These wages and work conditions represent the opportunity cost of Industrial Revolution wages and work conditions. And, the evidence clearly indicates that during the Industrial Revolution the average laborer benefited from moving from the farm to the factory (see, for instance, Hayek, 1963).

What is difficult to understand is why economists who readily accept and rely on this logic when discussing the Industrial Revolution are incapable of doing so when it comes to discussions about the prosperity-enhancing capacities of private order. The first objection on the lips of every person who believes spontaneous order could never be as efficient, let alone more efficient, than government, is that none of the historical examples we have of spontaneous social order demonstrate high levels of wealth.

My question is, relative to what? Relative to today's highest-performing governments this is certainly true. But relative to the actual political governance alternatives these societies faced at the time, it may not be. This is an empirical question and one that economists should explore rather than simply announcing the obviousness of the answer without ever considering the evidence. In any event, when this benchmark is used instead of the quite irrelevant benchmark of wealth in countries with government today, even in the worst-case scenario for spontaneous order, the "wealth gap" between what spontaneous order and government can provide becomes considerably smaller than that suggested by most of spontaneous order's critics.

This brings me to the final point I want to make about assessing the comparative effectiveness of spontaneous order for securing cooperation vs. using government for this purpose. As noted above, spontaneous order's critics are happy to point out that all but one of the world's countries have government. I have already addressed why this observation doesn't imply what these critics think it does. But much more curiously, what spontaneous order critics inevitably fail to point out is that among the approximately 200 countries and thus experiments with government in the world at the moment, more than half, if evaluated in terms of their ability to promote social cooperation, must be counted as abject failures. According to the Foreign Policy/Fund for Peace *Failed States Index*, nearly 14 percent of the world's countries (28) have officially "failing states" (Failed States Index, 2006[4]). In them, governments are on the verge of total collapse. Another 39 percent of the world's countries (78) have states in imminent danger of failing. This is not exactly a track record to write home about.

The fact that only a minority of experiments with government actually produce social order along the lines that spontaneous order's critics imply government routinely produces has tremendously important, but totally neglected, implications for evaluating the potential effectiveness and thus desirability of spontaneous- vs. government-created social order. Of course, government's failure to effectively produce social order in most of the world doesn't necessarily mean that spontaneous order would do any better. But at the very least, the advocates of state-created order need to understand that what they have in mind when discussing the indispensability of government for wealth and prosperity is in fact a minority of remarkably successful governments – namely those located in North America and Western Europe. What they have in mind is the exception, not the rule.

Further, while to date we have but one example of a failing state that ultimately collapsed altogether leaving utter anarchy in its wake – Somalia – the evidence here favors the superiority of privately created as opposed to politically created order in this case. Somalia is not a nice place to live. It is one of the poorest countries in the world and has many other severe problems. Still, spontaneously ordered Somalia has performed better on nearly every welfare indicator for which data are available than it performed under government. The reason for this is not necessarily the amazing job that spontaneous order in Somalia has done at creating improvements.[5] Primarily, it seems that Somalia's improved welfare under statelessness is the result of a truly horrendous government that preceded anarchy.

This is not to detract from the superiority of spontaneous order in this case, however. Numerous factors, especially those cultural and historical, severely constrain the extent of development Somalia could likely enjoy, at least in the short run, under any governance regime. Thus, it would be unreasonable to expect a wealthy Somalia regardless of its reliance on government or spontaneous order. But spontaneously ordered Somalia appears to be wealth*ier* in terms of overall development than centrally ordered Somalia was.[6] And this is the relevant comparison.

Note that the relevant comparison is *not* spontaneously ordered Somalia vs., say, the United States with government. Those who emphasize the urgency of re-establishing government in Somalia often invoke this comparison (oftentimes implicitly), similar to the way that spontaneous order critics illegitimately invoke comparisons between wealth in historical spontaneously ordered societies and wealth in modern government-ordered societies, to suggest that a centrally ordered Somalia would outperform a spontaneously ordered Somalia. But like its cousin, discussed above, this comparison is illegitimate unless a United States-quality government – that is a transparent, highly constrained government that protects citizens' private property rights and provides important public goods – is a genuine institutional option for Somalia. If it is not, then this comparison is irrelevant. Being the United States is not Somalia's opportunity cost of relying exclusively on spontaneous order. But being Sierra Leone – a country with a similar history to Somalia and thus similar institutional constraints – or Somalia when it was under government, is. And the evidence suggests that spontaneously ordered Somalia is superior to these institutional alternatives (see, for instance, Leeson, 2007; Powell et al., forthcoming).

10.5 Concluding remarks

In this chapter, I have investigated the question of how much order spontaneous order can create by considering three "classes" of spontaneous order's emergence and operation. These classes corresponded to what

I have called the "easy," "harder," and "hardest" cases for spontaneous order. The first is spontaneous order in the shadow of the state. The second is spontaneous order outside this shadow under anarchy. The third is spontaneous order outside the shadow of the state that generates as much wealth and cooperation, or even more, than the amount that government generates. Although my discussion was brief, a few broad insights can be drawn from this analysis.

First, as is commonly acknowledged, spontaneous order can emerge and successfully function in environments in which: (1) a well-functioning state exists to provide meta-institutions of social order, such as an overarching legal system that addresses both violence and theft, and to provide a method of legal enforcement including courts and police; and (2) the state legal system covers contractual violations such that in the event a spontaneously ordered institution of contractual compliance fails, government can pick up the slack. In short, spontaneous order can emerge and operate where it is helpful but, strictly speaking, it is not really needed. The reason such orders may emerge under these circumstances nonetheless is because of the advantages of spontaneously ordered institutions of contractual compliance over state institutions in some cases, such as being faster, more reliable, and more cost-effective.

Second, a more controversial conclusion: spontaneous order does not require the shadow of the state to emerge or function. When, because of pockets of anarchy, which lead to a genuine absence of government law creation/enforcement for certain kinds of interactions, or because of utter anarchy, which leads to a genuine absence of government law/enforcement in general, individuals cannot rely on state-made meta-institutions to facilitate cooperation, they do not simply avoid one another or wind up in a Hobbesian Jungle equilibrium of violence and plunder. Instead, individuals devise private meta-institutions precisely to realize the benefits of avoiding this outcome. These institutions emerge to regulate contractual opportunism, violence, theft, and other manner of anti-social behavior as needed depending upon the particular situation and kind of anarchy (i.e., "pocket" or "utter") involved. Foreign trade, both historically and today, is an example of such private institutions spontaneously emerging in the face of a large pocket of anarchy – the international arena. Early eighteenth-century pirate societies and the American West are two examples of such institutions emerging to provide more encompassing social order in the face of the situations of utter anarchy that these environments presented. Spontaneous order, then, is capable of producing considerably more order than conventional wisdom traditionally permits.

Finally, and most controversially: although we have no examples of purely spontaneously ordered societies generating levels of wealth commensurate with what modern societies governed by highly functioning governments generate, this doesn't mean, as is commonly supposed, that spontaneous order is incapable of generating such levels of wealth. We must remain agnostic on the question of the comparative efficiency of spontaneously created social order vs. government-created social order as a general proposition. Theoretically, there are conditions under which spontaneously created social order can outperform government-created social order and vice versa. In practice what matters is the specific situation that spontaneous order or government operates in, the particular variety of spontaneously emerged social institutions or state institutions that exist, and so forth. It would be foolish to contend that all cases of spontaneous social order will outperform all cases of government-created social order. Switzerland, for example, would clearly not improve its situation by moving toward the institutions of Igbo self-governance in pre-colonial Africa.

But economists are in no danger of coming to such an erroneous blanket conclusion. The far more imminent danger is coming to the equally erroneous blanket conclusion to the opposite effect: all cases of government are superior to all cases of spontaneous order. This idea, though commonly suggested, is patently false, not only theoretically, but also empirically, as the case of Somalia highlights. The key factor to consider when evaluating the efficiency of spontaneously created vs. government-created institutions of social order is the kind of government that represents the institutional opportunity cost of spontaneous order. Switzerland's government is quite a different bird from the government that currently rules the Democratic Republic of Congo. If the government alternative to spontaneous order in a particular case looks like, or is more likely to look like, the latter variety than the former variety, spontaneous order may very well produce superior outcomes even if under idealized conditions it does not facilitate as much cooperation as government can under such conditions.

In other words, a "first-best government" – one that successfully protects private property rights, supplies important public goods, and does not use its power to prey on citizens – may outperform a "first-best spontaneous order." But this is irrelevant for assessing the comparative efficiency of spontaneous order and government unless the institutional alternative to spontaneous order in a particular case is in fact a first-best government. Second-, or even third-best spontaneous order, for example, may outperform second- or third-best government, even if spontaneous order loses in the efficiency contest when comparing first-bests. Stated differently, deviations from first-best government may involve larger welfare losses than deviations from first-best spontaneous orders, even if first-best government outperforms first-best spontaneous order.

If this is so, the question: "Where are the wealthy spontaneously ordered societies?" is the wrong one to be asking and not at all useful for evaluating the desirability of actual spontaneous order vs. actual government. Instead, the relevant question is: "In this particular case of x-best government and y-best spontaneous order, which will produce the superior outcome?" Since most of the world's governments are far from first-best, here, the prospects for spontaneous order's superiority are quite strong indeed.

Notes

1. Though, there is reason to possibly reject this dichotomy. See Wagner (2007). Carl Menger, for example, suggested that the state itself was a spontaneous order ([1883] 1963).
2. Of course, if the reason individuals rely on spontaneously ordered mechanisms of contract enforcement is the prohibitive cost of state contract enforcement, even the "shadow of the state" cannot ensure contractual compliance. However, for those contracts where a spontaneously ordered institution of contract enforcement is used because it is cheaper than state enforcement (when the former is effective), though state enforcement remains cost-effective if it has to be relied upon, the "shadow of the state" can secure contractual compliance even if spontaneous order breaks down.
3. On medieval Iceland's spontaneous order, see David Friedman's (1979) superb study.
4. See http://www.fundforpeace.org/web/index.php?option=com_content&task=view&id =104&Itemid=324; accessed 27 January 2010.
5. Though, as Tim Harford and Tatiana Nenova's (2004) important paper discusses, private sector actors have been remarkably innovative in anarchic Somalia.
6. I emphasize wealth*ier* here to highlight the fact that, as I try to make clear above, I'm not claiming that Somalia is wealthy. Hopefully this is clear from my entire discussion in the section – that the benchmark is not one of wealthy or poor from some idealized, unattainable (i.e., modern North American or Western European) and thus irrelevant benchmark, but rather, in the case of Somalia, what preceded spontaneous order, which was a brutal and predatory government – Somalia's institutional alternative. If history is any indicator, only a small percentage of readers will "get this." The much larger part will wrongly infer that I'm saying Somalia is grand or that Somalia is evidence that spontaneous order is always better than any government.

References

Anderson, Terry L. and Peter J. Hill. 2004. *The Not So Wild, Wild West*. Stanford: Stanford University Press.
Benson, Bruce L. 1989. "The Spontaneous Evolution of Commercial Law," *Southern Economic Journal* **55**(3): 644–61.
Craig, W.L., William Park, and Ian Paulsson. 2000. *International Chamber of Commerce Arbitration*. New York: Oceana Publications.
Dykstra, Robert R. 1996. "Overdosing on Dodge City," *Western Historical Quarterly* **26**(winter): 505–14.
Ferguson, Adam. [1767] 1966. *An Essay on the History of Civil Science*, edited by Duncan Forbes. Edinburgh: Edinburgh University Press.
Friedman, David. 1979. "Private Creation and Enforcement of Law: A Historical Case," *Journal of Legal Studies* **8**(March): 399–415.
Harford, Tim and Tatiana Nenova. 2004. "Anarchy and Invention," *Public Policy for the Private Sector*. World Bank, note no. 280.
Hayek, F.A. 1948. *Individualism and Economic Order*. Chicago: University of Chicago Press.

Hayek, F.A. (ed.) 1963. *Capitalism and the Historians.* Chicago: University of Chicago Press.

Hayek, F.A. 1973–79. *Law, Legislation, and Liberty.* 3 vols. Chicago: University of Chicago Press.

Leeson, Peter T. 2007. "Better Off Stateless: Somalia Before and After Government Collapse," *Journal of Comparative Economics* **35**(4): 689–710.

Leeson, Peter T. 2008. "How Important is State Enforcement for Trade?," *American Law and Economics Review* **10**(1): 61–89.

Menger, Carl. [1871] 1950. *Principles of Economics.* Glencoe, IL: Free Press.

Menger, Carl [1883] 1963. *Problems of Economics and Sociology.* Urbana: University of Illinois Press.

Powell, Benjamin, Ryan Ford, and Alex Nowrasteh. Forthcoming. "Somalia After State Collapse: Chaos or Improvement?," *Journal of Economic Behavior and Organization.*

Smith, Adam. [1776] 1976. *An Inquiry into the Nature and Causes of the Wealth of Nations.* Chicago: University of Chicago Press.

Stringham, Edward P. 2006. "Overlapping Jurisdictions, Proprietary Communities, and Competition in the Realm of Law," *Journal of Institutional and Theoretical Economics* **162**(3): 516–34.

Volckart, Oliver and Antje Mangels. 1999. "Are the Roots of the Modern Lex Mercatoria Really Medieval?," *Southern Economic Journal* **65**(3): 427–50.

Wagner, Richard E. 2007. *Fiscal Sociology and the Theory of Public Finance.* Cheltenham, UK and Northampton, MA, USA: Edward Elgar.

Williamson, Oliver E. 2005. "The Economics of Governance," *American Economic Review* **95**(2): 1–18.

PART IV

CONCLUSION

11 Back to the future: Austrian economics in the twenty-first century

Peter J. Boettke

At the time of writing, the market economies of the world are suffering through a financial crisis of significant proportions. The capitalist system is under intellectual attack to an extent it has not been subjected to since the Great Depression. And the discipline of economics, and in particular, orthodox models of rationality and perfect competition, are often held up for ridicule. And modern macroeconomics is subjected to particular disdain for its inability to predict the current crisis, and modern financial theory is often pinpointed as the culprit behind the entire mess.

This is not just evident in the rhetorical excesses of left-wing politicians and journalists. Even rather skilled economic commentators (both inside and outside of academia) make this assessment of the state of economics and public policy. The era of Reagan/Thatcher laissez-faire must come to an end, and a return of Keynesian style economics and public policy must be ushered in.

The fate of the Austrian school of economics in all of this is – to put it bluntly – rather strange. The Austrian school is often held up for ridicule by those on the left for having provided the intellectual justification for the laissez-faire policies of Reagan/Thatcher, while the ideas in modern economics and finance that are held up for special scrutiny are in direct opposition to the methodology and methods of the Austrian school of economics. In addition, commentators who know that the Austrian school is at odds with modern mainstream economics, use that tension to dismiss the unique Austrian position in the economic debate as not being scientifically legitimate. So if one is paying close enough attention, they should notice that the Austrian school is criticized for being responsible for the transformation of economics and public policy to such an extent that an era of laissez-faire was ushered in throughout the world, and criticized for being irrelevant and outside of the mainstream of economic thought. If this were in fact true, the phenomenon of the Austrian school of economics would be worthy of serious study not only by economists but by all social scientists. How could an intellectual movement, so small and so out of step, transform the world of public policy? And keep in mind what we actually witnessed world-wide since the late 1970s – the collapse of the

Keynesian hegemony in thought and policy; the collapse of communism in East and Central Europe and the former Soviet Union; the widespread recognition of the failure of development planning in Latin America, Asia, and Africa; and the integration into the world economy of some of the poorest nations in the world through liberalization and globalization.

Those are some amazing facts to contend with even if at the backend of that era we also witnessed growing tensions over the threat of terrorism resulting in military conflict; increased debate over the consequences of development on the environment and the demand for policies to address global climate change; and a world-wide financial crisis that threatens to bankrupt nations. How powerful exactly are ideas of economists supposed to be? Keynes perhaps said it best when he simply stated about the power of ideas that "Indeed the world is ruled by little else".[1]

This volume had a more humble ambition than to counter the rhetoric of our age, or to trace out the ultimate influence of Mises' and Hayek's idea on the global transformation toward market-oriented policies, or to set the academic record straight once and for all on the contributions of the Austrian school vis-à-vis neoclassical models of omniscient and hyper-rational agents interacting in perfectly competitive market environments, or the representative agent models of modern macroeconomics. Instead, it was simply to set out the modern Austrian school of economics as prac-ticed at the beginning of the twenty-first century as a progressive research program in contemporary economics and political economy. Taking the lead from my Introduction, the idea was to "reduce" the Austrian claim to a unique approach to economic scholarship to a set of ten propositions and to tease out the implications of those propositions.

The authors are all part of the next generation of Austrian school economists and represent that third generation since the resurgence of interest in the Austrian school following Hayek's Nobel Prize in 1974 and the organizational efforts of Israel Kirzner and Murray Rothbard to create a modern Austrian school of economics starting with a conference in South Royalton, VT in the summer of 1974. Kirzner and Rothbard (and also Ludwig Lachmann) gave a series of lectures on methodol-ogy, market process analysis, and money, capital, and macroeconomics. Those in attendance formed the first generation of the modern Austrian school, and included individuals such as Don Lavoie, Mario Rizzo, Gerald O'Driscoll, Jack High, Randy Holcombe, Karen Vaughn, Roger Garrison, Joe Salerno, Walter Block, and Richard Ebeling, amongst others. Other conferences followed, a book series was established, and a PhD fellowship program was established at NYU for students interested in studying Austrian economics. Richard Langlois, Peter Lewin, Bruce Caldwell, Bill Butos, and Lawrence White all joined that first generation of economists in the modern Austrian tradition in the mid- to late 1970s and early 1980s.

As these individuals established themselves within the economics profession, new PhD programs were established at Auburn University and George Mason University that provided intellectual space for studying the modern Austrian school of economics. With these new programs, journals were also established such as *The Austrian Economics Newsletter* and *Market Process*, and then the *Review of Austrian Economics*, *Advances in Austrian Economics*, and the *Quarterly Journal of Austrian Economics*. The latter three are still publishing, the former two are now defunct (but I believe available online). That first generation, with the guiding help of Kirzner and Rothbard along the way, and the help of several foundations and enterprising individuals established an Austrian community of scholars within the economics profession. The Ludwig von Mises Institute was established in the early 1980s as was the Center for the Study of Market Processes, and this was in addition to the existing institutional infrastructure of The Foundation for Economic Education, The Institute for Humane Studies, Liberty Fund, and The Cato Institute.

A new generation of economists committed to advancing the ideas of the modern Austrian school emerged in the mid- to late 1980s and early 1990s. This second generation of the modern Austrian school consisted of the products of these new programs[2] and includes names such as George Selgin, Roger Koppl, Dan Klein, Don Boudreaux, Mark Thornton, Steve Horwitz, Emily Chamlee-Wright, David Prychitko, and myself. As we established ourselves in the 1990s with our teaching and research, a new group of students emerged in the early 2000s and they are who I have tapped for this volume. Among this group are emerging superstars within the economics profession in general, while others are fast becoming recognized intellectual leaders in the Austrian and classical liberal/libertarian movement. The oldest is in his early forties, the youngest is still in his twenties. Yet we have journal editors, past presidents of professional societies, department chairpersons, center directors, and publishing machines. In other words, while young this new generation is already making a professional impression.

The contemporary Austrian school is not a unified body of thought, and it would be a big mistake to suggest it was.[3] And, in reality it has not been since the mid-1970s. Kirznerian, Rothbardian, and Lachmannian have been various labels that have been used to characterize individuals and their contributions. Misesian and Hayekian are meta-labels that have often been used by friends and foes of the respective strands of thought within the modern Austrian school. The way I see it, contemporary Austrian economics is a progressive research program, not a settled body of thought, and that is the only way forward – which means we should not worry about fidelity to the works of any past or present thinker and instead only pursue truth as we see fit and grab productive ideas wherever we may find them. I also think that this was in fact the way that Mises and Hayek did social science so this is not anything new to the Austrian school. Cross-fertilization of the ideas of Menger and Böhm-Bawerk with those of English economists such as Wicksteed, Swedish economists such as Wicksell, and US economists such as Knight was the way Mises and Hayek thought about the intellectual activity of an economist. Cross-fertilization is not about complete consistency, but about selective blending to improve economic reasoning. Many contemporary Austrians have studied with and/or have continuously learned from the work of: Alchian, Baumol, Becker, Boulding, Buchanan, Coase, Demsetz, Friedman (Milton, Rose, and David), Leijonhufvud, Loasby, McCloskey, North, Olson, Phelps, Schelling, Vernon Smith, Tullock, and Williamson. Other influences from the fields of politics, law, sociology, philosophy, as well as economics could also be listed.

As the editor, I am sure that the volume takes off from my perspective on the Austrian school and my summary in the Introduction of the ten propositions that I see as key to the Austrian contribution to modern economics. In this sense, the volume is framed by my interpretation even though none of the contributors are expected to agree with me on that broader perspective, nor did I impose on them any requirement that they pursue the implications of the propositions as I see them. In fact some of them push the argument in directions I would not, but that is the point of a progressive research program – nobody has control of it, and attempts to control it merely thwart creativity and growth.

Let me add one important note on certain terms associated with the Austrian school of economics; namely praxeology and the aprioristic nature of economic reasoning. These terms were not used in my Introduction, but I personally believe that nothing I have said contradicts Mises' methodological position, rightly understood. First, the subject matter of praxeology is human action. Second, apriorism is an epistemological position justified by Mises on neo-Kantian grounds, but as Rothbard demonstrated it can be philosophically justified on Aristotelian grounds as well. The economists *qua* economists need not take a strong stand on the philosophical justification of the a priori nature of economic theory to deploy the logic of economics for theoretical and applied purposes. Third, Mises argued that praxeology was not new, and neither was his insistence on the a priori nature of economics. In fact, he insisted that all good economics was done in this way both prior to him and among his contemporaries. Smith to Knight, in other words, were counted as in that basic same tradition even if they did not always understand that – the way they did their economics was the same way Mises did his. This is an approach that puts the choosing actor (with his/her purposes and plans) at the center of the analysis, and builds out from that to understand the complex social structures of an economy. Fourth, while economics, or catallactics, was the best developed branch of praxeology, further developments of praxeology in fields outside the realm of economics proper should be expected.

The common parlance in modern academia for praxeology is "rational actor" approach. Now praxeology does not reduce the means-ends calculation of individuals to the machine-like behavior of automata. Many rational choice models do in fact commit the fallacy of treating the choosing agent like a robot. Mises, instead, emphasized rational choice theorizing with human choosers. This led him in his day to reject ideas of *Homo economicus*, as did Hayek. But this did not mean in their work that the "rational actor" is not at the center of all analysis. Anyway, where one reads "rational actor" or "rational choice" in the contemporary Austrian literature, understand it as praxeology and the methodological individualist approach to social science.

The epistemological issue Mises sought to address with his insistence on apriorism, while more exotic in its philosophic treatment than his predecessors, boils down to the claim that theory comes prior to observation. We use theory to make sense of the economic world around us. The choice for the analyst is never theory or no theory, but instead always theory that has been articulated and defended or theory that remains inarticulate and hidden from critical examination. The analyst does not confront the "data" pure and simple. Stated this way, nothing in Mises' claim for the aprioristic nature of economic reasoning is new and startling. Menger, of course, made this argument against the claims of historicism, but one can also read them throughout the classical period of political economy in various authors. But it is a mistake to believe that these arguments either claimed that the entire field of economics was a priori or that economics is completely insulated from criticism of an empirical nature.

Economics as a field of inquiry can be divided into (1) pure theory, (2) applied theory, and (3) economic history and/or contemporary history (i.e., public policy). The realm of pure theory is an essential element of economics, but it is limited in range. It is often referred to as the pure logic of choice. Mises' first 100 pages of *Human Action* (1949) are the essential reading on this point for Austrians, but one can also get systematic statements of this position in Menger, Böhm-Bawerk, and of course Mises' *Epistemological Problems* ([1933] 1960).[4] Lionel Robbins' *Nature and Significance of Economic Science* (1932) could also be usefully consulted,

as could a careful reading of Knight's *Risk, Uncertainty and Profit* (1921).
The realm of applied theory, on the other hand, moves well beyond the
pure logic of choice and makes up the bulk of economic reasoning. In
this area, the pure logic of choice is combined with various institutional
assumptions (empirically verifiable) to explain both the manifestations of
rationality under alternative contexts and the efficacy of exchange relationships within those environments. Hayek's 1937 paper "Economics
and Knowledge" is the primary reading on this point for Austrians.[5]
Often interpreted as a break with Mises' praxeological understanding
of economic science, the position in the paper that Hayek carves out is
actually consistent with Mises in the reading I am suggesting. The pure
logic of choice is a necessary, but not sufficient, component of the theory
of the market economy and the price system. Subsidiary arguments of an
empirical nature are in fact required to work in combination with the pure
logic of choice to provide an explanation of how markets work, and when
the system is able to successfully coordinate economic activities and when
the system may face coordination problems.

   The realm of economic history and/or contemporary history is where the
analyst takes the arguments one constructs in pure and applied theory, and
then develops a framework of analysis that aids empirical interpretation
of events and provides an economic assessment of those events. Economic
assessments are limited to strict means/ends analysis, and not normative
statements about the "goodness" or "badness" of the situation. Socialism,
for example, fails on its own terms, not due to a moral assessment of col-
lectivism versus individualism. The means of socialism do not permit the
ends of socialism to be realized from the point of view of the advocates
of socialism. Collective ownership by in effect eliminating the ability of
economic actors to engage in rational economic calculation destroys the
ability of the socialist system to meet its end of advanced material production and thus harmony among the classes through post-scarcity. If
socialism was to change either its means or its ends, Mises' demonstration
would need to be modified as his argument is in fact the rather specific one
that rational economic calculation is impossible without private property
in the means of production. When socialism means private property in the
means of production, rational economic calculation may indeed be now
possible, provided a market for the means of production is permitted. And
when the goal of socialism is no longer advanced material production so
rationalized as to usher in post-scarcity, but instead a vow of poverty then
the argument *against* socialism made by Mises loses much of its force.[6]
Economic analysis has its limits, but it also provides essential knowledge
to the broader project of social and moral philosophy.[7]

   Nothing I have argued above should be interpreted as insulating

Austrian arguments from refutation, but instead clarifying the terms under which refutation is to occur. Statistical tests in themselves do not provide guidance here. But arguments can be proven to be false, and are, at each step if one can demonstrate a logical error in the theorist's derivation. Moreover, theories can be demonstrated to be logically valid, but not sound. Theories can be inapplicable to a situation because the empirical subsidiary assumptions are not true for the case to be examined. And finally, there is always the issue of magnitude. In a complex world, many factors may be at play and some more important than others. Consider the current financial crisis; there is evidence that contributory factors include credit expansion (deviations from the Taylor Rule) by the Fed, perverse incentives in the housing market, and confusion caused by changes in the regulations governing high finance. Can we say any one of these is *the* cause, or do we have to simply admit that a perfect storm of perverse incentives and distorted information resulted in a massive cluster of errors that required massive adjustments to capital and labor to get back on the correct economic track? As Deirdre McCloskey has continually stressed, the two most important questions the economist must ask of their own and others' work are: (1) so what?; and (2) how big is BIG? Austrian economists need to ask those questions just as much as anyone else doing economics and political economy.

Praxeology, apriorism, and value-freedom all remain core claims of the Austrian school of economics, though the argument must be restated and restructured to meet the counter-arguments of this generation of thinkers and directed toward the interests of one's contemporaries. To put this another way, Mises developed his argument to meet objections that were raised to economics and its teachings by intellectual opponents of the nineteenth and early twentieth century; Hayek developed his argument to meet the objections raised by mid-twentieth-century intellectual opponents; similarly Kirzner was addressing his arguments to opponents of the 1960s–80s; Rizzo and Lavoie to opponents of the 1980s and 1990s, and so on. And this new generation of economists will need to address their arguments to the challenges offered by modern day historicists, formalists, and positivists (even more difficult to do given that the philosophic self-awareness of the mainstream of economists seems to have actually declined since the 1980s).

At the same time that this discussion of the methodological foundations of contemporary economics and political economy are difficult to engage, the field of economics and political economy have opened up to new ideas and new methods. In many ways, economics has entered a new era of intellectual excitement. The analytic narrative approach to economic history associated with Avner Grief and Barry Weingast, the behavioral and cognitive economics and political economy of Timur Kuran and Bryan Caplan, and the agent-based models of complex systems associated with Rob Axtell and Peyton Young should all be seen as great opportunities for those interested in the ideas of Mises and Hayek to develop them in the context of contemporary social science. Topically, the work on colonial origins, legal origins, constitutional and political economics, organization and management, and entrepreneurial studies also opens great opportunities for a new generation to bring the ideas of Mises and Hayek to the forefront of professional discourse. Many of the authors in this volume are in fact doing this and developing their own voices in the context of contemporary economics and political economy.

Finally, we must recognize the great opportunity provided to economists of all stripes by the pressing practical problems of the world that demand explanation and understanding. We find ourselves in the midst of a global financial crisis, the root cause of which appears to be a credit-induced boom-bust cycle (i.e., the Austrian Theory of the Business Cycle). Furthermore, we live in a time where a large segment of the world suffers under the yoke of failed and weak states. In such a world, the traditional economic approach of treating institutions as given is not appropriate. Instead, progress in economics must seek to endogenize institutions; to examine situations in which institutions within which economic activity takes place are in fact being constructed either through design or evolution. This is true whether we are talking about development in Africa, or reconstruction in the Middle East. We are in fact confronted with issues of life and death, and issues that may even touch on the survival of civilization as we know it, and the economist is uniquely situated to provide the necessary philosophic understanding and the public policy knowledge to both grasp the essential problem and offer the requisite solution.

When I was at the same stage of my career as the contributors to this volume, I once described Austrian economics as humanistic in its method, and humanitarian in its concern. This is what attracted me to the school. It promised philosophic understanding of the complex world around us, and when combined with some basic concepts of morality produced a powerful argument for a society of free and responsible individuals. Twenty years later I still find this description to be apt. It is my sincere hope that students of economics and political economy will read this volume, see the common-sense wisdom of the Austrian approach to economics, as well as the intellectual power of the Austrian school as a framework of analysis for the most pressing problems of our age. The volume is not an opportunity for indoctrination into a settled body of economic thought, but an invitation to inquiry to the next generation of students guided by a new generation of scholar/teachers who have learned from past thinkers, think hard about what the discipline as a whole has to offer, and are now pushing economic arguments in new and novel directions to advance our understanding of the economic and social world.

Notes

1. Keynes, John M. *The General Theory of Employment, Interest and Money.* London: Macmillan, 1936, p. 383.
2. There were several other young scholars emerging who were not products of these programs, such as Tyler Cowen, Peter Klein, Nikolai Foss, Paul Lewis, and Guido Hülsmann to name a few.
3. The Austrian school, like all vibrant bodies of scientific thought, always had its internal disputes amongst its members from its founding and maturing in Vienna and continuing through its dispersal in the 1930s throughout Europe and the United States. Mises, Hayek, Machlup, Morgenstern and Habeler, for example, are all very different scholars of economics, but there is also something quite similar in their work that can be recognized in their respective arguments in methodology, method, and application of economic reasoning to problems of public policy. Vociferous debate about economic theory and its philosophical foundations has been evident throughout the long history of the Austrian school of economics.
4. Mises, Ludwig von. *Epistemological Problems of Economics.* New York: D. Van Nostrand Co., [1933] 1960.
5. Hayek, Frederic von. "Economics and Knowledge." *Economica*, 4(13), 33–54.
6. Mises' argument concerning rational economic calculation would remain but the implication would be different. Collective ownership of the means of production precisely because it eliminates the ability to engage in rational economic calculation may in fact be the most efficacious means to obtain the ends of poverty, squalor, and destruction.
7. Economics, in other words, cannot tell you whether profits are deserved or not, but economics can inform you on what the consequences will be of your answer to that question on just desert.

Index

equilibrium
  allocation paradigm as equilibrium
    exchange 16
  capital 126, 128
  entrepreneurship in 99
  market equilibrium and
    entrepreneurial discovery
    88–9
  monetary, and money, non-
    neutrality of 113, 119
  price 71, 72
Evans, Anthony J. 3–13
exchange and coordination *see*
  economics as study of
  coordination and exchange

Ferguson, A. 136
Fisher, F. 104
Fogel, R. 25–6
Foss, N. 20
free market
  social utility maximizing 61–3
  and spontaneous privatization *see*
    under private property and
    rational economic calculation
Freeman, S. 122
Friedman, D. 152
Friedman, M. 79, 114, 121

game theory 6, 18–19, 20
Garrison, R. xvii, 120, 130, 134
Garrouste, P. 21, 26
Geertz, C. 34–5, 37–8
Glaeser, E. 24

Haberler, G. 121
Harcourt, G. 134
Hardin, G. 77
Harford, T. 152
Harper, D. 105, 106
Hayek F. xi, xiv, 5, 9, 14, 22, 26, 46, 61,
  74, 77, 78, 79, 89, 90, 111–12, 113,
  115, 116, 118, 121, 122, 163, 164
  Capitalism and the Historians 147
  "Competition as a Discovery
    Procedure" 16, 48, 49, 104
  The Constitution of Liberty 20–21
  The Counter-Revolution of Science
    31, 36–7
  "Economics and Knowledge" 162

*The Fatal Conceit: The Errors of
  Socialism* 25
Individualism and Economic Order
  xvi, 6, 30, 136
"Individualism: True and False" 6
"Investment that Raises the Demand
  for Capital" 132
Law Legislation and Liberty 17, 18
"The Meaning of Competition" 104
Prices and Production 114, 117, 134
Pure Theory of Capital 134
The Sensory Order 117
"The Use of Knowledge in Society"
  19, 72–3, 97, 129
Heath, J. 3, 5
Hicks, J. 15
High, J. 105
Hill, P. 83, 144
Hodgson, G. 3, 5, 8–9, 10, 11
Hollis, M. 8
Holmes, S. 83
Horwitz, S. 116–17, 119, 120, 124–5,
  127, 130
human welfare
  and economic value and costs,
    subjectivity of 53–6
  social order harmony, and markets 90
Hume, D. xi, 14, 112, 115
Humphrey, T. 115

Ikeda, S. 106
individualism, methodological 3–13
  as building blocks of the social
    sciences 3–5
  and conception of reality 7–9
  and Homo economicus 5–7, 10
  institutional form of 9–11
  and purposeful actor 6
inflation
  and capital heterogeneity
    implications 131
  and money, non-neutrality of 114,
    116, 117
institutions *see* economics as study of
  coordination and exchange,
  institutions

Jarvie, I. 10
Jevons, S. xi, 44–5
Johnson, S. 23